GREAT NEGROES
PAST AND PRESENT

by
RUSSELL L. ADAMS

Illustrations by
EUGENE WINSLOW

DAVID P. ROSS, JR.
Editor

AFRO-AM PUBLISHING COMPANY
INCORPORATED
CHICAGO

LIBRARY OF CONGRESS CATALOG CARD NUMBER 64-22914

Fourth Printing of Second Edition

© 1963, 1964, BY

AFRO-AM PUBLISHING COMPANY, INC.

PREFACE

The publication of this book, *GREAT NEGROES— Past and Present*, is a culmination of searching inquiry into the need for a popular rendering of historical source material on the American Negro—material which hitherto has been unavailable to the public.

The multiple contributions of the Negro people and their African antecedents in the context of the American culture and material wealth have never been popularized. They have been accorded arid scholarly treatment in documents that were intended to satisfy the intellectual curiosity of a highly specialized group.

Such documents, by their very nature, are limited in number and inaccessible to the uninitiated. Even public libraries, repositories of general information, carry few titles on their shelves dealing in a popular vein with the subject-matter of the Negro and his contribution to the stream of the American culture. Thus, the paucity of relevant descriptive data, and the scarcity of pictorial representations are the compelling motives that actuated the production of this book.

The swift tide of events incidental to the black revolution on civil rights, and the sudden transformation of colonial Africa into imposing independent sovereign states create greater urgency for the need for comprehensive information on the Negro.

The text is documented. Source notes at the end of each biographical sketch guide the reader to additional information on the subject in the text. An extensive bibliography is included for those interested in pursuing a broader knowledge and more detailed information.

Introductions to the chapters provide background information and place the sketches in their historical perspective. Here, also, an attempt is made to project important individuals, in each field, who are not featured in the biographical sketches. Although every effort was made to give recognition to persons who have made significant contributions, doubtless there are some who have been omitted. The field of sports was omitted mainly because of the abundance of available material on sports personalities.

The author, Russell L. Adams, did a thorough, painstaking job of research in documenting the data and presenting the events. Governed by the limitation of space, the author condensed vital information into interesting reading, highlighting the essential facts.

The portraits and illustrations by Eugene Winslow represent a major contribution, in that they are the results of extensive research. Many of the personalities pictured here are seen for the first time. Graphic details in the composite illustrations give the pictorial story academic interest and local color. Using a variety of illustration techniques, the artist seeks to re-capture the spirit and character of the personalities.

The idea of this pictorial-biographical presentation was conceived by the editor as one which would have broad appeal and reader-interest for all age groups. The book, starting as it does at 720 B.C., acquaints the reader with the heritage of the African and his American descendants.

GREAT NEGROES—Past and Present is the end result of close collaboration of three individuals who recognized the need and timeliness of a publication which would serve to acquaint people of all ethnic backgrounds with many important achievements of the American Negro, and give an insight into the vital role which persons of African descent have played in shaping history in the context of world culture.

David P. Ross, Jr.
Editor-Publisher

ACKNOWLEDGMENTS

The author wishes to thank the individuals and institutions who contributed to the publication of this book. He is especially indebted to Dr. Metz T. P. Lochard, W. Louis Davis and Mrs. Geraldine Scott, to Consolidated Book Publishers of Chicago and the George Cleveland Hall branch of the Chicago Public Library. The author is deeply indebted to his wife Eleanor for her assistance and encouragement.

Grateful acknowledgments are made to:

Alfred A. Knopf, Inc. for permission to quote lines from "The Negro Speaks of Rivers" in *The Big Sea* by Langston Hughes (Alfred A. Knopf, 1940)

Dodd, Mead and Company for permission to quote lines from "Little Brown Baby" and "Ode to Ethiopia" in *The Collected Poems of Paul Laurence Dunbar* (Dodd, Mead and Company, 1954)

Harper & Row, Inc. for permission to quote lines from "Heritage" in *Color* by Countee Cullen (Harper & Brothers, 1925); from "Black Majesty" in *On These I Stand* by Countee Cullen (Harper & Brothers, 1947); from "The Ghosts at the Quincy Club" in *The Bean Eaters* by Gwendolyn Brooks (Harper & Brothers, 1960)

Twayne Publishers, Inc. for permission to quote lines from "If We Must Die" in *The Selected Poems of Claude McKay* (Bookman Associates, 1953)

The volumes of *The Journal of Negro History*, *The Negro History Bulletin*, the *Dictionary of American Biography*, *Current Biography*, *Ebony* and *Negro Digest* were of inestimable value to this writer.

RUSSELL L. ADAMS

CHICAGO, ILLINOIS
NOVEMBER 3, 1963

TABLE OF CONTENTS

TABLE OF CONTENTS

TABLE OF CONTENTS

TABLE OF CONTENTS

GREAT NEGROES ꙮ Past and Present

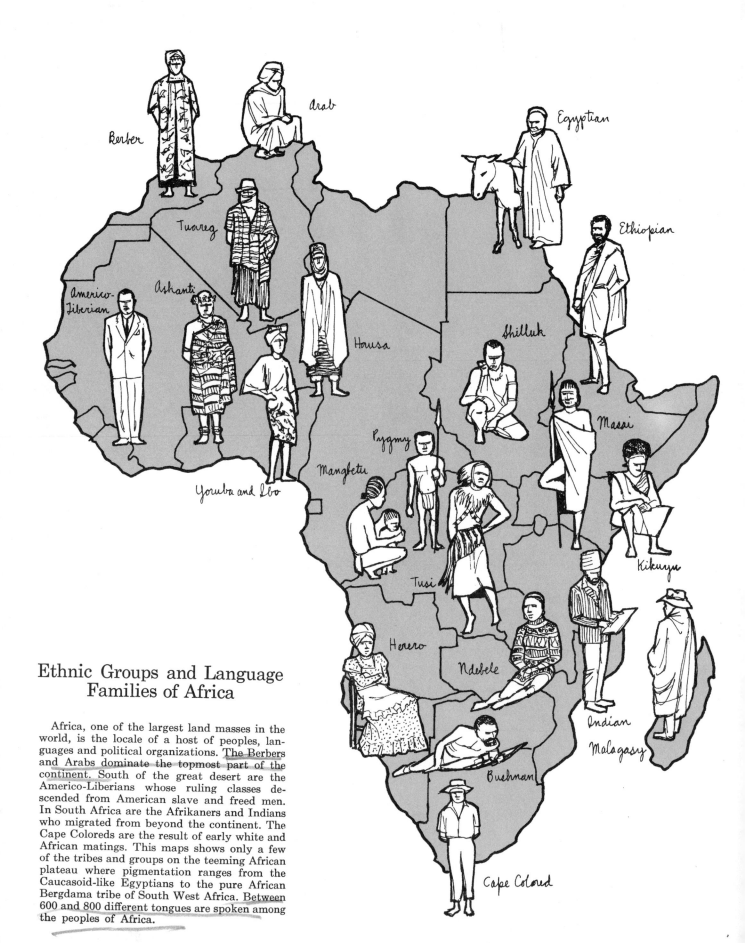

Ethnic Groups and Language Families of Africa

Africa, one of the largest land masses in the world, is the locale of a host of peoples, languages and political organizations. The Berbers and Arabs dominate the topmost part of the continent. South of the great desert are the Americo-Liberians whose ruling classes descended from American slave and freed men. In South Africa are the Afrikaners and Indians who migrated from beyond the continent. The Cape Coloreds are the result of early white and African matings. This maps shows only a few of the tribes and groups on the teeming African plateau where pigmentation ranges from the Caucasoid-like Egyptians to the pure African Bergdama tribe of South West Africa. Between 600 and 800 different tongues are spoken among the peoples of Africa.

Berber

Arab

Egyptian

Ethiopian

Tuareg

Americo-Liberian

Ashanti

Hausa

Shilluk

Massai

Pygmy

Mangbetu

Kikuyu

Yoruba and Ibo

Tusi

Herero

Ndebele

Indian

Malagasy

Bushman

Cape Colored

X

I   CONTRIBUTORS TO EARLY HISTORY

Out of the Mists of Time

The history of the black man began long before the voyage of the *Mayflower*. It stretches back into the dim mists of time. Compared with the history of other cultures and peoples, our historical knowledge of Africa is rather sparse. Until the present century, Africa remained as dark a continent to most historians as it had been to the geographers in the early nineteenth century. Only now is the real story of the black man coming to light.

As the study of Africa proceeds, archaeologists and anthropologists are leaning more and more to the idea that the first human beings evolved on the African continent. The remains of, possibly, one of man's oldest ancestors has been found in northern Tanganyika. There the archaeologist L. S. B. Leakey found remnants of human prototypes nearly two million years old.

There is in Africa evidence of a human society which existed almost 50,000 years ago. This society was remarkably similar to the stage of human development in Europe at the same time. As early as eight thousand years ago, the Ishongo people in the Congo were using an abacus or primitive multiplying device. In the Sahara desert are to be found rock paintings of human beings by Negroid people who lived three thousand years ago.

Long called the "cradle of civilization," Egypt has been regarded as the source of the early beginning of western civilization. Historians are not certain of the physical appearance of the ordinary Egyptian in the days of the ancient Greeks, although Herodotus, the father of history, called them "black and curly-haired." Homer and other Greek observers described the Egyptians as "men of burnt faces."

Many of the physical representations of the early Egyptians show them as being full-lipped with broad noses and woolly or kinky hair. These characteristics can be seen in the Sphinx and other sculptured figures. There are many other representations showing them to be of a Caucasoid type. Since the valley of the Nile was most hospitable to human habitation, people from different parts of the Mediterranean area migrated there and formed a mixed society.

Four thousand years before Christ, Egypt was united under a single ruler, the Pharaoh. In the third millenium B.C. the country was having difficulty repulsing the Nubians who descended upon the growing state. By 2000 B.C. Nubians had gained positions of power and influence in Egypt. During these dawning years of Egyptian history a Nubian, Ra Nahesi, sat on the throne of the Pharaohs.

In the first millenium B.C. during Egypt's 25th Dynasty, the ancient Ethiopians of the Sudan gained control of the country. In 751 B.C. the mighty Piankhi fell upon Egypt from Ethiopia and subdued the country. His reign was followed by that of his brother, Shabaka. For more than one hundred years Ethiopians ruled Egypt. The greatest of the Ethiopian rulers of this pioneer civilization was Taharka who ascended the throne of the Pharaoh in 688 B.C. His mastery of Egypt was so complete that he called himself "Emperor of the World."

By the year 670 B.C. the ancient Ethiopians were driven out of Egypt only to retreat to their own highly civilized land in the region of the Sudan. At the Ethiopian capitals of Napata and Meroe black kings reigned in splendor. One of the most outstanding Ethiopian rulers was Metekamane who built monuments to himself and his queen, Amanetari, at many places along the Nile. He also set up two huge statues of himself on Argo Island. In 590 B.C. Napata was sacked by the Assyrians who were now overrunning the Fertile Crescent that nourished ancient Egypt.

Centuries after the decline of ancient Ethiopia in the Sudan, another civilization of black men rose on a broad stretch of land south of the Sahara. Here flourished ancient Ghana, Melle and Songhay. Possessing a history traceable to the fourth century A.D., Ghana reached its apogee in the eleventh century under one Tenanenin. When Ghana began to decline in the twelfth century, Melle, a Mandingo empire, rose to prominence and achieved its zenith under Kankan-Mussa who ruled it from 1307 to 1332. Melle's influence extended from the Atlantic ocean on the west to Lake Chad on the east. The fabled empire of Songhay took its place in the fifteenth century.

Accounts of these three states indicate that, in many respects, they were as advanced as those of Europe during the same epoch. Trade and commerce formed the bases of their economies. Religion and education were promoted. Timbuctu and the University of Sankore were the mecca of Sudanese savants and scholars. Historians such as Ibn Bututa, Mohammed Koti, and Adberrahaman Sadi left vivid acounts of these states. Many lesser states thrived in the same general region.

Down to the sixteenth century, the history of Africa unfolded independently of that of Europe. The Caucasians saw Africans first as curiosities and had no particular personal attitude towards them. Slavery was an old institution in the ancient world and involved people of every race. Then the explosive release of European economic energy occasioned by the Renaissance led to the modern traffic in men which ended only with the coming of the Civil War in America.

John Hope Franklin. *From Slavery to Freedom* (2nd Ed.), 1956, pp. 5-22; Roland Oliver and J. D. Fage. *A Short History of Africa*, Baltimore, 1962, pp. 44-65; Lerone Bennett. "The African Past," *Ebony*, July, 1961, pp. 34-40.

Piankhi (720 B.C.)
CONQUEROR OF EGYPT

Standing on a wharf and shaded by huge umbrellas held aloft by slaves, Piankhi, the black king of Nubia, seethed with rage and frustration as he watched ships loaded with casks of gold, scores of slaves and bands of fighting men, float down the Nile enroute to Osorkin III, King of Egypt. For 1800 years other Nubian kings had witnessed the same sight, the payment of tribute to the Egyptians who dominated the fertile Crescent. But unlike others, Piankhi decided that he would make war on the Egyptians and put an end to the ceaseless and annoying greed of his powerful neighbor.

For years Piankhi plotted, watched and waited, but sent his yearly tribute to Egypt. All the while he planned his strategy and built his army. Smug in their domination of the subjected countries and lulled into carelessness by the steady payment of tribute, the Egyptians paid no attention to Piankhi.

Finally, Piankhi decided that the time was ripe to make war on Egypt. Again the sleepy Nile was loaded with ships headed for Egypt. This time however, instead of tribute, they carried soldiers and warriors. With disciplined skill, Piankhi's soldiers captured town after town until at last they arrived at the first large Egyptian fortress of Hermopolis and laid siege to it. With crushing power, Piankhi defeated Namlot, the Egyptian commander. Prostrating himself before Piankhi, Namlot begged for mercy, explaining that he was one of the king's slaves, paying duty into the treasury.

Piankhi pressed on, capturing one city after another until he came to the great city of Memphis, which was at that time the capital of Egypt. Memphis was surrounded by a high wall, the western wall being higher than the eastern one which faced the open sea.

Word of Piankhi's victories had preceded him and the Egyptians at Memphis planned their defence. They expected to defeat this Nubian who was placing much of their country under his rule. But Piankhi did the unexpected. Strategically deploying his fleet, he soon had control of the harbor and then the eastern sea wall which, as he suspected, had been neglected.

Before the western defences of Memphis could come to the aid of the seaward side of the city, the Nubians had scaled the sea walls from their ships and were soon in control of the city. Tefnakhte, the commander of Memphis, meekly surrendered. With Memphis conquered, Piankhi continued his triumphal march toward Heliopolis where King Osorkon waited. The king had grown fat and indolent from years of ruling and had no desire to fight. He gave up without resistance and Piankhi became master of Egypt.

Following the adage of "to the victor belong the spoils," Piankhi sailed for home. Again hundreds of ships covered the Nile laden with treasures of gold and silver. This time they were bound for the vaults of Egypt's new master, the mighty Piankhi.

J. A. Rogers. *World's Great Men of Color — 3000 B. C. to 1946 A. D.*, I, New York, 1947, pp. 36-38; *Encyclopædia Britannica*, 1957 Edition (vol XVI) p. 586.

Antar (615 A.D.)
AFRO-ARABIAN POET-STORY TELLER

Africa and the land of Arabia blend into one another, separated mainly by the desert. Peoples of Africa and the desert are unlike in many ways; yet they also have much in common. The love of story-telling and poetry and the love of personal adventure are only two of a host of things they share.

One of Arabia's greatest story-tellers and warriors was the legendary Antarah Ibn Shaddad in whose veins flowed both African and Arabian blood.

Antarah Ibn Shaddad, known to history simply as Antar, wrote many poems based on the great love he had for his high-born wife Abla. No one knows just how many poems were composed by Antar, for most of his compositions were handed down through the generations by oral tradition. In 1889 some thirty-two volumes of *The Romance of Antar* were published at Cairo, Egypt.. A few years later, ten volumes were published at Beirut, Labanon.

Antar was born of an African slave, Zabuba and an Arabian prince and warrior, Shaddad. He soon grew into a very intelligent and sensitive young man of great physical strength. Other chieftains competed for the ownership of this strangely dark youth who killed a wolf when he was ten years old.

Herding sheep, tending camels and doing a variety of things left for slaves alone, Antar met the love of his life, Abla, the hauntingly beautiful daughter of his father's brother. Smitten beyond caring, Antar began composing odes to Abla's beauty to express his love for her. Abla, herself a princess, slowly developed a kindred but carefully guarded affection for Antar, the slave boy. Antar's skill and bravery in combat and skill in verse won his freedom and the hand of Abla. His love for her inspired many of his finest odes.

Antar's poems were regarded as models of Arabic style. Inscribed in gold and hung high in the Kaabah at Mecca is one of his poems. At Aleppo, Bagdagh or Constantinople his poems are still recited in coffee houses and around glowing fires. Arabian poetry lovers have an adage which claims that "'The Thousand and One Nights' is for the amusement of women and children. Antar's is a book for men."

In the verses of Antar, the Arabian may find reflected virtues he admires: personal courage, pride, fierce love and the grand gesture. Antar himself embodied many of these virtues. He died in battle in 615 AD but his poems live on in *The Romance of Antar*.

J. A. Rogers. *World's Great Men of Color — 3000 B.C. to 1946 A.D.*, (vol I), New York, 1947, pp. 70-73; A. O. Stafford. "Antar, The Great Arabian-Negro Warrior", *Journal of Negro History*, vol. I (January, 1916), pp. 151-162.

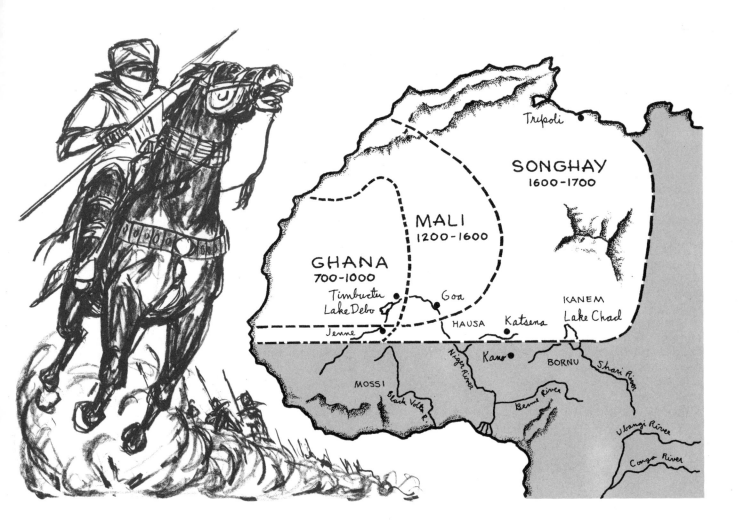

Sonni Ali (-1492)

WARRIOR-KING OF SONGHAY

Enshrouded in myth and legend, the old African empires of Ghana, Mali and Timbuctu are little known to the world today. Yet between the 11th and 16th centuries, they rivalled Europe both in size and sophistication. Their capital cities of Goa, Jenne and Timbuctu were centers of trade, commerce and learning. Of all the Mellestine and Songhaese rulers, Sonni Ali, in the words of W. E. B. DuBois, was among the "last and the greatest." Beginning his career as a common soldier, by 1464 A.D. Sonni Ali found himself master of all the territory "from Timbuctu to the blue waters of the Atlantic."

Sonni Ali was a native of Songhay. When he came of age he was forced into the army of the Mellestine king Mansa Musa and had to fight against his own people. But in time he shrewdly managed to rally enough soldiers to overthrow Mansa Musa and set himself up as ruler of Jenne and Timbuctu. He was able to consolidate his revolution by intermarriage between the people of Mali and those of Songhay.

Aware of the tremendous wealth sent to Mecca by the Mohammedian Mansa Musa, Sonni broke the grip of the Moslem faith in the empire by bringing the priestly class under his control and by exercising a more direct control over the University of Sankore, the Mecca for Sudanese and Arabian scholars. To those who did not understand his motives in restricting the University of Sankore, Sonni Ali said, "Without learning, life would be neither pleasure nor savour."

After Sonni captured Jenne and Timbuctu, "The Humburi, the Fulbes, the Mossi, the Teska, the Ghana and the Bara came to acknowledge him as their lord. His armies then captured the Housas, the Senhadata, the Dias, the Fulbes" and even marched as far as Lake Debo to capture the strongly fortified city of Chiddo. Sonni Ali has been acclaimed "one of the born soldiers of the world." His empire covered more territory than Napoleon's during his apex. In the south it reached as far as Lake Chad and in the north it touched the present-day Tripoli.

The date of Sonni Ali's birth is uncertain, but it is recorded that he died in 1492. The ruler who succeeded him was Mohammed Askia.

W. E. B. DuBois. *Black Folk: Then and Now*, New York, 1937, p. 47; Anna Melissa Graves. *Africa: The Wonder and the Glory*, Baltimore, 1961, pp. 35-36.

Askia The Great (1494-1538)
BUILDER OF TIMBUCTU

Timbuctu, the capital city of the Songhay Empire, was built by Askia the Great, a former general in the army of Sonni Ali, the founder of this fabled domain. Overthrowing Abu Kebr, heir of Sonni Ali, Askia presided over Songhay whose easternmost "boundary reached to Lake Chad and in the northeast to the south east corner of what is Tripoli today." Under Askia, the Songhay empire became one of the most enlightened and wealthy countries of the sixteenth century.

Askia began his rule by consolidating his empire and unifying the various political and religious elements within it. Like Alexander the Great, Askia and his officials intermarried within the diverse tribes so that most of the influential families were in some way related to him and to one another. Since military force was the basis of his empire, Askia maintained the loyalty of his troops by making them partners in the wealth and glory of Songhay and Timbuctu. So tranquil was the country under Askia that many travelers marveled at the safety and hospitality of the people.

On the banks of the Niger river, located nine miles from the city of Timbuctu, Askia had canals dug and a merchant fleet created to handle trade and commerce. Mainstays of the economy were salt, gold, woods and hides. Caravans arrived and departed in great numbers. The University of Sankore was a gathering place for scholars from all over the African and Arabic world.

Located at the center of this busy activity was Askia whose subjects virtually worshipped him. As a conqueror and unifier, he was possessed of a "good heart, well-inspired and was endowed with a generosity that God had placed in him." No one spoke directly to Askia but only through intermediaries. When he travelled, his retinue was preceded by trumpets and by many outriders.

In the midst of his wealth and glory, Askia began to lose his eyesight and was forced to abdicate by one of his sons. However, Askia recouped and was able to spend his last years in his palace as ruler. For thirty-six years Askia ruled over Songhay, Timbuctu, an empire of culture learning and wealth. He died in 1538 . . . and Songhay began to die a half century later.

J. A. Rogers. *World's Great Men of Color — 3000 B. C. to 1946 A.D.*, I, New York, 1947, pp. 134-137; A. O. Stafford. "The Tarik e Soudan", *Journal of Negro History*, II (April, 1917), pp. 139-146; Basil Davidson. *The Lost Cities of Africa*, Boston, 1959, pp. 71-81.

Abderrahaman Sadi El Timbuctu (1596-1660)
EARLY HISTORIAN

Ancient Ghana, Mali, Kanem, Songhay—all melodious names—have been part of the ancient memories of Africans transplanted to the new world. For hundreds of years, vague recollections of the glory were the only consolations of slaves toiling in the Americas; these slaves were dimly aware of a high civilization of black men behind them in Africa.

To their masters and to European scholars as a whole, only Ethiopia and Timbuctu had a sort of incredulous reality. Mali, Songhay, Kanem, Ghana and other places meant little. One Ibn Buttuta in the 14th century had travelled through some of the flourishing African kingdoms and wrote glowing accounts for an unbelieving Europe emerging from the stagnation of the Middle Ages. Timbuctu and Ethiopia brought to mind far away places and hazy glories, but more than anyone else in the 17th century, one Abderrahaman Sadi el Timbuctu made real the African kingdoms then flourishing along the Niger river.

In one of Sadi's books, the famous *Tarishk el Sudan*, he says, "I shall speak of Timbuctu, of its foundation, of the princes who have wielded power in that city. I shall mention the learned and pious men who dwelt there." For years, Abderrahaman worked on his Tarishk, using his position as secretary to a high-ranking official to study men, places and documents which gave his work the convincing details of truth.

Through his eyes we see Timbuctu as a busy city where camel caravans come from all over the Sudan, bearing items and objects of trade. Arriving and departing with the caravans are students and scholars bound for or leaving the University of Sankore in Timbuctu. We see salt and gold, the basis of economy, exchanged for leather and embroidery; we see cultural exchange in the form of manuscripts on parchment, the works of learned men. In Abderrahaman's pages Timbuctu glows as the hub of the Sudan to which men from Africa and Spain come to trade and learn.

Born in 1596, Abderrahaman grew up in a religious household which was devoted to discussions of poetry and science of his day. Beyond doing his job as a notary, a secretary and a minor diplomat, Abderrahaman had only one ambition—to preserve for posterity the memories of the great African civilizations that flourished in this part of the so-called "Dark Continent."

Recent studies have confirmed the revelations of *Tarsihk el Sudan*, the truth of ancestral memories of blacks in the new world.

Arna Bontemps. *Story of the Negro*, New York, 1948, pp. 34-36; A .O. Stafford. "The Tarik e Soudan", *Journal of Negro History*, II (April, 1917). pp. 141-146.

Abram Hannibal (1697-1782)
SOLDIER, COMMANDER IN RUSSIA

Captured in Africa at the age of eight and sold to a Russian nobleman in Constantinople, Abram Hannibal was given as a slave to Tsar Peter the Great of Russia. Peter grew fond of him and he soon became a court favorite. The young black captive was brought up in the Russian Orthodox Church, where he was baptized Abram Hannibal.

When Abram completed his early schooling in 1716, the Tsar sent him to Paris to study military engineering with the expectation of him joining the Tsar's army. In Paris, Abram repeated his earlier social success by becoming a preferred intimate of the Duc d'Orleans, then Regent. A strikingly handsome young Hannibal was permitted to join the French Army and soon attained the rank of commander. After seven years, to the regret of the Duc, he returned to Russia and joined the Tsar's own guard regiment as an engineer lieutenant.

He became a good military man and grew very fond of Russia. When his brother in Africa learned of his whereabouts and offered the Tsar a rather generous ransom for his return, Hannibal turned it down, saying "Convey my thanks to my brother. May God bless his good intention on my behalf. But tell him that I am happy here in the land of my adoption. I will remain here."

For a time Hannibal enjoyed favor and esteem in his adopted country; however, at the death of Peter the Great, Hannibal discovered that Queen Catherine was not so interested in him. Peter II was even less fond of Abram and with the connivance of Abram's enemies, sent him to Siberia where he suffered greatly. Abram managed to escape but was eventually captured and returned to Siberia.

By 1741, under still another ruler, Abram was forgiven and reinstated in the Russian army, and made many military contributions to the Tsar. Honors began to come his way. In a border conflict between Russia and Sweden, Abram was commissioned to fix the disputed boundary line. After this, he was appointed a member of the Logoda Canal Commission and a member of the inspection staff of the Russian Forts. His crowning honor was his appointment as commandant of the city of Reval, and as major in the garrison at Tomesk where he had been held captive many years before.

Abram Hannibal married a German girl who gave him five sons; one of these sons became the father of Russia's greatest poet, Alexander Pushkin.

Albert Parry. "Abram Hannibal, the Favorite of Peter the Great", *Journal of Negro History*, *VIII* (October, 1923), pp. 359-366; Beatrice Flemming and Marion Pryde. *Distinguished Negroes Abroad*, Washington, 1946, pp. 166-170.

Chaka (1787-1828)
18TH CENTURY ZULU KING AND WARRIOR

Out of a chance encounter between an African warrior prince and a beautiful commoner was born Chaka. Being an outcast from birth, Chaka developed a drive for power and revenge which carried him to the head of the Zulus.

As a solitary, brooding youth, he was ridiculed by his fellows because of his illegitimate birth. He saw his father, Zenzangakona, drive his mother, Nandi, and himself into exile where he grew up with a rival tribe. But instead of being crushed by the hardships he and his mother endured, Chaka sharpened his native intelligence and conditioned his body to win recognition and acceptance as a warrior. It is upon his military skill and leadership that his fame rests.

Dingiswayo, leader of Chaka's tribe and his father's rival, quickly took note of Chaka's unusual courage and intelligence and groomed him to become a leader of the Mtetwas, a small tribe numbering between two and three thousand people. In this part of Natal, South Africa, different chiefs, sub-chiefs and plotters were usually engaged in a daily round of wars and assassinations, and the Mtetwas were no exception. Dingiswayo successfully plotted the death of Chaka's father. Then Zwide, who was another aspirant for power, tricked Dingiswayo, causing his early death. Chaka ascended to leadership of the Mtetwas and set out to destroy Zwide. Chaka met and defeated Zeide's army. Zwide escaped but was later assassinated.

Under Chaka, the Mtetwas began a series of conquests which brought most of Natal under their control. His armies used a special kind of stabbing knife known as an assegai, instead of the spear. It enabled them to subdue many times their number. He also employed tactics of the old Greek and Roman phalanxes in battle.

In 1824 Chaka saw his first white men. Among them was H. F. Fynn, a Britisher who was exploring this section of Natal. Fynn successfully treated Chaka for a battle wound. In gratitude, he made a grant of Port Natal to Fynn and his compainion, Farewell.

Chaka brought together many tribes of his region and they learned to live together in harmony. However, he was not without enemies, for in 1828 he was assassinated, but left a proud people in their unity.

E. A. Ritter. *Shaka Zulu*, New York, 1955.

Jacques Eliza Jean Captein

(1745-   )

ORATOR, PHILOSOPHER

Jacques Eliza Jean Captein holds a curious place in the history of the Negro. At a time when the Dutch were getting an increased share of the African slave trade, by chance it was Captein who was used to prove that the African was capable of understanding the tenets of Christianity and hence had a soul to save. Slavery, through the Dutch, would be one method of saving these heathens from hell-fire.

When Captein was bought at the age of eight by a fellow African, little did he realize that he would be a guinea pig to "prove" to the Dutch populace that a human being stood behind the dark skin of men greedy business entrepreneurs saw as a source of great profits. Captein found himself in the hands of a Dutch Captain who, for amusement, began teaching him the rudiments of his native language and was startled at the brilliance of his little pupil. Soon Captein was given books to pore over and, in short order, he became familiar with their contents. His owner was convinced that he had made a most unusual purchase. This conviction was re-inforced when one day he chanced upon his dusky scholar holding a small painting which he had done without any instruction.

Convinced that he would profit even more from systematic training, Captein was sent to the Hague where he was placed under a teacher familiar with languages. Greek, Hebrew, Latin, and Chaldean he soon learned to read. By now Captein was a young man and his patron made it possible for him to enter the University of Leyden where he took a degree in theology.

News of his proficiency and brilliance spread and Captein, upon graduation, was sent back to Elmina, on the Gold Coast, to work among his people as a missionary. However, it was soon apparent that the natives of Elmina had not heard of the great experiment, for Captein was much less successful as a missionary than as a scholar. He soon returned to Holland where he made a name for himself, first as a curiosity and still later for what he had to say about Christianity and the institution of slavery.

Strictly a brilliant product of his training and the designs of his master and teacher, Captein was misled to use his intellect in a defense of the institution of slavery, arguing that slavery was one way for his fellow Africans to save their immortal souls. He was unable to see the deeper design of the Dutch, which was to provide a rationale for pursuing the slave trade with ever-increasing vigor.

In addition to his prose work, Captein wrote poems in Latin which have endured much better than his defense of the peculiar institution of slavery. Misguided though he was, his intelligence as pure brain power would have made him conspicuous anywhere.

Beatrice Flemming and Marion Pryde. *Distinguished Negroes Abroad*, Washington, 1946, pp. 141-146.

Gustavus Vassa (1745-1801)
SEA-FARER, COLONIZER

On March 21, 1788, Her Royal Highness, Charlotte, Queen of England received a petition containing among other things, these words:

"I presume . . . your gracious Queen, to implore your interposition with that of your royal consort (King George III) in favor of the wretched Africans, that by your Majesty's benevolent influence, a period may now be put to their misery; and that they may be raised from the condition of brutes to which they are at present degraded to the rights and situation of free men . . ."

The petitioner was Gustavus Vassa who had risen from the rank of kidnapped slave to that of "commissary of the government," superintending part of a plan to return Africans to their native lands.

Born in the Essaka Valley of Guinea, he was kidnapped and hustled aboard a slave ship headed for the Barbadoes, British West Indies. After a fearful Middle Passage, Vassa, only eleven years old, was sold at a slave auction and became the property of a Virginia planter. This worthy gentleman sold Vassa to a sea captain, one Pascal, who commanded a ship called the *Industrious Bee*. Aboard the ship was a young American who taught Vassa the rudiments of the English language.

After two years, Captain Pascal sent his little slave to England to be the household servant of two pious ladies who insisted that he learned to read the Bible. Over the next few years, Vassa changed hands as owners saw fit and again he found himself at sea. Shipped again to the West Indies, Vassa fell into the hands of a Quaker merchant from Philadelphia who permitted him to earn extra money to purchase his freedom. Within a few years, Vassa was a free man.

Gustavus Vassa desired to go to England where he had spent the best years of his life and after much voyaging reached London only to find it impossible for him to complete his haphazard education without any funds. In 1773 Vassa joined an expedition seeking a northwest passage to India and wound up on the coast of Greenland. Still deeply addicted to the sea, Vassa travelled to Spain and India and made occasional journeys to the United States.

In 1785, the Crown was trying to return Africans to their native land. Vassa was appointed to a post with the government and was placed in charge of the commissary which supplied the Africans with clothing and other items deemed necessary for the voyage home. Vassa reported the dishonesty and the thievery among his English co-workers who wasted little time securing his dismissal from his post. Vassa continued to work for the emancipation of his fellow Africans and made his famous appeal to Queen Charlotte.

In 1789, Vassa published his autobiography, *The Interesting Narrative of the Life of Olaudah Equiana or Gustavus Vassa*. This was the first and to us, the fullest account of the life of a free Negro during this period. The book was so popular that it went through eight editions in five years.

Benjamin Brawley. *Early Negro American Writers*, Chapel Hill, 1935, p. 56.

Joseph Cinque (1811-1852)

AFRICAN PRINCE AND REVOLUTIONIST

Few stories of heroism and bravery hold greater interest than that of Joseph Cinque, an African prince kidnapped and sold into slavery in Havana, Cuba. It is a story of mutiny and revolt, a story of court room drama and freedom. It really began in 1839 in Havana.

After being prodded, poked, and pinched by Spaniards who were buying slaves, Cinque and thirty-eight other hapless people were packed into the hold of a 120-ton schooner called the *Amistad* whose destination was the Island of Principe. Two days out from Havana, a raging storm hit the ship. The regular crew fought to keep the ship moving against the elements until they fell into a deep sleep near midnight. Stuffed in the hold below, Cinque and his fellow slaves plotted their escape. Cinque dominated this group as he had dominated nearly every other. He gave the instructions. The others listened carefully, feeling that a man as self-confident as Cinque must be fully aware of what he was planning.

On board the *Amistad* were machetes and knives, placed out of reach of the chained slaves. Yet Cinque and the slaves got free of their irons. Peering up toward the deck, they could see no one but a solitary helmsman trying to keep the ship on its proper course. Silently spreading out, Cinque and his men fell upon all the whites at once. Señor Don Jose Ruiz and Señor Don Pedro Montez, their owners, were spared; the rest, including the Captain and the crew, were slain.

Cinque was now in complete control of the ship but knew nothing about navigation. Using Ruiz and Montez as helmsmen and navigators, Cinque directed them to steer the schooner eastward toward Africa, the land of his fathers, the land where his wife and three children were still mourning his absence.

The two Spaniards had not amassed the wealth to buy almost forty slaves by being dull-witted. During the day, they kept the ship going in an easterly direction, but at night they slowly headed the *Amistad* in a northwest direction. Days passed. Cinque and the others did not have the slightest idea of the ruse being pulled on them by Ruiz and Montez, for, by steering a cleverly zig-zagged course, the wily Spaniards worked the *Amistad* all the way from the Caribbean to Long Island, New York.

A sensation was created when Ruiz and Montez told of the revolt and of the killings on board the ship. Never had a slave been so brazen as Cinque who promptly sat down to negotiating with the Americans for passage to Africa. But he and all of the Africans were taken prisoner. The Abolitionist fever was running high. Quickly a committee was formed to defend the legal rights of the slaves. The U. S. District attorney for New York moved that the rebels be turned over to the Spanish government.

Through a maze of claims and arguments, the case of the *Amistad* revolt began its tortuous journey up through the courts with each succeeding court deciding that Cinque and his cohorts were free men. The U. S. Justice Department fought this view all the way up to the United States Supreme Court where John Quincy Adams, now an old man, defended the *Amistad* revolt, basing his argument on the inherent right of every human being to be free, regardless of legal arrangements to keep him in fetters. The U. S. Supreme Court ruled in favor of Cinque and the other Africans, declaring them free to return to Africa, their native land.

William Owens. *Slave Mutiny The Revolt on the Schooner Amistad*, New York, 1953.

Menelik II (1844-1913)
FOUNDER OF MODERN ETHIOPIA

Ethiopia for more than two thousand years has been a place and a symbol. Of all the African countries, it is the only one with a record of continuous independence, unbroken except for the Italian occupation of 1935-40. No monarchy on earth can match that of Ethiopia in tenure, for it is said to have begun with the Queen of Sheba and her son, Menelik I. Although Ethiopia is a part of the African continent, one does not think of the country as really a part of Africa. In reality, this country is neither black nor white nor even yellow. It is in part Semitic and in part Arabic, with a very strong Negroid mixture. For hundreds of years, the rest of the world has thought of Ethiopia as some sort of exotic jewel, shining on the east coast of Africa. Little does the world realize that until the 19th century Ethiopia was not a united country, but a collection of tribes from the same racial stock under the name of Ethiopia. The Gallo, the Tigre, the Shoa and the Harar tribes embraced a great mass of the people. Serious conflict and rivalry existed among these tribes, aggravated by the Madhists and Somalis to the south and east, and other tribes and countries. Internal strife and chaos were the rule until the advent of one man, Menelik II.

During his early years, Sahala Mariem or Menelik, as he later called himself, aspired to be the Negus Negusti, the King of Kings, leader of all the tribes in the land. Brought up in splendor befitting a prince of a Shoa king, Sahala was made a prisoner in 1855 of one Kassai, the governor of Shoa. Kassai then seized power over all the tribes. After a rather debauched five-year reign Kassai died in 1868. Sahala Mariem (Menelik), by this time a young, ambitious, extremely energetic and intelligent man of 24 years, once more tried to succeed to the high throne of Negus Negusti, but again was unsuccessful. Instead, the Ras (King) of Tigre emerged victorious in the struggle for supreme power, taking the name of John IV. Sahala then decided on a more subtle tactic. He married his daughter, Zaudith, to John IV's son, the Ras Area. This move caused Sahala to be regarded as a remote claimant to the throne, but few people had any idea that within three years Sahala would be the emperor. In a campaign against the Madhi, a stray bullet ended the life of John IV, and with the help of the colony-minded Italians, Sahala at last ascended to the throne.

With the ascension of Menelik, as Sahala called himself, the tribes began to close ranks. Unwittingly helping to unify the country were the Italians, joined by the British and the French, each seeking some type of concession.

Menelik II

Italy was intent on grabbing all of the territory it possibly could and played the various aspirants for the throne against one another.

Menelik had no serious rival. He was the most outstanding personality among the Ras and had the full support of the Shoan army. Immediately after his ascension, the Italians rushed to have him sign the Treaty of Ucialli, a treaty which was the seed of much trouble for both Ethiopia and Italy. The terms of the treaty, in the Italian view, gave Italy complete control over the country's relations with foreign powers, in effect, making the country subservient to Italy. Menelik viewed the treaty differently, claiming that it left full control and sovereignty with himself. As a part of the treaty settlement, the Italians gave Menelik 38,000 rifles and twenty-eight cannons and loaned him 4,000,000 francs with the Harar province as collateral. The first thing Menelik did was to repay the loan but the question of Ethiopia's sovereignty continued to fester. Meanwhile, the Italians got a foothold in the north-eastern part of the country and christened the area Eritrea.

Menelik, ever alert to the question of his country's independence, began to rally the populace behind him. He slowly added arms and equipment to his arsenal. He made peace with most troublesome of the minor Ras. However, Italy also started moving men and material into the country. Finally in 1896, 14,500 Italian officers and soldiers moved toward Adowa, the Ethiopian holy city. With over-extended lines, unreliable maps and a false estimate of Menelik's strength, the Italians were attacked and routed on the plains of Adowa. They left behind some 12,000 killed and over a thousand prisoners. Finally, in October, 1896, the Italians sued for peace.

Menelik had startled the world, for never before had an African nation so decisively defeated a would-be colonizer. There were no further questions of sovereignty. Britain, France, Turkey and Russia sought concessions and monopolies in the country. The French built a railroad and tried to turn control of it over to the British until Menelik stopped them. During all of these transactions, Menelik had two goals uppermost in his mind: the continued sovereignty of the government and the extension and consolidation of borders within and without the territory. He used the greed of the foreigners to his and his country's advantage. With one major exception, most of the border disputes were settled. The exception led to the Italo-Ethiopian War of 1935.

Up to 1906, Menelik rode herd on the Ras, tribes, provinces and the host of foreigners in the country and succeeded in bringing Ethiopia into a more or less unified whole. In this year and in 1908, Menelik suffered strokes and gave active control of the country to others. In 1913, worn out by his strenuous labors, he died, paving the way way for Haile Selassie some seventeen years later.

A. H. M. Jones and Elizabeth Monroe. *A History of Ethiopia*, Oxford, 1955.

II EARLY AMERICAN HISTORY

Heralds of a New Day

From the very beginning Negroes have been part and parcel of American history. They were present during the exploration of the American continent. Negroes took part in the American Revolution, in the abolitionist movement and in the agitation preceding the Civil War.

Doubtful legend has it that a Negro, Alonzo di Pietro, was a pilot on one of Columbus' ships. Historians are agreed that since 1501 Negroes have been present in the New World. In 1513, thirty Negroes, including Nuflio de Olan, were with Balboa when he discovered the Pacific Ocean. They helped him build the first ships made on the Pacific Coast. Cortez, the explorer of Mexico, was accompanied by Negroes. Three Negroes accompanied the explorer, Velas, in 1520. Negroes were with Alvarez when he went to Quito, the oldest city in the New World. They were with Pizarro when he went to Perú in 1541.

The best known of Negro pioneers in the Americas was Estevanico or Estevanillo—one of the four men to live through the expedition of Narverez. Little Stephen, as Estevanico was called, explored for Spain the land which is now Arizona and New Mexico in 1527.

Negroes were present when the French explorers wandered in the Canadian wilds. Jean Baptiste Pointe de Sable was only one of hundreds of Negroes who settled in the Mississippi Valley in the eighteenth century. By the end of the eighteenth century, approximately 500,000 Negroes were living on the North American continent. Virtually all of them were slaves, although here and there were to be found free Negroes.

Five thousand Negroes participated in the American Revolution. Some of them served on the navy's galleys and brigs; others fought with the Continental army. A Negro from Connecticut, known simply as George, was active on a brig, the *Defense Colony Service*, in the spring of 1776. In that same year the galley *Trumbull* carried three Negroes known only as Peter, Brittain and Daniel. The *Aurora*, captained by the famous David Porter, carried Negro seamen. One Cato Blackney served on three Massachusetts brigs, the *Hazard*, the *Deane* and the *Prospect* during 1778 and 1779.

A large number of these early Negro seamen were pilots as indicated by a letter written by George Washington on July 26, 1779 ,wherein he stated that, "I have granted a Warrant of 1,000 dollars promised the Negro pilots." The Virginia legislature bought the freedom of a slave known only as Caesar because he had "entered early into the service of his country, and continued to pilot the armed vessels of this state during the late war."

As the colonists became more desperate for able-bodied men, even slaves were accepted for military duty. Many slaves received their freedom as a result of their service during the Revolution.

Caesar Ferrit and his son John, Samuel Craft, Peter Salem, Pomp Blackman and Lemuel Haynes were at the battles of Lexington and Concord in April of 1775. At the battle of Bunker Hill, Caesar Brown lost his life in action. Peter Salem fired the shot that killed Major Pitcairn, leader of the British troops during this battle. Lemuel Haynes, Primas Black, and Epheram Blackman took part in the battle of Ticonderoga. Prince Whipple was with George Washington when he crossed the Delaware on Christmas Day, 1776. Tack Sissons was one of the raiders who captured the British General, Richard Prescott at Newport, Rhode Island on July 9, 1777.

During the course of the War for Independence, Negroes fought in all of the major battles, including Brandywine, Boonesborough, Yorktown, White Plains, Saratoga, Trenton, and Monmouth. Almost all of the colonies supplied Negroes who took part in the war. Vermont, New Hampshire, Rhode Island, New York and Connecticut had especially heavy enlistments.

After the War for Independence ended, Negroes began taking part in the general development of the country. Prince Hall organized the first Masonic Lodge among Negroes in this country in 1774.

In 1791 the St. Thomas Episcopal Church was organized by Absalom Jones. Andrew Bryan was preaching to a congregation of two hundred persons in Savannah, Georgia in the late 1780's. Fifty of his communicants were able to read. Benjamin Banneker was publishing his Almanac between the years 1792 and 1803. James Derham was beginning to practice medicine as the first Negro physician in America.

In the abolitionist movement were men such as William Still in Philadelphia, Stephen Myers in Albany, New York, J. W. Loguen in Syracuse, New York, Martin R. Delany in Pittsburgh, Pennsylvania. In the year immediately preceding the Civil War, Negro writers and orators were expressing themselves on such matters as colonization of Negroes, the institution of slavery and the progress of the Negro as a group. Negro conventions devoted to these subjects were meeting in different parts of the North.

The early history of the Negro shows him as an explorer, a settler, a slave and as a patriot, beginning his vigorous pursuit of freedom, liberty and equality. In these days he saw himself as an American. As the nation developed and expanded, the Negro developed into an ardent supporter of the nation's highest ideals.

Benjamin Brawley. *A Short History of the American Negro*, New York, 1931, pp. 2-3; John Hope Franklin. *From Slavery to Freedom*, New York, 1956, pp. 44-45; Herbert Aptheker. *The Negro in the American Revolution*, New York, 1940, pp. 27-41.

HAITI: THREE WHO MADE REVOLUTION

Toussaint L'Ouverture
Jacques Dessalines
Henri Christophe

Toussaint's victories earned him the name "The Opener" among the blacks.

La Citadel, looming high above Cap Haitien like some hand-carved Gibraltar, is a monument to the lives of three men and a slave revolution. Still piled row after row are 12 pound cannon balls and hundreds of huge cannons scattered about the ramparts of La Citadel as though waiting for the return of Henri Christophe, its builder.

Before Toussaint L'Ouverture, Jacques Dessalines and Henri Christophe, the history of Haiti, then called Saint Domingue, could be summed up in one word: slavery. African slaves were first brought to Saint Domingue by the Spaniards in 1512 and at the turn of the 17th century they out-numbered their masters.

In 1630 the French came to the island and took control of the western side of Saint Domingue. With the sweat of the blacks they made their territory the richest European colonial possession, sending to France a steady stream of sugar, cotton and indigo. By the end of the 17th century, some 20,000 Frenchmen, 50,000 mulattoes and 2,000,000 blacks lived there in an uneasy balance. Caste and class separated the three groups. Complicating these divisions was the presence of the Spanish rule on the eastern half of the island. High, well-nigh impassable mountains sliced Saint Domingue in two parts.

While France itself was astir with talk of the rights of man and of freedom, equality and fraternity, autocratic governors-general held absolute sway over thousands of slaves who produced the wealth of Saint Domingue and over dissatisfied mulattoes who could own land, but had no political or social standing. When the Bastille fell in 1789, the island trembled as though in anticipation of some dreaded catastrophe. In this same year the mulattoes revolted. France then loosened its rule a bit and allowed the mulattoes to have seats in the new colonial assembly.

12

Warned of the plot by a native maid, Dessalines escaped by leaping through the window.

But the enslavement of the blacks continued, harsh and cruel as ever. As the revolution in France gained momentum, the far away island of Saint Domingue became increasingly restless. The blacks became fired with the desire for freedom and deep in the forest at night they gathered and plotted. The tom-tom language of the Africans told the blacks of the planned uprising.

On August 1, 1789, in the late night hours Boukmann, a voodoo priest, whose name and reputed deeds struck terror in the hearts of slaves, held a meeting of leaders. Among them was Francois Domingue Toussaint, known for his wisdom and respected for his learning. That night the conspirators plotted their revolt.

Eight days later, the entire 2,000 miles of French territory reverberated to the rhythm of hundreds of drums. The whites were terrified. With a mad sweep the blacks moved from village to village putting the torch to everything that would burn, and killing every white encountered. For weeks the sky glowed with the flames. More than 6000 coffee plantations and 200 sugar refineries went up in smoke. The French rallied their forces and finally routed the slaves. Boukmann, leader of the revolt, was captured at Cap Francois and his head was impaled on a pole to put fear in the hearts of the slaves.

Toussaint succeeded Boukmann as leader of the slaves and sought an honorable peace for the blacks, who had taken refuge in the forests. At the same time, across the ocean, France had declared war on Spain and England. Thus the French and Spanish halves of Saint Domingue were at war. Following the Arab dictum that "he who is the enemy of my enemy is my friend," Toussaint collected his forces and joined the Spaniards to war against the French army.

Second in command to Toussaint was Jacques Dessalines, a homely African who had been brought to the island as young slave but was virtually free because his master feared him.

The Spaniards equipped the slave rebels and they began attacking the French from the northern and eastern portion of the island. Aided by the Spanish, Toussaint drove the French forces from the area. France sent 3,000 soldiers to subdue Toussaint and his black Spartans, but they were soon overcome by the forces of Toussaint or the fever which spread throughout the island. Recognizing that it was helpless to control the revolt, France proclaimed an end to slavery.

Toussaint was not satisfied with the proclamation. He abandoned his Spanish allies and fought his way through the French territory, routing the enemy town after town. His victories won for him the nickname of L'Ouverture (the Opener) and the title of "General of Saint Domingue" for life. All of the blacks praised him and when he conquered Cap Francois, called him the "Deliverer." It was here that he was joined by Henri Christophe, a slave who was born in Grenada in 1767. As a mere boy Henri worked as a mason and later was bought by a Negro master who operated an inn where Christophe served as a waiter. In the army of L'Ouverture, Henri used his native ability to promote himself to the rank of Sergeant in short order.

After conquering all of the French territory, Toussaint established himself as Governor-General of Saint Domingue. Dessalines, his comrade in arms was made Governor of the province. Christophe had been elevated to the rank of General by this time and was made Governor of Cap Francois and the surrounding region. To the south of the island, a region predominately inhabited by the mulattoes, Alexander Sabes Petion ruled the prosperous peninsula.

Toussaint turned his attention to the tasks of peace, developing the island's natural resources and foreign trade. The island began to prosper. Trade with France was begun, for the revolt as seen by Toussaint, was not directed so much against the French as against the institution of slavery. Proving his lack of blind hatred for France, he sent his two sons to study in Paris.

Under Emperor Napoleon, France was conquering all Europe. Napoleon held a very low opinion of the black rulers of the former colony. He was determined to regain France's former rich possession. He saw the blacks as only savages whose numbers made their rule of the island possible. To reconquer the island, Napoleon ordered eighty-six ships built to carry 22,000 fighting men.

With Captain-General LeClerc in command, the mighty armada arrived in the waters of Saint Domingue in February, 1802. Its main force was directed at Cap Francois; other ships were stationed around the island to await the attack. LeClerc sent word to Christophe, Governor of Cap Francois, to prepare for his formal reception. Not having the approval of Toussaint, Christophe refused his entry.

The French forces attacked. Henri's veterans put up a valiant but fruitless fight. The peasants did not support the resistance, having been made indolent by the successes of their armies. Christophe, determined to leave Cap Francois a smoldering ruin, signalled the burning of the the city by first putting a torch to his own fabulous palace. He then fled with his troops to the hills. LeClerc, taking command of the Cap, decreed that all plantations be returned to their former French owners, and that slavery be re-instituted for all blacks. The latter decree jolted the peasants out of their indifference and they rushed to join Christophe.

Sensing that his military success was meaningless without the blacks, LeClerc declared all blacks free forever. He also offered Christophe and Dessalines general-ships in the French army and they accepted. The aged Toussaint L'Ouverture was retired with honor. But, LeClerc was insincere. On the pretext of having Toussaint meet with the French to discuss the final disposal of his troops, LeClerc had him captured and taken to France where in 1803 he died in prison. Then LeClerc planned to destroy Dessalines, but the plan failed when a maid learned of the plot and warned Dessalines, telling him of the plot in African sign language in the presence of his enemies.

News of the attempt on the life of Dessalines set off a new revolt. Saint Dominigue was again the scene of burnings and killings. This time the mulattoes joined the blacks and drove the French into the sea. Saint Domingue was proclaimed a Republic and given the Indian name of Haiti. Dessalines had himself named Governor of Haiti for life and his first act was to have all Frenchmen on the island put to death.

The blacks had no idea that Dessalines could be almost as cruel to them as he had been to the French. In short order his cruelty and tyranny proved too much for his own people and resulted in his assassination in 1806.

Henri Christophe became the new ruler of Haiti. He found himself the head of a poor war-torn country virtu-

He resumed construction on La Citadel which was started by Dessalines.

ally prostrate with strife and aimlessly floundering ex-slaves. Christophe negotiated with the United States and several European powers and offered them opportunities for commerce and trade. Declaring all green gourds the property of the state, Henri converted them into a medium of exchange. Before the end of 1807 the Gourds had been replaced by metal coins, which until this day are called Gourds.

Convinced that Haiti would gain more respect if it had a king, the assembly named Christophe, King Henri I in 1811. Moving ahead with his plans to rebuild and stabilize the kingdom, he created ranks of nobility and based the retention of titles on the productivity of the individual. Every boy over ten years of age was compelled to learn a trade. The state furnished the tools and technicians. Every facet of the economy was under central control.

Haiti prospered and within one year the new kingdom produced ten million pounds of sugar, twenty million pounds of coffee and five million pounds of cotton. These goods were exchanged with foreign powers for gold and made the economy of Haiti stable. Christophe built a small merchant fleet to transport the nation's produce.

Henri I was a master builder and within a short time seven of his palaces were built on his vast personal property. The most elaborate was Sans Souci. He resumed construction on La Citadel which was started by Dessalines. La Citadel was constructed on the highest mountain in the region of Cap Haitien some 300 feet above sea-level. This great fortress was built in the shape of an irregular square, with walls between 20 to 30 feet thick, towering skyward 130 feet. Three hundred and sixty-five bronze cannons capable of firing 12-pound balls surrounded the ramparts of La Citadel. The huge fortress was capable of accomodating 10,000 soldiers. To provide water, an enormous underground cistern was built and rain falling on the structure was collected in it.

Into the palace of San Souci went the most elegant furnishings and art treasures available from around the world. Although King Henri learned only to sign his name, he placed importance on education.

Christophe imitated Napolean in manner and dress...

With the fields glistening with abundant crops and palaces shining in the sun, Haiti again could be called the "Pearl of the Antilles." Beneath the outward show and activity, however, was dissatisfaction and resentment. Henri could not understand why every Haitian did not work as hard as he did. His increasing presure for production (and penalties for the lack of it), was resented by many. In addition, it was rumored that the King was motivated by ambition for personal gain. As before groups of malcontents plotted the death of Henri I.

Gaffie, Henri's chief executioner, beheaded so many of the plotters that he became adept to the point that he could remove the head of the condemned without soiling his shirt. Haitians swore that Henri was drunk with power and neither the bloody sword of Gaffie nor the high walls of La Citadel would stop the resistance.

King Henri I, while earning a grudging respect from other nations, had alienated himself from his own subjects, and his drive had taken its toll on him. In 1820 his body collapsed and he suffered a stroke which paralyzed his lower limbs. Rumors of his illiness swept the island. At Saint Marc, Henri's army officers on hearing the news of his illness felt themselves no longer bound by their oath of allegiance. Most islanders rejoiced that the King was disabled. The royal guards deserted their post at La Citadel on Cap Francois.

Christophe sensed that the end was near. He got his wife and daughters out of danger, but his son, Prince Victoire, was captured and murdered to put an end to the royal line of inheritance. On October 8, 1820 Henri had his worn-out body placed on a stretcher and secretly carried to La Citadel. Here, virtually alone, he put a pistol to his head and fired a silver bullet into his brain.

Toussaint L'Ouverture, Jacques Dessalines and Henri Christophe, all extraordinary men, loom like a triple-peaked mountain in the history of Haiti. La Citadel stands today as a monument to those champions of freedom and independence.

John W. Vandercook. *Black Majesty*, New York, 1928.

Crispus Attucks (-1770)

FIRST TO DIE FOR INDEPENDENCE

In 1775 Patrick Henry declared, "Give me liberty or give me death" . . . and died in bed 14 years later.

Earlier, in 1770, Crispus Attucks, a runaway slave, ex-seaman and common laborer, cried, "Do not be afraid" . . . and minutes later fell dead on the frozen ground of Boston Commons before the bullets of British soldiers— the first to die for independence.

The occasion of the death of Attucks and several other American colonists that night became known to history as the Boston Massacre. However, little is known about the first Negro patriot prior to that fateful night except that he had escaped from his master some 20 years earlier and secured work as a seaman. An account of his burial in the *Boston Gazette and Country* refers to him as a "stranger." He was described by the same paper as being "6 feet two inches high, short curl'd hair, his knees nearer-together than common," and was known to the townspeople as "the mulatto."

The Boston Massacre marked the turning point in the relations between England and the thirteen colonies from smoldering resentment and riots to open hostility and conflict. George III and his minions understood little of the frontier America and failed to see that it was not an English borough but a budding nation. In the manner of all tyrants, they dispatched troops to quell the rebellious colonists. Soon Boston and other cities were filled with British troops, and tension began to mount. The spring of 1770 was marked by street brawls and tavern fights.

At approximately nine o'clock on the night of March 5, 1770, as a result of a call for help from a beleagured British sentry, seven soldiers representing the might of King George III paraded toward the Commons with bayonets fixed. Crispus Attucks and 40 or 50 patriots waited at the head of the street armed with clubs and sticks. As the soldiers drew near Attucks yelled, "The way to get rid of these troops is to attack the main guard."

The Americans let loose a shower of sticks and stones. "Do not be afraid." they shouted, "They dare not fire."

The soldiers fell back. Suddenly there was the crackle of rifle fire. Tall, distinguishable by his color, and in the front ranks, Attucks was the first to fall.

As a symbol of resistance to tyranny, Attucks' death placed him among the immortals. Today his name tops the names of the five carved in the monument of granite and bronze erected to commemorate that historic night in Boston Commons.

Crispus Attucks. "The Story of Crispus Attucks," *Negro Digest*, July 1, 1963, pp. 46-49.

Jean Baptiste Pointe De Sable (1745-1818)

CHICAGO'S FIRST SETTLER

LAKE MICHIGAN

ESCHIKAGOU-1779

"A handsome and well educated Negro..."

Chicago, the city with the broad shoulders, a deep laugh and a twinkle in its eye, grew from a small settlement started in 1772 by Jean Baptiste Pointe De Sable, "a handsome, well-educated Negro," on the north bank of the Chicago River near the present location of the Wrigley building. De Sable was born in 1745, in St. Marc, Haiti and educated in France. He came to America in 1765, stopping first at New Orleans. With him came a lifelong friend and former classmate, Jacques Clemorgan, a native of Martinique.

De Sable and Clemorgan came to America seeking new business for the thriving company of De Sable and Son, in Haiti. Jean Baptiste was the son of a successful Haitian emigrant father from Marseilles, France and an ex-slave mother. New Orleans, a thriving city then under French control, funnelled furs and pelts of the midwest through the neck of the Mississippi to be carried abroad. Shortly after De Sable landed, the fortunes of war shifted New Orleans to Spanish control. He immediately left the city and went to St. Louis, another French controlled settlement up the Mississippi.

After two years in St. Louis where he and Clemorgan developed a bustling business with the Indians, a British take-over of this city led De Sable to move still farther north, near Peoria. Settling among the Peorias and Pota-watomis he took an Indian wife and came to know the great Indian chief, Pontiac.

In the course of his business, De Sable frequently traveled past Eschikagou (Chicago) to Detroit and Canada. In 1772 he decided to build a trading cabin on the Chicago River near Lake Michigan. After completing the cabin, he led his wife and a small band of Indians from Peoria to the settlement in Eschikagou. At the time Potawatomi Indians roamed the area. French fur traders passed through on their way back and forth between St. Louis and Canada. Indian trails were the only roads in this huge, virgin plain country. Indian canoes and French boateaux skirted the rim of Lake Michigan. French and English troops were skirmishing among the Indians, who, under the leadership of Pontiac, were unsuccessful in resisting them.

The settlement of Chicago grew and several structures were built. By 1800 the infant United States of America was claiming and parcelling out the Northwest territories. Dissatisfied with the changes brought about by the new government, De Sable sold his holdings and went back to Peoria for a short time. Later he moved to St. Charles, Missouri where he died on August 29, 1818.

A. T. Andreas. *History of Chicago*, Chicago, 1884; Shirley Graham. *Jean Baptiste Pointe De Sable*, New York, 1953.

Benjamin Banneker (1731-1806)

MATHEMATICAL WIZARD AND INVENTOR

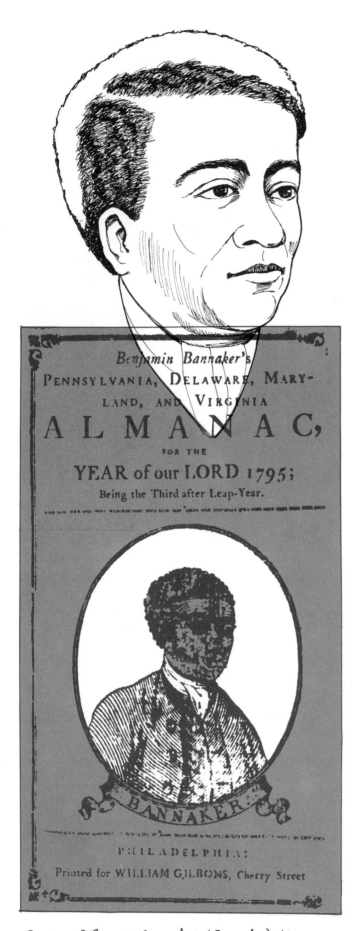

Cover of "Benjamin Bannaker's (Banneker) Almanac

Banneker, a free-born Negro, was an essayist, inventor, mathematician and lay astronomer, and because of his intellect, was called a "sable genius." Born on November 9, 1731 in Ellicott, Maryland, Benjamin Banneker was a self-taught mathematician and astronomer. While still a youth, he made a wooden clock which kept accurate time until he died. This clock is believed to be the first clock wholly made in America. In his forties, with the aid of books lent to him by the Ellicotts of Maryland, he became a proficient mathematician, able to solve any problems which were submitted to him. Deeply interested in natural phenomena, Banneker started publishing an almanac in 1791 and continued its publication until 1802. He published a treatise on bees, did a mathematical study of the cycle of the 17-year locust and became a pamphleteer for the peace movement.

His style of life was unusual. By night Banneker could be found wrapped in a cloak, studying the stars until dawn; by day he slept or worked on mathematical problems and received the curious, who came from near and far to see this strange genius. He never married but was always a most charming host, receiving one and all in his full suit of drab cloth and wearing his beaver hat and carrying his cane while showing visitors about his large farm which he subsequently sold in order to devote all of his time to his scientific pursuits.

Banneker was aware of slavery and its evils. In 1791, he wrote his famous letter to Thomas Jefferson in which he declared that if Jefferson's reputed liberalism were true, "I apprehend you will embrace every opportunity to eradicate that train of absurd and false ideas and opinions which so generally prevail with respect to us (Negroes); and that your sentiments are concurrent with mine which are: that one universal Father hath given being to us all; that He not only made us all of one flesh, but that He hath also without partiality afforded us all with the same faculties and that, however variable we may be in society or religion, however diversified in situation or color, we are all the same family and stand in the same relation to Him."

The intellect, insight and ability of this untrained and unschooled genius caused Jefferson, as they had others, to spread the name of Banneker across the seas. Banneker died in 1806, with the shadow of slavery deepening across the land. The significance of Banneker's life lay in it's dramatization to a slave-holding nation that Negroes are a part of the human family. This sable genius' life did not end slavery, but it did indicate to even the most skeptical the possibilities within the Negro when left free and unfettered.

Benjamin Brawley. *Negro American Writers*, Chapel Hill, 1935, pp. 74-77; Sauran Morris. "A Sketch of the Life of Benjamin Banneker", *Proceedings of the Maryland Historical Society*, 1854, Baltimore, 1854.

Paul Cuffe (1759-1817)

EARLY BUSINESSMAN AND COLONIZER

Paul Cuffe was one of the most unusual of all the men from New Bedford, Massachusetts who went down to the sea in ships. Unlike most Negroes who sailed in those days, Cuffe was no mere deck-hand or roustabout, but a ship-owner and businessman. He owned several ships and made his living hauling cargo to different parts of the world.

Starting with a small boat built with his own hands, Cuffe became the owner of sloops, schooners, brigs, and several other ships of various sizes, the largest being the 268-ton *Alpha* which, in 1806, he and a crew of nine Negroes sailed from Wilmington, Delaware, to Savannah, Georgia and thence to Gothenburg, Sweden. Six years before this, Paul Cuffe sailed the 162-ton *Hero* around the Cape of Good Hope.

Fearless, capable and energetic, Paul Cuffe at one point owned one regular ship, two brigs and several parcels of land. After spending considerable sums of money on various projects, Cuffe was able to leave an estate of over $20,000.

However, Cuffe was not solely interested in making money. As a free Negro whose father had been a slave, the status of Negroes in New Bedford and elsewhere was of paramount concern to him. One of Cuffe's earliest acts was to have the family name Slocum changed to Cuffe, for Slocum was the name of his father's master. At this time Cuffe was seventeen years of age. Two years later he and a brother, John Cuffe, sued in the Massachusetts courts for the right to vote. The suit was unsuccessful but it did help make possible legislation to achieve the same end several years later.

Going to sea at the age of sixteen, Paul Cuffe was able to purchase a $3500 farm in 1797 for himself and his Indian wife, Alice Pequit. While granting the vote by this time, New Bedford still had no schools for the off-spring of free Negroes. At his own expense Paul Cuffe built a school on his farm and with money out of his own pocket, hired a teacher for free Negro children.

A Quaker and a Negro, Paul Cuffe had a double interest in the freedom of the Negro. Enlightened opinion at this time generally favored colonization as the answer to the incipient racial problem. In 1811 Paul Cuffe sailed one of his ships, the *Traveller*, from Westport, Massachusetts to Sierra Leone, Africa where he founded the Friendly Society for the emigration of free Negroes from America. The War of 1812 interrupted his colonization plans, but in 1815 he took thirty-eight Negroes to Sierra Leone at a cost of $4,000 from his personal funds.

Cuffe planned many more trips with black colonists but his health failed and he died in 1817.

H. N. Sherwood. "Paul Cuffe", *Journal of Negro History*, VIII (April, 1923), pp. 153-229.

Prince Hall (1735-1807)
FRATERNAL LEADER

Prince Hall was the founder of the oldest social organization among Negroes in America. Today's Prince Hall Masonic order goes back to the seedtime of the Republic. While almost all Negroes are acquainted with the Prince Hall Masons, and their social and charitable activities, very little is known about Prince Hall.

Prince Hall, the founder of the first Masonic Lodge, came from Barbadoes, British West Indies. Born in 1735, he was the son of an English father and a free Negro woman, At the age of twelve, he was apprenticed to a leather merchant. After a few years, Hall gave up his apprenticeship and, following a variety of jobs, finally came to Boston, Massachusetts in 1765. Working in and around Boston, he saved enough money to buy property and to become a voter. During his spare time he educated himself.

In 1774, Prince Hall joined the Methodist church and eventually became a minister and the leader of the small Negro community then in Boston. When the American Revolution reached the shooting stage, he petitioned John Hancock of the Committee of Safety for the Colonies to allow him to join the Continental Army. This petition was approved by George Washington himself.

On March 6, 1775, at Hall's initiative, he and fourteen other Negroes were inducted into a British Chartered Lodge of Freemasons at Boston Harbor. After the Revolutionary War in 1787, Prince Hall and his fellow Masons were chartered as African Lodge No. 459. Four years later, an African Grand Lodge was formed and Prince Hall elected Master. In 1797, Hall organized African Lodges in Philadelphia and Rhode Island. After Hall's death in 1807, Negro Masons decided to change the name of their organization from the African Grand Lodge to the Prince Hall Grand Lodge.

Hall's interests were not restricted to Lodge activities. He took a deep interest in the general status of Negroes in Boston and elsewhere. As early as 1776 he urged the Massachusetts legislature to support the cause of emancipation. He successfully prodded the city of Boston to provide schools for free Negro children in 1797.

The hundreds of Lodges throughout the country may be seen as a monument to Prince Hall who adopted America as his home.

Harold van Voorhis. *Negro Masonry in the United States*, New York, 1940, pp. 7-13; Harry E. Davis. "Documents Relating to Negro Masonry in America", *Journal of Negro History*, XXI (October, 1936), pp. 411-432.

James Forten (1766-1842)
FORGOTTEN ABOLITIONIST

A powder boy in the infant American navy at fifteen, foreman in a sail loft at twenty, James Forten was one of the vigorous opponents of colonization and slavery during the early years of the 19th century. He was one of the driving forces behind the Negro Convention movement which gave voice to the opinions and ideas of free Negroes in the North long before Frederick Douglass.

James Forten's opposition to slavery and colonization was implacable, and unbending. Within twenty years after being made the foreman in the sail loft, Forten was its owner, employing forty men, white and Negro. Amassing over $100,000 from his business, he threw his great energy and shrewdness into the struggle for the rights of free Negroes. His loyalty to the United States was unquestioned, for during the War of 1812, he personally recruited 2,500 Negroes to help guard Philadelphia when the city appeared threatened by the British. In 1813 he wrote "A Series of Letters by a Man of Color" opposing proposed legislation requiring the registration of all Negroes in Philadelphia.

When William Lloyd Garrison started his newspaper, *The Liberator*, James Forten solicited many of its 1700 Negro subscribers. Although Richard Allen's name appears as Chairman on the record of the first Negro Convention (held in Philadelphia in 1830), Forten was one of the prime movers making the convention possible.

On several occasions James Forten used Richard Allen's church, Bethel, to address the city's Negroes on issues of the day, including proposals made by the American Colonization Society which was trying to interest free Negroes to return to Africa. Over and over he drove home the idea that America was now the home of the Negro.

Although uneducated in a formal sense, his writings reveal a vigorous mind and his deeds show him as he was —an uncomprising advocate of freedom and equality for men of color. Due to his influence, anti-slavery groups had a clear idea of what most Negroes of his era desired: the right to live as truly free men in America.

Roy Allen Billington. "James Forten: Forgotten Abolitionist", *Negro History Bulletin*, November, 1949, pp. 1-6; Benjamin Brawley. *A Short History of the Negro in America*, New York, pp. 36-37; Richard Bardoplh. *The Negro Vanguard*, New York, 1961, pp. 40-41.

David Walker (1785-1830)
"APPEAL TO THE SLAVES"

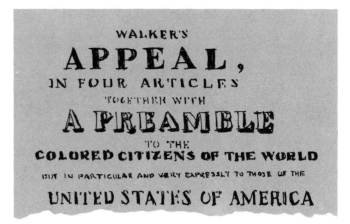

In 1829, David Walker published his first edition of *Appeal*. In it he proclaimed to the slaves, ". . . it is no more harm for you to kill the man who is trying to kill you, than it is for you to take a drink of water."

The *Appeal* exploded with shattering force in the North and in the South. Anti-slavery leaders of both races rejected the violence advocated in Walker's publication and he was forced to circulate it at his own risk and expense. In the South its circulation was deemed a capital offense but this did not stop it. The Governor of Massachusetts, the state in which Walker lived, was asked to supress it, but refused. A reward was then offered for Walker; $1,000 dead or $10,000 delivered alive.

"I will stand my ground. Somebody must die in this cause. I may be doomed to the stake and the fire or to the scaffold tree, but it is not in me to falter if I can promote the work of emancipation." Thus spoke David Walker in answer to the pleas of his wife and friends who urged him to go to Canada to escape the wrath brought upon himself by his stirring publication.

His courage and determination had deep roots. David was born in Wilmington, North Carolina, a border state, in 1785 while the Revolutionary War phrases of "liberty" and "pursuit of happiness" were still echoing faintly in the air. His mother was free, which entitled him to the status of free-born, but his father, Merel Walker, was a slave. Young David hated slavery with all his heart. He finally left home and wandered to Boston where he became a permanent resident and in 1827 opened a second-hand clothing store.

David Walker was self-taught and read extensively the literature on human slavery, concentrating on the history of resistance to oppression. *Appeal* became one of the most widely read and circulated books written by a Negro. Following its third edition in 1830, Walker died and foul play was suspected. The *Appeal* was the only work produced by Walker, but up to that time it was the boldest attack by a Negro writer against slavery in America.

Herbert Aptheker. *A Documentary History of the Negro People in the United States*, New York, 1962 (Paperback), pp. 90, 93-97; Richard Bardolph. *The Negro Vanguard*, New York, 1961, pp. 41, 55.

Denmark Vesey (1767-1822)
ANTI-SLAVERY INSURRECTIONIST

Telemarque—known to history as Denmark Vesey—is one of those leaders who made history because of his hopes and not because of his deeds. Denmark Vesey is popularly known as a leader of a slave "revolt" in Charleston, South Carolina—a "revolt" which never got beyond the planning stage. For his plan and ideas, Telemarque and thirty-four other Negroes were hanged.

Telemarque's life was filled with melancholy irony. As a slave, for over twenty years he sailed with his master, one Captain Vesey, to the Virgin Islands and Haiti, which was then ruled by free black men. Telemarque was Captain Vesey's property but moved about the streets of Charleston like a free man. He secured his own freedom by winning a $1,500 lottery, $600 of which he used to buy himself from his master. He tried to purchase his children but was unable to do so.

Born in 1767, at an early age Telemarque was sold by Captain Vesey but later was re-purchased because he suffered from epilepsy. As Captain Vesey's constant companion, Telemarque learned much about the nature of freedom and of business. When he became free, he applied his experience and knowledge to his own business ventures and soon prospered.

Telemarque wanted more than anything to secure the freedom of his people. Partly because of his ability to read and write, and partly because the church was the one place where one could speak to large numbers of Negroes without questioning by the whites, Telemarque became a Methodist minister. In short order his home was made a regular meeting place. Money was collected to buy arms. Telemarque had a blacksmith make a large number of daggers and bayonets. A white barber sympathetic to his plans was engaged to fashion wigs and whiskers out of European hair, so that his mulatto conspirators could penetrate the heart of the city and seize control when the time came. Zero hour was set for the second Sunday in July of 1822.

Everything was in readiness, when suddenly the whole scheme had to be advanced to June 16. The plans which were two years in the making had been revealed to the whites by a Negro whom Telemarque had felt he could trust. In a twinkling, Charleston was an armed camp. The whites rounded up hundreds of Negroes believed to be involved in the plot. Telemarque went into hiding, but after two days was discovered and taken captive.

A local tribunal, operating as judge and jury heard condemning testimony from scores of witnesses. Telemarque had a good lawyer and during the trial showed himself adept at cross-examining witnesses, but there was no doubt that he was planning the overthrow of the city. For this he was sentenced to be hanged along with thirty-four other Negroes. Four whites who had aided them were fined and imprisoned.

Two days before Independence Day, 1822, Telemarque—Denmark Vesey—died on the gallows.

Herbert Aptheker. *American Negro Slave Revolts*, New York, 1943, pp. 268-272.

Nat Turner (1800-1831)
ANTI-SLAVERY REVOLUTIONIST

Nat Turner, the Black Prophet, was a strange man, given to seeing visions and hearing voices, to feelings of religious exaltation and dire prophecies. From his earliest years, he felt himself to be destined for great deeds. He was intelligent and experimented with making paper, gunpowder, pottery and the like. A strangely mystical turn of mind led him to fast and pray; he learned to read the Bible; he reported visions of black and white angels locked in fatal combat high in the heavens. Voices constantly told him that he was too wise to be a slave. All of these abilities and ideas came to a head one day in August of 1831.

After months of secret meetings in churches, at picnics, and in swamps, Nat Turner and a small band decided to strike. Southampton, Virginia was a lazy, placid community where thousands of seemingly contented slaves toiled in the hot August sun. Nearby was the great Dismal Swamp, a densely foliaged bog. Turner's plan was to conquer Southampton county, as the white men did in the Revolution, and then retreat, if necessary, to the Dismal Swamp.

A short, powerfully built person of dark mulatto complexion, Turner was then almost thirty years old. The year of his birth had witnessed the Haitian Revolt, and he had heard hushed talk of Denmark Vesey's revolt in South Carolina. Now Turner's hour of destiny was at hand. His co-conspirators now numbered six. These six set out to conquer Virginia from within. With the righteous determination of a zealot, Turner and his band began moving from one house of whites to another, killing everyone in sight. The little band of black insurrectionists increased to fifteen, forty and finally sixty, armed with muskets, axes and scythes. Household after household felt the swing of axes, the sweep of the scythes and the blasts of the muskets, as the group made its awesome way across Southampton county. For forty-eight hours, Turner and his men roamed the plantations, leaving dead a total of fifty-five whites. Finally, he decided to attack the county seat, Jerusalem, where he hoped to find additional arms and ammunition, plus money. Enroute, he reluctantly agreed to pause for reinforcement. This pause proved his undoing, for a posse of whites met and dispersed the daring insurgents. Fleeing in many directions, Turner's group was later re-assembled. Again they were discovered and routed, this time never again to be reunited except at their trial. Nat Turner fled to the Dismal Swamp where he stayed for over six weeks, before he was at last spotted and captured.

All of Southampton was terror stricken. All slaves were suspects; hundreds were shot down at random. No plantation felt itself safe. Turner and those of his band who were captured alive were brought to trial. Seventeen were hanged, including Nat Turner; twelve convicted and sent out of state, twenty were acquitted, and four free Negroes were dismissed as being innocent.

Rayford Logan. "Nat Turner, Fiend or Martyr", *Opportunity*, IX, 1931; "Denmark Vesey", *Dictionary of American Biography*, XIX, 1936, pp. 258-259.

William Still (1821-1902)
UNDERGROUND RAILROAD LEADER

LIBERTY LINE.
NEW ARRANGEMENT---NIGHT AND DAY.

The improved and splendid Locomotives, Clarkson, and Lundy, with their trains fitted up in the best style of accommodation for passengers, will run their regular trips during the present season, between the borders of the Patriarchal Dominion and Libertyville, Upper Canada. Gentlemen and Ladies, who may wish to improve their health or circumstances, by a northern tour; are respectfully invited to give us their patronage.

SEATS FREE, *irrespective of color.*

Necessary Clothing furnished gratuitously to such as have "*fallen among thieves.*"

"Hide the outcasts—let the

☞For seats apply at the conductor of the train.

N. B. For the special benefit Officers, an extra heavy wagon f nished, whenever it may be nece will be forwarded as dead freight, t cals," always at the risk of the ow.

☞Extra Overcoats provided for are afflicted with protracted *chilly-pho*

Of all the Underground Railroad stations dotting the North, perhaps the busiest and most efficient was run by William Still, Secretary of the Pennsylvania Society for the Abolition of Slavery. During his fourteen years as an official of the Society, William Still was awakened hundreds of times in the middle of the night to give refuge to escaping slaves. He kept his big house stocked with food and clothing for the runaways bound for freedom.

Because secrecy was an absolute necessity, information is vague and imprecise regarding the extent of the underground railroad. However, Still kept meticulous records of the fugitives so that relatives and friends might locate them. For a time these records were hidden in a cemetery and later published in a book, *The Underground Railroad*. By his own count, he aided 649 slaves to freedom.

Extremely able and vigorous, William was the last of eighteen children of slaves Levin and Sidney. Levin Steel bought his own freedom and left his native Maryland for New Jersey. His wife, Sidney, escaped and on joining her husband, changed the family name to Still and her given name to Charity. She left two young children in bondage during her escape.

This family experience made a deep impression on William. In the year 1844 he left the family farm in New Jersey and went to Philadelphia, arriving with no friends and only five dollars in his pocket. He taught himself to read and write. Three years after arriving, he was named Secretary of the Pennsylvania Abolition Society, then a very small group of whites. In order to offer practical aid to the slaves, the Society needed someone who knew the Negro community well. Still performed his chores so well that the Society elected him chairman in 1851 and he served for ten years.

Acting as a conductor of the Underground Railroad was only part of Still's activities. He helped organize and finance a "social, civil and statistical association" to collect data on the Negro. Through his efforts an orphanage for the offspring of colored soldiers and sailors was set up in Philadelphia. The energetic Mr. William Still was one of the organizers of the first Y.M.C.A. for his people in America.

In 1860 after retiring from the chairmanship of the Abolition Society, he went into the stove business with great success. Later he branched out into the coal business as a retailer in 1865 and earned a modest fortune. An indication of financial and business acumen is evident in the fact that he was elected to the Board of Trade in Philadelphia. He remained active until his death in 1902.

"William Still", *Dictionary of American Biography*, XVIII, 1935, p. 22; William Still. *The Underground Railroad*, Philadelphia, 1872.

Harriet Tubman (1826-1913)

"BLACK MOSES OF HER RACE"

Strong as a man, brave as a lion, cunning as a fox was Harriet Tubman who, unable to read or write, made nineteen journeys into the Deep South and spirited over 300 slaves to freedom. Harriet Tubman, a medium-size, smiling woman, was the leading "conductor" of the Underground Railroad over which countless thousands of nameless slaves fled from bondage. The Underground Railroad was neither a railroad nor underground, but a system for helping slaves to escape. By moving from one friendly hand to the next, from house to house, from church to church, on foot, by horseback, wagons, trains, passing through slave state after slave state they reached the freedom of Ohio, New England or Canada. By day and by night, summer and winter, escaping slaves took the Underground Railroad to the North.

It was dangerous for anyone to help the slaves as most states had severe penalties for aiding "property" to escape. It was doubly dangerous for a Negro female to go South and lead slaves North, for she could lose her own freedom and herself become enslaved. To the dauntless Harriet Tubman, these considerations were as nothing. Every possible trick and disguise were used by her to help the slaves. On several occasions, at gun-point, Harriet forced wavering slaves onward. "You'll be free or die," she quietly commanded.

Slaveowners and their agents looked high and low for her but she always managed to elude them. Once on a train she was almost caught but, pretending to read a newspaper and hoping that she held it right side up, Harriet Tubman was overlooked, for her pursuers knew she could not read. Her luck held and she remained free.

Born in Maryland in 1826, Harriet Tubman herself escaped from her master and went to New York. In her own words, she described her first taste of liberty: "I was free and I couldn't believe it. There was such a glory all around and the sun was shining through the trees and on the hills. I was free!"

During the Civil War, Harriet Tubman served both as a nurse and a spy for the Union. When she died in 1913 she was buried in Ohio with military honors.

Sarah Bradford, *Harriet Tubman: The Moses of Her People.* New York, 1961

Sojourner Truth (1797-1885)
"A PILGRIM OF FREEDOM"

PROCLAIM LIBERTY T̶ THE
LAND UNTO ALL THE IN̶ ̶OF

She began life as Isabella but lived it as Sojourner Truth. She was the first Negro woman orator to speak out against slavery. Although unable to read or write, she traveled through Connecticut, Massachusetts, through Ohio, Indiana, Illinois and Kansas, speaking to tens, hundreds and thousands of people, both Negro and white. Sojourner felt herself a "Pilgrim of God" whose one mission was to free her people from slavery.

At a time when oratory was a fine art, Sojourner Truth, through her strong character and acid intelligence, was among the best and most famous anti-slavery speakers of her day. She met most of the outstanding white abolitionists such as Gerit Smith, Parker Pillsbury, Lyman and Harriet Beecher Stowe, she was received by Abraham Lincoln at the White House. Only Frederick Douglass outshone her in eloquence.

She began life as a slave and, after running away to freedom, worked as a domestic. Not until 1843 did she feel an overpowering urge to speak out against slavery. Already deeply religious, Sojourner, in the spring of that year, suddenly felt reborn. In her own words she declared, "I felt so tall within—I felt as if the power of the nation was with me." Isabella then renamed herself Sojourner Truth, and on foot, set out to "gather in the flock," speaking out against slavery and for women's suffrage. Her deep, bass voice, her fierce intelligence, sense of drama and the utter sincerity of her speeches quickly spread her fame throughout the North and astounded an unbelieving South.

Frequently efforts were made to silence her. She was beaten and stoned but nothing could stop her. Sleeping where she could, working only enough to keep soul and body together, Sojourner thundered against slavery from countless rostrums. She wore across her chest, a satin banner bearing the words, "Proclaim liberty throughout the land unto all the inhabitants thereof." Because of her daring, strength, and almost hypnotic control over an audience, some doubted her, the mother of five children, to be a woman. Once when a heckler, in the middle of one of Sojourner's speeches dared her to prove that she was a woman, Sojourner ripped her blouse to the waist and declared that it was to his shame, not hers, that such

a question should be raised. Deeply compelled to wander from state to state, Sojourner lived up to her new name, staying in one place only long enough to proclaim the truth and move on.

Hertha Pauli. *God's Faithful Pilgrim*, New York, 1958; Saunders Redding. *The Lonesome Road*, New York, 1958, pp. 65-74.

Frederick A. Douglass (1817-1895)

GOLDEN TROMBONE OF ABOLITION

The first day of 1863 was bitter and cold. The 3,000 abolitionists and free Negroes gathered in Tremont Temple, Boston were excited and waited impatiently for news from Washington, D. C. Among those in the hall were Harriet Beecher Stowe, William Wells Brown and Frederick A. Douglass, people whose lives had been dedicated to bringing about this moment. The crowd had gathered early and passed the time with oratory and singing. Douglass, the greatest orator of them all, had spoken and now he, too, was waiting with the rest. Into the hall burst a man shouting, "It is coming, it's on the wires, the Telegram is coming in!" The Telegram was news of the Emancipation Proclamation, now taking effect. The crowd quickly translated the Telegram into song:

Sound loud the timbrel o'er Egypt's dark sea
Jehovah has triumphed: His people are free!

Four million black men and women would soon be free. Not all of them and not all at the same time but, inevitably, all one day would be free.

For Frederick A. Douglass, already a free man, this night was the high point of his life. From Tremont Temple, Douglass could look back on a life which had begun in slavery and obscurity. Rising like some bronze Phoenix, Douglass for years had been the golden trombone of abolition, ever pressing for the freedom of his fellow Negroes. No one knows just how this ex-slave, ship caulker, wood cutter, coal handler and odd job man, almost over-

night, became the spokesman of his race. Born in 1817 on Maryland's hard scrabble, Eastern shore, Frederick Augustus Bailey as a child often had to fight with dogs over bones in order to get enough food. His rebellious spirit kept him in trouble with his master and once he was whipped each week for six months in an effort to break his indomitable spirit. Exasperated, his master sold him when he was ten years old. When Frederick Augustus Bailey was 21, he escaped and went to New Bedford, Massachusetts, the city of Paul Cuffe. Here he finally learned to read and write and to know that there were many others who felt slavery to be wrong.

In 1841, now a married man, Frederick Augustus Bailey changed his name to Douglass and began to attend meetings of the various anti-slavery societies, telling of his experiences as a slave. The Massachusetts Anti-slavery Society engaged him as lecturer and expected him to tell simply what had happened to him and leave the broader issues to others, such as William Lloyd Garrison and the society general agent, William Collins. But like Garrison, Douglass determined that he would be heard. "It did not entirely satisfy me to narrate wrongs. I felt like denouncing them." From this point forward, Douglass traveled all over New England and much of the North. His travels were not without hardship and danger, for he was still a fugitive slave. Nor was the North itself completely sympathetic with his cause. In Pendleton, Indiana for example, he was beaten unconscious and left for

Frederick A. Douglass

Home of Frederick Douglass, Washington, D.C.

Anna Murray Douglass, Wife

dead by a white mob. Undaunted, Douglass continued to denounce the evils of slavery.

It was perhaps in the crucible of the anti-slavery lecture circuit that the real education of Douglass was earned. So great was Douglass' skill as an orator, his fame soon overshadowed that of other able Negro spokesmen such as Charles Remond and Henry Highland Garnett, and even caused tension between himself and some of his white colleagues. Three things contributed to his success as a spokesman: the inherent justice of his cause in a North growing increasingly doubtful of the wisdom of slavery, the vigor of his oratory, and the drama of his person. A powerfully-built, strong-featured mulatto with a huge leonine head, Douglass' bearing was nobility itself. James Russell Lowell said that "the very look of Douglass was an irresistible logic against the oppression of his race."

In 1845 against the advice of his friends, Douglass decided to write an account of his life, fully aware of the possibility that this would mark him as the "Bailey, runaway slave of Thomas Auld." When his *Narrative of the Life and Times of Frederick Douglass* appeared in this same year, Douglass went to England and continued to speak out against slavery. English friends raised money to secure his formal freedom from his old master and two years later Douglass returned to America to start a newspaper, first called *The North Star*, and later *Frederick Douglass' Paper*. In his own words, Douglass managed "to keep my anti-slavery banner steadily flying during all the [slavery] conflict from the autumn of 1847 till the Union of the states was assured and Emancipation was a fact accomplished."

Shifting slowly from the spoken to the printed word, Douglass now moved even closer to direct action. In 1848 he joined the short-lived Liberty Party. During the early winter of 1850, he met with John Brown before his raid on Harper's Ferry and cautioned the latter, declaring that "from insurrection nothing can be expected but imprisonment and death." Douglass' prediction came true and Douglass himself had to live in Canada for a while.

When the impending crisis finally erupted in outright war, Frederick Douglass urged Lincoln to free the slaves and arm Negroes. He also recruited Negroes for the Union armies, among them his own sons.

When the Union emerged victorious, Douglass turned his attention to the status of the freedmen, urging education as a way out. Many of these ideas were read by Booker T. Washington and embodied in Tuskegee Institute. Douglass was also quite interested in universal suffrage, women's rights, and world peace. He held a variety of offices with the U. S. government, including that of Recorder of Deeds, Washington D.C. and Minister to Haiti.

Frederick Augustus Douglass lived until 1895 and saw the pendulum of history swing from slavery toward the beginning of freedom.

Frederick Douglass. *Narrative of the Life of Frederick Douglass, An American Slave*, Boston, 1845; Frederick Douglass. *Life and Times of Frederick Douglass*, Hartford, 1887.

III FROM THE CIVIL WAR FORWARD

They Lift Their Heads High

When the Civil War began Frederick Douglass boldly voiced the sentiments of many free Negroes and slaves. He declared that "never since the world began was a better chance offered to a long-enslaved and oppressed people. The opportunity is given us to be men." Douglass went further to urge that "colored troops from the North be enlisted and permitted to share the danger and honor of upholding the government."

In less than a year the First South Carolina Regiment was organized by Major General David Hunter in May of 1862 and later made a memorable record under the leadership of Thomas Wentworth Higginson. This regiment was composed of ex-slaves. The Fifty-Fourth Massachusetts Regiment, composed of free Negro volunteers, under the command of Colonel Robert Gould Shaw, is mentioned in all accounts of the Civil War because of the exceptional valor of its personnel. Serving with the Fifty-Fourth Massachusetts was Sergeant William H. Carney, a standard bearer who kept the Union flag from touching the ground during the furious attack on Fort Wagner. In the Union attack on Fort Hudson in Mississippi, the eight Negro regiments involved were conspicuous by their bravery. Here another standard bearer, Anselmas Plancianois, made his famous remark: "Colonel, I will bring these colors to you in honor or report to God the reason why."

The Negro troops were not all standard bearers. They performed a variety of tasks. Many of them were spies who knew the Southern terrain better than their white counterparts. Some of them built fortifications. Tens of thousands of Negroes fought as soldiers not only at Fort Wagner in South Carolina, and Fort Hudson but also at Petersburg, Virginia, Milliken's bend in Louisiana, Fort Pillow in Tennessee and many other places.

The consequences of the Negro's participation in the Civil War went far beyond combat. The Negro soldier learned military discipline. He became accustomed to giving and executing orders. Many learned to read for the first time. For many, also, the military banks, which served as depositories for their pay, gave them their first opportunities for systematic saving.

Nearly 200,000 Negroes served in the Union Army; three-fourths of them were ex-slaves. As a group they were competent soldiers. Abraham Lincoln's appraisal of their effectiveness, made on December 8, 1863, has been borne out in the reviews of later historians: "So far as tested, it is difficult to say they are not as good soldiers as any." Ulysees S. Grant was enthusiastic in his praise of the courage and bravery of these troops. Over thirty-six thousand Negro soldiers gave their lives in the fight for the abolition of slavery and the salvation of the Union.

The Northern victory in the Civil War was the end of slavery in America and the beginning of freedom for the Negro. Representing the aspirations of the four million ex-slaves were hundreds of Negroes who rose to positions of leadership during the Reconstruction era. Most of them were ministers. Many of them had been soldiers. Some had been school teachers; others had been employees of the Freedmen's Bureau. Some were ex-slaves as in the case of Robert Smalls of South Carolina. They were all concerned with the situation of the Negro and the future of the South.

At the national level, several Negroes, notably Henry Highland Garnet, Frederick Douglass, John Smyth and Ebenezer D. Bassett represented the United States abroad. Two able Negroes, James Matthews and James Trotter, were Recorders of Deeds in Washington, D.C.

Twenty-two Negroes were elected to Congress from the South. In addition to those treated in this book, Jeremiah Haralson, Henry P. Cheatham, Robert C. DeLarge, John A. Hyman, Alonzo J. Ransier, Thomas E. Miller, Charles E. Nash, James O'Hara, Joseph T. Rainey, Benjamin S. Turner, Joseph T. Walls, George H. White and George W. Murray sat in the nation's highest legislative body. (Brief biographical sketches of these men may be found in the comprehensive *Biographical Directory of the American Congress: 1774-1961.*)

The belief that the Negro dominated Southern politics after the Civil War has been more of a myth than a reality. Only in the state of South Carolina did the Negro approach anything resembling control. The state's first legislature following the Civil War consisted of eighty-seven Negroes and forty whites. Two Negroes were lieutenant governors —Alonzo Ransier in 1870 and Richard H. Graves in 1874. Francis L. Cardozo was successively secretary of state and state treasurer. Jonathan J. Wright was an associate justice of the state supreme court for seven years. Six Negroes went to Congress from South Carolina.

On the other hand, in the state of Mississippi where the Negroes were a majority of the population, there were forty Negro lawmakers in a state legislature of 115 men. In Louisiana three Negroes served as Lieutenant Governor; Oscar J. Dunn, P. S. B. Pinchback and C. C. Antoine. W. G. Brown was superintendent of public instruction and Antoine Dubuclet was state treasurer.

Most of the Negroes who came to public notice already had some experience in civic affairs. Many of them had been members of constitutional conventions in states seeking re-admission to the Union. Others had been state senators, representatives, sheriffs and tax assessors. As a group they did yeoman service in a chaotic South. Northern neglect and Southern hostility drove them from public life by the end of the nineteenth century. Speaking of the Negro's performance during these early years of freedom, James G. Blaine declared that "the colored men who took seats in both the Senate and the House did not appear to be ignorant or helpless. They were as a rule studious, earnest, ambitious men, whose public conduct . . . would be honorable to any race."

Dudley Taylor Cornish. *The Sable Arm,* New York, 1956, pp. 27, 285-291; John Hope Franklin. *Reconstruction—After the Civil War,* Chicago, 1961, pp. 84-103, 127-173; John Hope Franklin. *From Slavery to Freedom* (2nd Ed.), New York, 1961, pp. 267-275, 286-290.

Robert Smalls (1839-1915)

The *Planter*, a dispatch and transport vessel of the Confederacy, lay at anchor in Charleston Harbor. Its captain and officers, weary from a full day of hauling guns from Cole's Island to James Island, had gone ashore to relax amid the merriment occasioned by the outbreak of war between the North and South. Captain Ripley left Robert Smalls and eight members of the crew on board the *Planter*. Smalls and his fellow crewmen were slaves, pressed into service as deckhands and laborers aboard ships of the Southern fleet. Robert Smalls knew well the treacherous waters between Morris Island and Fort Royal where the vessels of the infant Southern fleet operated. As soon as the captain left the decks, Smalls began to put into operation a plan which had long been fermenting in his active mind.

He waited until four A.M. during which time his wife and two children were smuggled aboard. Putting the crew to work, Robert Smalls got the *Planter* underway. He was sure that if any errors were made in any portion of his plans, certain death was the only possible outcome. His plan was simple: deliver a vessel to the Union fleet and he would have his freedom. The odds were high, but so were the possible rewards. Fort Sumter was heavily armed. Successfully running a gantlet of cannons was no guarantee that he would safely reach the blockading Northern fleet. Between him and the nearest Yankee vessels stood the guns of Fort Sumter and Morris Island.

Even if Smalls succeeded in getting the vessel past these two obstacles, there was the chance that the ship would be mistaken for a hostile southern vessel and be fired upon. This was a chance he chose to take.

As the ship neared the Fort, cannons could be seen, silhouetted against the night. The night watch idly glanced at the passing vessel. No one could mistake the huge straw hat worn by Captain Ripley or the manner in which he leaned out the window of the pilot house with his arms folded. On the other hand, no one on the Fort had the slightest idea that, under the hat, was not the *Planter's* captain but an audacious slave of twenty-two, stealing one of their most valuable ships from under their very noses. When it became clear that Captain Ripley was not on the ship, the Fort frantically signalled Morris Island to intercept the *Planter*, but by this time, the ship was beyond the reach of shells. As the *Planter*, with its slave captain and crew, neared the Federal squadron, Robert Smalls ran up a small white truce flag and drew near enough to explain his mission.

The *Planter* was thus turned over to the Northern forces. Smalls was taken aboard another ship, the *Crusader*, where a few months later, at Simmons Bluff, he served as pilot. Subsequently both the *Planter* and the *Crusader* engaged in a sharp battle with Confederate artillery and infantry and the southerners were completely routed.

NAVIGATOR, SLAVE-HERO, CONGRESSMAN

The capture of the *Planter* itself was the war's most daring exploit up to this point. The ship was invaluable to the North. It was in good condition and worth over $60,000. Flag Officer Dupont said of Robert Smalls, "This man Robert Smalls is superior to any who have come into our lines—intelligent as many of them have been." The *Dictionary of American Biography* states; "This daring exploit gave him national fame. He was made a pilot in the U.S. Navy and given a share of the prize money."

Smalls continued to pilot both the *Planter* and the *Crusader*. When the *Planter* was sailing through heavy Confederate fire, the Captain panicked and deserted the ship. Pilot Smalls calmly took command of the vessel and carried it out of danger. For this particular feat, Smalls was promoted to Captain and served on the *Planter* until the end of the war.

Robert Smalls was born in slavery in Beaufort, S. C. on April 5, 1839. He was moved to Charleston by his master in 1851 and became quite familiar with every brink and shoal in Charleston harbor. Weathering many engagements, Robert Smalls served out the war as blockading pilot of the Union Navy.

Not only did this brave and intelligent man serve with distinction during the war itself, but he also went on to achieve fame as a legislator. Although meagerly educated by an indulgent master, Robert Smalls "was good humored, intelligent, fluent and self-possessed." He was a delegate to the South Carolina Constitutional Convention in 1868 and from that year to 1870 he was in the South Carolina House of Representatives. From 1870 to 1874 he served in the South Carolina State Senate.

Robert Smalls took his seat in the United States House of Representatives in 1875 and served until 1887. The ex-slave and former pilot was a good orator, eloquently speaking out against dishonest election tactics of the southern Democrats and for bills to provide equal accommodations for Negroes in interstate conveyances. His major legislative accomplishment was his introduction and support of the immediate post-Civil War Civil Rights bills, making clear the right of the freedmen to make contracts, to hold property and to enjoy full protection of the laws.

Robert Smalls was active in behalf of the Negroes during the remaining years of his life. His last major public effort to alleviate the conditions of the freedmen was as a delegate to the South Carolina Constitutional Convention in 1895 where he made a gallant but futile attempt to prevent the disfranchisement of Negroes in the state. From that time on, he lived quietly in Beaufort, giving counsel and advice to whites and Negroes alike until his death in 1915.

Dorothy Sterling. *Captian of the Planter; The Story of Robert Smalls*, New York, 1958; *Biographical Directory of the American Congress: 1774-1961*, Washington, D.C., 1961, p. 1611.

John Mercer Langston (1829-1897)

U. S. CONGRESSMAN FROM VIRGINIA

In 1855 at a meeting of the American Anti-slavery Society, gathered in New York City, a slim, debonair mulatto went to the speaker's rostrum and uttered these words:

"A nation may lose its liberties and be a century in finding it out. Where is the American liberty? ... In its far-reaching and broad sweep, slavery has stricken down the freedom of us all . . ."

The speaker was John Mercer Langston, the first Negro elected to public office in the United States. The young lawyer whose remarks were quoted throughout the anti-slavery press was destined to be among the last Negroes elected to Congress during the 19th century.

The road from the plantation of his master and father, Ralph Quarles of Virginia, to the United States House of Representatives was long and arduous, yet it was filled with significant achievement. John Mercer Langston, was at various times a member of the city council of Brownhelm, Ohio (1855-1860), member of the Oberlin, Ohio Board of Education (1867-1868); school inspector general of the Freedmen's Bureau (1868-1869); Dean of the Law school at Howard University (1869-1876); an able and successful minister-resident to Haiti (1877-1885); President of Virginia Normal and Collegiate Institute (1885-1888). John Mercer Langston was elected to the U. S. Congress as a representative from Virginia in 1889 and served until 1891.

John Mercer Langston was also very active in the various movements and organizations devoted to enlarging the area of freedom for the American Negro. He opposed the objectives of the emigration movement of the 1850's; he was a prime mover in the various Negro Conventions which met in different parts of the country. In 1865 he was president of the National Equal Rights League; in 1870 Langston became a guiding spirit of the Negro National Labor Union which sought to grapple with the economic problems facing the freedman.

After his congressional career came to an end, John Mercer Langston became a very popular lecturer. He maintained his interest in political and economic affairs until his death in 1897.

Williams J. Simmons. *Men of Mark*, Cleveland, 1887, p. 515; *Biographical Directory of the American Congress: 1774-1961*, Washington, D.C., 1961 p. 1191.

Blanche K. Bruce (1841-1897)

SENATOR FROM MISSISSIPPI

The time: March 4, 1875. The place: the Senate of the United States of America. The occasion: swearing-in ceremonies of new Senators for the 44th Congress. The roll call of states had been going on for some time. The new Senators were escorted to and from the rostrum by the senior Senators from their states. The roll call and marching to-and-fro finally reached Mississippi. All eyes turned to Blanche K. Bruce, a light-skinned, 36-year old Negro, who had been elected to the U. S. Senate from the sovereign state of Mississippi. As he started his proud march towards the rostrum, expectant eyes shifted from him to Mr. Alcorn, the white senior Senator from Mississippi. Mr. Alcorn was terribly busy with his newspaper and did not look up. Walking alone as though Mr. Alcorn did not exist, Bruce was half way up the aisle when Roscoe Conkling, Senator from New York stepped up and said, "Excuse me, Mr. Bruce. I did not until this moment see that you were without escort. Permit me. My name is Conkling." Together the two Senators completed the round trip. Thus began a career in the Senate which lasted longer than that of any other of the twenty-two Negroes who served in Congress during the last thirty years of the 19th century.

Bruce had been born in slavery, the natural son of his master and a slave woman. When but a small lad, he was made the body servant of his white half-brother and was schooled along with him. When his half-brother joined the Confederate army, Bruce escaped from him and made his way first to Missouri, where he started a school for Negroes, then later to Ohio to complete his own education at Oberlin College.

After the Civil War ended, Bruce began his life of public service as a sergeant-at-arms in the Mississippi Senate. Following this, he was appointed tax assessor in Bolivar County, Mississippi and served two terms. In 1873, Bruce was urged to run for the Senate of the United States where two senatorships were at stake: one for a full term and one for a year. The last was the incompleted portion of Jefferson Davis' term. Bruce was elected for the full term. Bruce's term ended in 1881, but he later was appointed Registrar of the Treasury and twice Recorder of Deeds in Washington D.C.

William J. Simmons. *Men of Mark*, Cleveland, 1887, p. 701; *Dictionary of American Biography*, III. 1929, pp. 180-181.

Robert B. Elliott (1842-1884)

U. S. CONGRESSMAN
FROM SOUTH CAROLINA

As a Congressman, most of his energies were spent in trying to stem the flood of anti-Negro legislation advocated by the Southern states. One memorable encounter between Elliott and his Southern foes concerned the Civil Rights bills. Elliott, naturally supported the bills which were designed to put teeth into the 14th Amendment. Many Southern Senators including Alexander Stephens of Georgia, opposed them. To this unrepentant racist, Elliott had this to say

> "I meet him only as an adversary, nor shall age or any other consideration restrain *me* from saying that he now offers this government, which he has done his utmost to destroy, a very poor return for its magnanimous treatment, to come here to seek to continue, by the assertion of doctrines obnoxious to the true principles of our government, the burdens and oppressions which rest upon five million of his countrymen, who never fail to live their earnest prayers for the success of this government, when the gentleman was seeking to break up the Union of their states and to blot the American Republic from the galaxy of nations."

Following his resignation from the House of Representatives, Elliott in 1876, made an unsuccessful bid for the position of Attorney General of South Carolina. He subsequently moved to New Orleans and resumed the practice of law until his death on August 9, 1884.

William J. Simmons. *Men of Mark*, Cleveland, 1887, p. 468; *Biographical Directory of the American Congress: 1774-1961*, Washigton, D.C., 1961, p. 856.

Few men, black or white, in the 42nd and 43rd Congresses were able to match the polish and brilliance of Robert B. Elliott, who represented the state of South Carolina from 1871 to 1874. Elliott was not an ex-slave, but a free-born Boston-bred Negro so dark of complexion that his law partner once affectionately called him "an undoubted African." His parents were of West Indian extraction.

Elliott's education was obtained at private schools in Boston and in the British West Indies, at Highbon Academy in London, and at Eton where he graduated with high rank in 1853. In 1868, he was a member of the State Constitutional Convention. After the adoption of South Carolina's new constitution, Elliott was elected to the lower house of the South Carolina state legislature and served from 1868 to 1870. Elliott was then elected to the 42nd and 43rd Congresses.

Richard H. Cain (1825-1887)

U. S. CONGRESSMAN FROM SOUTH CAROLINA

Another outstanding individual from South Carolina was Richard H. Cain, who served two terms in the U. S. House of Representatives. He was also one of the outstanding Methodist ministers and church organizers of his time. It has been estimated that under his influence roughly 100,000 people joined the Methodist Church in South Carolina.

A free-born Negro, Richard H. Cain was licensed to preach in 1844 at the age of 19, was ordained a deacon in 1859 and then entered Wilberforce (now Central State College) at the age of 35. After two years at Wilberforce he left Ohio for New York where he began the real labors of his career. After heading several churches in New York, he was sent to South Carolina in 1865 to minister to the newly freed slaves there. Using his Charleston Church of 10,000 members as a base, Cain covered the state in a manner reminiscent of the great founder of Methodism, John Wesley.

When the Constitutional Convention met in Charleston in 1868, Cain, like Elliott, was elected to the South Carolina House of Representatives after serving in the State Senate for four years. During his political career, he served two terms in Congress, one term lasting from 1873 to 1875, and the other from 1877 to 1879.

Richard H. Cain has been described as an unmixed black who took an active part in everything which would advance his race and shelter them from exploitation. In 1868 he started a newspaper, *The Missionary Record*, which soon became the most influential paper in the state. He even served as president of a small Methodist institution, Paul Quinn College in Waco, Texas. In 1880 Cain was appointed Bishop of the AME Church and served until his death in 1887.

Biographical Directory of the American Congress: 1774-1961, Washington, D.C., 1961, p. 646.

SOUTH CAROLINA

John R. Lynch (1847-1939)

U. S. CONGRESSMAN
FROM MISSISSIPPI

John R. Lynch was one of the few Negro Congressmen during the Reconstruction era to be elected three times to Congress from Mississippi as a Republican. John Lynch was elected to the 43rd, 44th, and 47th Congress, but served only two full terms. His last election to the 47th Congress in 1877, the end of the Reconstruction era, was contested and he was not allowed to take his seat. There is some belief that the state defrauded him of his rightful term. Lynch was aware of this and declared among other things that "The Republicans . . . and I am pleased to be able to say, thousands of honest Democrats as well, are anxious that this agitation will cease, upon such conditions as will secure to all citizens the equal protection of the laws, and a willing acquiescence in the lawfully expressed will of the majority."

Nevertheless Lynch remained active in public life. He was Chairman of the Mississippi Republican State Executive Committee (1881-1889), and towards the close of his political carreer, he was apponted fourth auditor for the Treasury in the Navy. In 1898, he was appointed a paymaster in the regular army and served until his retirement in 1911.

Lynch was born a slave and was promised eventual freedom, but his father and owner died before he could be freed and he was sold to a Mississippian. Freed by the ending of the Civil War, Lynch, after educating himself, came to the attention of politicians, one of whom appointed him a Justice of the Peace for Natchez County, Mississippi. In 1869, Lynch was elected a member of the Mississippi State House of Representatives, which led to his being elected to the 43rd Congress.

The success of Lynch's self-education can be seen in this excerpt from a speech where he stresses the patriotism of the Negro immediately after the Civil War. "They were faithful and true to you there; they are no less so today. And yet they ask no special favors as a class; they ask no special protection as a race. They feel that they purchased their inheritance, when upon the battlefields of their country, they watered the tree of liberty with the precious blood that flowed from their loyal veins. They ask no favors, they desire and must have—an equal chance in the race of life."

These words were to be echoed in the demands of Negro spokesmen from the time of John R. Lynch to the present.

William J. Simmons. *Men of Mark*, Cleveland, 1887, p. 1044.
Richard Bardolph. *The Negro Vanguard*, New York, 1961, p. 88; *Biographical Directory of the American Congress: 1774-1961*, Washington, D.C., 1961, p. 1232.

Jefferson Long (1836-1900)

U. S. CONGRESSMAN
FROM GEORGIA

When Jefferson Long took his seat in Congress in 1870, he became the first Negro to be elected to the United States House of Representatives. The day he was elected, white Georgians killed seven Negroes and chased Long to a courthouse where he remained until friends sneaked him to an uncompleted sewer.

Throughout the state Negroes were intimidated, beaten, and abused by whites who could not stomach the idea of a Negro representing a district of that state in the U. S. Congress. Jefferson Long had been a leader of Negroes in Macon, Georgia where he had a thriving business as merchant tailor. When the white Congressman-elect was denied a seat in the House because of doubt about the honesty of his election, Long was persuaded to run for the vacancy. The merchant tailor won by only nine hundred votes, although it has been said that the votes for him would have been much larger had not many Negroes been terrorized into staying away from the polls.

Jefferson Long's first speech in Congress was devoted to ways and means of protecting Negroes who were qualified to vote, but who were unjustly prevented from voting by unreconstructed whites. The disheartening experience of Long's election made such an impression on him that he declined to stand for re-election, but he did retain an active interest in Republican politics. In 1880 he attended the Republican National Convention which met in Chicago and nominated James A. Garfield for President.

Upon the completion of his term in Congress, Long returned to his tailoring business in Macon, Georgia. His early training was typical of many other Negro Congressmen who followed him. He was largely self-educated, learning to read and write the best way he could. Born in Crawford County, Georgia, Long worked at a variety of odd jobs and occupations until he decided to open a tailoring business in Macon. This prospered and left him time and money for politics. Years after his leaving Congress , Republican politicians, Negro and white would seek him for advice which he dispensed freely.

Jefferson Long's term in Congress was very short, but he was the second Negro to ever enter that body in other than a menial capacity.

Richard Bardolph. *The Negro Vanguard*, New York, 1961, p. 88; *Biographical Directory of the American Congress: 1774-1961* p. 1232.

Hiram Revels (1822-1901)
U.S. SENATOR FROM MISSISSIPPI

Just ten years after the Confederates fired on Fort Sumter, Hiram Revels sat in the Senate seat of Jefferson Davis. Revels had the distinction of being the first of the only two Negroes ever to sit in this, the "world's most exclusive club." Completing the term commenced by Jefferson Davis, the expresident of the Confederate States of America, Hiram Revels represented the state of Mississippi from February 25, 1879 to March 3, 1881.

Senator Revels had been a state senator in Mississippi and prior to this he had been an alderman. However, the basis of his activity in politics lay in his career as a minister of the gospel. In Natchez, Mississippi he had preached to a large congregation and was known as one of the most able and popular ministers in the Delta.

Hiram Revels was born in Fayetteville, North Carolina in 1822. Negroes, slave or free were forbidden to learn to read and write at this time and as soon as Revels was old enough, he left the state for Ohio where he studied at a Quaker Seminary. Later he was graduated from Knox College, Galesburg, Illinois.

Like many of his contemporaries, Revels decided to make a career in the ministry and entered the Methodist Episcopal Church. He served congregations in Indiana, Kentucky, Maryland, and Kansas. When the Civil War started he was preaching in Maryland but left the pulpit to recruit soldiers for the first colored regiment organized in the state.

During 1863-64, he taught school in St. Louis, Missouri and then worked with the U. S. Provost Marshall in handling the affairs of freedmen. In the chaos of Emancipation, Hiram Revels followed the Union Army, organizing churches, attempting to start schools and lecturing to the freedmen. He finally settled at Natchez, Mississippi where he started his second public career.

William J. Simmons. *Men of Mark*, Cleveland, 1887, pp. 948-950.

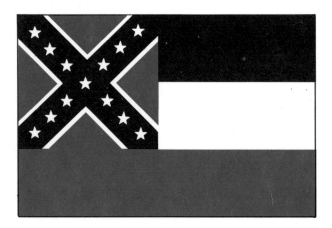

James T. Rapier (1839-1884)
CONGRESSMAN FROM ALABAMA

"I accept the civil and political equality of all men and agree not to attempt to deprive any person or persons on account of race, color or previous condition, of any political or civil rights." Repeating this pledge with other delegates at the Alabama Constitutional Convention in 1867 was James T. Rapier, then twenty-seven years old. The delegates were meeting to help Alabama re-enter the Union.

Wise beyond his years and looking like an older man in his long frock coat and with side whiskers, James T. Rapier had been sent to the convention by his neighbors both white and Negro even though he had lived in the state only two years after the Civil War. He was destined to represent them in the United States House of Representatives from 1873 to 1875.

James T. Rapier had returned to his native Alabama riding a horse and carrying in his saddle bags literature urging Negroes to unite themselves into labor unions where their scattered strength could be brought together and used in their own interests. It was James T. Rapier who called the first conclave of laboring men in Alabama. It was he who drew up the first Republican party platform in the state of Alabama. Far-sightedly, his platform called for a free press, free speech and a public school system. He even started his own newspaper, *The Sentinel*, to spread his views.

As a Congressman, Rapier was in the vanguard of those calling for strong enforcement of the civil rights legislation passed during the years following the Civil War. He felt that only by stringent application of this legislation could the average freedman be safe and learn to participate in public affairs.

Before the Civil War, Rapier's father and master sent him to Canada to be educated. He was tutored privately and then sent to Montreal College and the University of Glasgow, Glasgow, Scotland. Following his return to Alabama he became a planter and entered public life, becoming a notary public, tax assessor and unsuccessful canadidate for office of Sectretary of State in Alabama.

After his term of office in the U. S. Congress ended Rapier was appointed collector of internal revenue in Alabama, a post he held until his death in 1884.

Eugene Feldman. "James R. Rapier: 1839-1884", *Negro History Bulletin*, vol. XX. #2, 1956, pp. 62-66.

Alexander Crummell (1819-1898)
WRITER, ADVOCATE OF EQUALITY, MINISTER

One of the leaders who helped shape anti-slavery thought during the years preceding the Civil War was Alexander Crummell, a minister and orator who had careers on both sides of the Atlantic. "It was he above all others who, before Emancipation, preached an optimistic view of the Negro's prospects, a bouyant self-confidence as a challenge to the sense of inferiority to which the Negro in America had been so long conditioned."

As a youth Alexander Crummell wanted to be an Episcopalian clergyman and after a rather difficult time, was ordained a priest in the Episcopalian Church but received little encouragement from the church. His efforts to start congregations met with little success. In 1847 he went to England and studied at Queen's College, Cambridge, where he became interested in working in Africa as a Missionary. Graduating in 1853, Crummell went to Liberia where he served an Espicopalian parish and taught theology in Monrovia. He remained in Africa for twenty years, teaching and lecturing, and returned to America in 1873.

Going to Washington, D. C., Crummell laid the foundation of St. Luke's Espiscopalian Church and led its congregation for nearly two decades. His speeches and writings attracted considerable attention. Indicative of the appeal he had for readers, his speech, "The Black Woman of the South: Her Neglects and Her Needs" was printed for 500,000 readers. Crummell also published works on Thomas Clarkson, a pioneer English abolitionist, and a collection of speeches delivered in Liberia, stressing the possibilities of progress facing that country.

Born free, Crummell devoted his life to helping make freedom a reality for others.

W. E. B. DuBois. *The Soul of Black Folk*, New York, 1961 edition, pp. 157-161; William J. Simmons. *Men of Mark*, Cleveland, 1887, pp. 530-535.

Ebenezer D. Bassett (1833-1908)
FIRST DIPLOMAT

Although the relations between the United States and Haiti were relatively stable but tense, Haiti and San Domingo were having serious difficulties. Haiti had long followed a policy of opposing foreign domination of San Domingo. At this time, the United States was considering annexing it. Haitian awareness of this created strong anti-American feelings among the Haitians. In addition to these problems, the Haitians were faced with serious internal difficulties. Bassett was expected to carry out United States policy and to keep his country informed of developments on the island.

Bassett's dispatches to Hamilton Fish, then Secretary of State, and others indicated a firm grasp of political developments in his host country. Appraisals of Bassett's work unanimously agree that he did the best job possible in the rather tense atmosphere of the early 1870's. As a manuever in diplomacy, his appointment could hardly have been wiser, for the Haitians accepted Bassett with a confidence his predecessors never enjoyed.

Additional evidence of Bassett's success as a diplomat may be seen in the fact that after he completed his assignment in 1877, he was appointed a general consul *from* Haiti to the United States, a post he held for ten years.

In 1888, Bassett returned to Haiti to live as a private citizen. While there he collected materials which were subsequently published in a *Handbook of Haiti*, printed in French, English and Spanish.

In recognition of this work he was named a member of the American Geographical Society and the Connecticut Historical Society.

Born of a mulatto father and an Indian mother in Litchfield, Connecticut, Bassett studied at Wesley Academy, Wilbraham, Massachusetts, Connecticut Normal School and for a brief period, at Yale. At the time of his appointment as minister-resident, Bassett was principal of the Institute for Colored Youth, Philadelphia.

Ebenezer D. Bassett was the first Negro to officially represent the United States abroad. Appointed by President Ulysses S. Grant as minister-resident to Haiti, Ebenezer D. Bassett set a high standard of achievement. ". . . With honor to himself and satisfaction to his country, he filled the position from 1869 to 1877, which was as long as the combined terms of his white predecessors."

James A. Padgett. "Diplomats to Haiti and their Diplomacy", *Journal of Negro History*, XXV (July, 1940), pp. 265-330.

James Lewis (1832-1897?)

PORT of NEW ORLEANS tax COLLECTOR

Of the various figures who achieved prominence in Louisiana during the Reconstruction, James Lewis is one of the least known and appreciated. At various times, James Lewis was Surveyor-General for New Orleans, colonel of the second regiment, State Militia, collector of the New Orleans Port, naval officer, and superintendent of the U. S. Bonded Warehouse in New Orleans. He was also administrator of police for New Orleans, and administrator of public improvements for New Orleans.

Lewis was born in Wilkinson County, Mississippi. His early life was spent on the Mississippi River where he, like Pinchback, worked his way up to steward and, at the time of the outbreak of the Civil War, was serving as steward aboard a Confederate ship, *The DeSoto*. On hearing of the Emancipation Proclamation, Lewis jumped ship and made his way to New Orleans. At this time he was 31 years old and eager to fight. New Orleans had just fallen into the hands of the Union, and Lewis persuaded the commanding officer to allow him to raise regiments of colored volunteers. He succeeded in raising two companies, serving for a short time in the First Louisiana Volunteers Native Guards, and as captain of Company K.

In 1864, Lewis resigned his commission and joined the Freedmen's Bureau as a traveling agent, setting up schools for the ex-slaves. He found this work more dangerous than soldiering. On one occasion, as agent of the Freedmen's Bureau, he was mobbed in northern Louisiana, but was saved in the nick of time. After this work, he was appointed to the post of United States inspector of customs, making him the first Negro in Louisiana to hold Federal appointive office.

In 1870, he was appointed Colonel of the Second Regiment, State Militia, and in the same year was elected administrator of police for two years at the then considerable salary of $6,000 per year.

Becoming very active in Republican politics, Lewis in 1872 was nominated by the Louisiana State Convention for Congressman-at-large and served as chairman of the Louisiana Delegation to the National Republican convention.

Shortly afterwards he was elected administrator of public improvement for New Orleans, a post then regarded as one of the most important in the city government. He was the only Republican in local government, but an appraisal of his handling of the city's improvement department may be found in a report of the City Council for 1873. After listing the great economies effected by Lewis in his department, the report states: "Colonel Lewis has devoted himself to his duties with great energy and industry, taking constant care that every dollar expended should benefit the city."

William J. Simmons. *Men of Mark*, Cleveland, 1887, pp. 954-958.

Henry Highland Garnet (1815-1882)

ABOLITIONIST, MINISTER TO LIBERIA

GARNET

AFRICA

LIBERIA

Atlantic Ocean

"Brethren, arise, arise! Strike for your lives and liberties. Now is the day and the hour. Let every slave in the land do this and the days of slavery are numbered. You can not be more oppressed than you have been— you can not suffer greater cruelties than you have already. Rather die free men than to live and be slaves. Remember you are four million." This was the appeal of Henry Highland Garnet.

This was the year 1843. The occasion was a convention of free men of color gathered in Buffalo, New York. Over seventy delegates were present, among them Frederick Douglass, William Wells Brown, Charles Ray and Martin Delaney.

For years Garnet had held the belief that slavery would not be ended by peaceful means, and remembering Denmark Vesey and Nat Turner, he was an advocate of slave revolt. The convention was asked to adopt his remarks as a statement of sentiment of the delegates. Garnet's speech disturbed a number of abolitionists who did not favor violence. The vote was close, and Garnet's resolution lost by a single vote. While his speech attracted national attention, the vigor of his remarks to the slaves made Garnet increasingly ineffective as an anti-slavery worker, for the abolitionists had not yet moved to urge violence against slave holders.

Henry's grandfather was a Congolese brought to this country in chains. His father was a slave and had escaped to Delaware where Henry was born. As a boy he attended the African Free School in New York and the ill-fated New Canaan, Connecticut school for Negro youth which was destroyed. From there he went to Oneida Institute and later turned to the Presbyterian ministry. In 1842 he was licensed and the following year he began his ministry at Troy Liberty Street Presbyterian Church. He was highly successful as a minister. "His bright, unclouded eyes, large well shaped head, commanding presence, great courage, strong will and fiery personality" made him a standout in any gathering.

He was one of the most influential Negroes of his era— until he made his controversial Buffalo speech. From this point on, his public influence waned. However, he became very active in politics after the Civil War. He became Recorder of Deeds for a time, and in 1881 was appointed Minister to Liberia. While serving as Minister in Liberia he became ill and died in Monrovia.

"Garnet", *Dictionary of American Biography*, VII, 1931, pp. 154-155; J. W. Schulte Nordholt. *The People That Walk in Darkness*, New York, 1960, pp. 101-102. (Paperback). William M. Brewer. "Henry Highland Garnet," *Journal of Negro History*, XII (January, 1928), pp. 36-52.

John H. Smythe (1844-1908)

U.S. MINISTER TO LIBERIA

John H. Smythe was one of the earliest and ablest ministers to Liberia during the years immediately following the Reconstruction period of American history. A measure of his ability may be seen in the fact that he not only represented the United States government there but also the governments of Belgium, Germany, Sweden and Norway. His reports on Liberia were perhaps the most competent of his era. All accounts of his life emphasize his ability and skill.

John H. Smythe was the first colored newsboy in Philadelphia, and the first Negro artist to become a member of the Philadelphia Academy of Fine Arts. He studied at a Quaker Institute for Colored Youth, headed by Ebenezer Bassett, himself destined to be the first Negro minister to Haiti. After a short period of teaching John H. Smythe entered Howard University Law school in 1869 when John Mercer Langston was dean and, while attending this very recently established school, worked as a clerk in the Freedmen's Bureau. Later he was an internal revenue agent and an employee of the Freedmen's Bank.

In every position held by him, he served with obvious skill and soon came to the attention of highly placed politicians who felt him a perfect choice to represent the United States government in Liberia. As a result, in 1878 President Rutherford B. Hayes appointed Smythe minister to Liberia and President Chester A. Arthur again appointed him in 1882.

Following his second tour of duty, John H. Smythe practiced law in Washington where his fashionable home was a meeting place of all races.

Richard Bardolph. *The Negro Vanguard*, New York, 1961, p. 97; William J. Simmons. *Men of Mark*, Cleveland, 1887, pp. 872-878;

James Monroe Trotter (1844-1912)

RECORDER OF DEEDS

During the Reconstruction era, one of the government posts most prized by Negroes was the federal office of Recorder of Deeds, ranking only after ministerial posts to Haiti and Liberia. Frederick Douglass' first government post was in this office. The man who succeeded him was James Monroe Trotter, a writer, and former Assistant Superintendent in the Post Office Department, Boston, Massachusetts.

Born in Gulfport, Mississippi, James Trotter grew up in Ohio where he attended school and studied music. Bright, apt and alert, he enlisted in the famous 54th Massachusetts Regiment and in short order was promoted from sergeant to lieutenant. For his service in Boston politics, he was appointed assistant superintendent of the registered letter department in the Boston Post Office. He left this position in 1883 due to the creeping color line which was being drawn in the office and also because he was disgruntled with the way the Republican party had handled its victory at Appomattox.

During this time he continued his interest in music and wrote a history of music which elicited favorable comment from the critics.

However, his nomination for Recorder of Deeds at Washington provoked a storm which signaled the lack of concern over the role of the Negro in the federal government. His nomination was held up for a time, on the grounds that he was not a resident of Washington. However, the Negro press and fair-minded journalists were quick to point out that this and many other offices were filled with non-residents of the district. After much debate and procrastination, James M. Trotter was finally confirmed on March 4, 1887.

William J. Simmons. *Men of Mark*, Cleveland, 1887, pp. 656-661.

Johnathan J. Wright (1840-1885)
SOUTH CAROLINA JURIST

Sketch from 1863 cartoon commentary on racial injustice in South Carolina

From 1870 to 1877 Johnathan J. Wright was Associate Justice of the State Supreme Court of South Carolina. No other Negro rose to such a high judicial post during the whole of the Reconstruction era.

Wright was elected to fill out the few months left from the term of Solomon L. Hoge who had resigned to run for Congress. In the latter part of 1870, Wright was re-elected for a full six-year term. As an Associate Justice in the turbulent politics of South Carolina, Wright's decisions show evidence of considerable ability. Of the 425 cases heard by the State Supreme Court during his tenure, eighty-seven of the opinions handed down were written by him.

Born in Pennsylvania in 1840 Wright was the first Negro to be admitted to the bar in that state. In 1865, the American Missionary Society sent him to Beaufort, South Carolina to help organize schools for the freed men. From 1866 to 1868, he was a legal advisor employed by the Freedmen's Bureau to serve the legal needs of the ex-slaves.

In the roiling aftermath of slavery there was an acute demand for trained Negroes, particularly in politics. Realizing this, Johnathan J. Wright resigned his post with the Freedmen's Bureau and entered politics. He attended the South Carolina constitutional convention in 1868 and later was elected state senator from Beaufort, South Carolina. In the legislature, he was regarded as very "clear-headed, quick as a flash and could out-talk any man on the floor." Despite the corruption and vicious-ness of state politics at that time there was no proof of any dishonesty in his action, either in the legislature or on the bench.

As the restoration of white supremacy continued apace, Johnathan J. Wright resigned from the court in 1877, thus symbolizing the high water mark of Negroes in the courts until the twentieth century.

R. H. Woody. "Johnathan J. Wright, Associate Justice of the Supreme Court of South Carolina, 1870-1877", *Journal of Negro History*, XVIII (April, 1933), pp. 114-131; *Dictionary of American Biography*, vol. XX, 1936, p. 236.

George W. Williams (1849-1891)
SOLDIER, DIPLOMAT, HISTORIAN

Upon leaving the Army, George W. Williams enrolled in the Newton Theological Institution (now Seminary) where, in 1874, he became the first Negro to graduate. After a few years as a pastor of the 12th Street Chruch, Boston, Williams left Massachusetts for Washington, D.C. where he started a newspaper, *The Commoner*. John Mercer Langston and Frederick Douglass, among others, contributed articles to it, but, due to inadequate circulation, *The Commoner* failed.

Undaunted by this failure, Williams then went to Cincinnati, Ohio and was named minister of the Union Baptist Church which he served for two years. He continued his newspaper interests, having articles appear in the Cincinnati *Commercial* and the *South Western Review*. He even started reading law in the office of Alphonso Taft, a forebear of the present day Tafts. In 1879 Williams was admitted to the Ohio bar and also elected to the Ohio state legislature for a term of two years.

While in Ohio, Williams developed a deep interest in Negro history. From 1876 to 1883 Williams diligently carried on his investigations of the Negro's past and finally published his two-volume *History of the Negro Race in America from 1619 to 1880*. The work created great excitement in scholarly circles and was generally regarded as the best book on Negro history published during the 19th Century. Five years later Williams published his *History of Negro Troops in the War of Rebellion*.

In 1883 George Williams visited the Congo and wrote a very critical article of the Belgians' stewardship there. He served with distinction as United States Minister-Resident to Haiti in 1885-1886. Williams died in 1891 while living in Blackpool, England.

John Hope Franklin. "George Washington Williams, Historian", *Journal of Negro History*, XXXI (January, 1946), pp. 60-90; "George Williams", *Dictionary of American Biography*, XX, 1936, p. 264.

Into his brief forty-two years, George Washington Williams crammed several lifetimes. At the age of fourteen he was serving in the 6th Massachusetts Regiment of the Union Army. Because of his youth he was discharged but he promptly re-enlisted and became a sergeant-major on the staff of General N. P. Jackson. Serving in Texas, Williams was wounded, discharged again and then joined the Mexican Army. After less than a year in the Mexican Army, Williams resigned and joined the U. S. Cavalry and took part in the Comanche campaign where he served with conspicuous bravery. During each term of service Williams was noted for his courage and bravery. Because he was passed over as a candidate for the officer corps of the regular Army, Williams resigned from the Army altogether. He was only twenty years old and still saw his future before him.

Pinckney Benton Stewart Pinchback

(1837-1920)

LT. GOVERNOR OF LOUISIANA

Proud and imperious almost to a fault, Pinckney Stewart Pinchback rose from a canal boat cabin boy to the Lieutenant Governorship of the State of Louisiana. Like Robert Smalls before him, Pinchback's early life was molded through his meeting all types of men during many years on the lakes and canals which were the main highways of commerce in the 1840's. Pinchback was born a slave on a Mississippi plantation, but, along with his mother, was given his freedom and moved to Ohio. At the age of twelve, he found himself alone and soon obtained work as a cabin boy first on the Ohio, and later on the Missouri and Mississippi rivers. His natural skills and aptitudes carried him to the rank of steward at which time he was bluntly told that only his race prevented him from rising any higher.

In 1862 a few weeks after the Confederates fired on Fort Sumter, Pinchback gave up the river boat life and went to Louisiana where he enlisted in the Union Army. He even led volunteer efforts to recruit Negroes in Louisiana for the Union Army and by October, 1862, the Louisiana Native Guards, with Pinchback as captain, were mustered into service.

After this happy beginning, Pinchback ran into trouble, not with the Southerners, but with the Union troops who were openly hostile to him and his men. The Louisiana Native Guard was mistreated, despite all that Pinchback tried to do to avoid it. In disgust, Pinchback resigned his command. Still hoping to lead Negro troops, Pinchback again raised another regiment but was told by Union officials that, legally, no Negro could rise above the rank of non-commissioned officer. With his own desire to help the Union cause continuously frustrated, he gave up his military interests.

In 1865, he went to Alabama, (Mobile, Montgomery, and Selma) denouncing the treatment of the newly freed Negroes. Two years later, Pinchback organized the Fourth Ward Republican club of Northern Louisiana which elected him to the State Republican Caucus.

Pinchback as Captain, Second Louisiana Volunteers

Pinchback

... at the height of his political career

LOUISIANA

New Orleans

UNION JUSTICE & CONFIDENCE

Pinchback was later a delegate to the State Constitutional Convention. His major achievement was the successful introduction of the Thirteenth Amendment to the State's Constitution guaranteeing civil rights to all people of the state.

From this point onward, Pinchback's political career moved rapidly; in short order he became a state Senator, a delegate to the Republican National Convention in Chicago in 1868, School Director to the School Board of New Orleans, and president *pro tem* of the State Senate. At a time when the state government of Louisiana was in chaos, Pinchback was elected acting governor for forty-two days, succeeding Governor Warmouth who had been impeached. According to Simmons, "The brief period he occupied the gubernatorial chair was the stormiest ever witnessed in the history of any state in the Union; but the governor was equal to the emergency and displayed administrative capacity of a high order."

However, the greatest drama in the life of Pinchback occurred when, in a hotly contested race, he was elected to the United States Senate. Many other southern states in 1873 had disputed elections and the presentation of credentials to the clerk of the Senate was often a rather tense affair. In the case of Pinchback, the clerk had been instructed not to accept Pinchback's credentials until the Senate judicial committee had an opportunity to review them. An Alabama Senator-elect with the same problem had to wait only three days. After a three-year delay the Senate rejected Pinchback's credentials, thus denying him a seat in this conclave of gentlemen.

Pinchback was voted $16,666 of the Senate's contingent fund to cover the salary he would have earned up to the time he was finally denied his seat. In one of the rare flukes of politics, Pinchback was also denied a seat in the House of Representatives to which he had also been elected.

"Pinchback", *Dictionary of American Biography*, XVI, 1934, p. 611; John Hope Franklin. *Reconstruction After the Civil War*, Chicago, 1961, p. 134; William J. Simmons. *Men of Mark*, Cleveland, 1887, pp. 759-781.

IV SCIENCE and INDUSTRY
And They Studied Man and Nature

In science and, to a lesser extent, in industrial invention, Negroes have distinguished themselves. In 1770, the remarkable Benjamin Banneker of Maryland made the first American clock which struck off the hours. Henry T. Blair, also of Maryland, became the first Negro to receive a patent when his corn harvester was registered in 1835. Norbert Rillieux's work on evaporation and the liquid reduction process, in the opinion of some, has been "the greatest in the history of American chemical engineering."

The Negro has been active in the field of medical science for a long time. As early as 1667 one Lucas Santomée of New York was trained in medicine in Holland and practiced under the Dutch and the British. A slave by the name of Oneissimus provided Americans with an effective antidote for smallpox in 1721. In this same era, another slave, James Derham of Philadelphia, became the first American Negro medical doctor. As a freedman, he built up a large interracial clientele in New Orleans during the 1780s. James McCune Smith received a medical degree from Scotland's Glasgow University in 1837. David J. Peck had the distinction of being the first Negro to graduate from an American medical school when Rush Medical College of Chicago awarded him the M.D. degree in 1847. Two years after this John V. DeGrasse and Thomas J. White were graduated from Bowdoin College with degrees in the field of medicine. In recognition of his extraordinary ability, DeGrasse was admitted to the Boston Medical Society in 1854.

In the years following the Civil War the number of Negroes in the medical profession slowly increased. Twenty one years after Peck became a doctor, the Howard University Medical School opened its doors in Washington, D.C. Meharry Medical School in Nashville, Tennessee began training Negro physicians in 1876. By the year 1900 there were 1,734 Negroes licensed to practice the art of healing.

In the area of pure scientific research Negroes have only just begun to work in significant numbers. Yet, from the early days of this nation, a few Negroes have possessed the objective curiosity and opportunity to learn for the sake of learning, as in the case of the self-trained Banneker who calculated solar eclipses and the cycle of the seventeen-year locust. Edward Bouchet was among the first to pursue a scientific interest ("Measuring Refractive Indices") to the doctoral level when Yale University awarded him the Ph. D. degree in 1876. Beginning in the first decade of this century, Dr. Charles Turner published forty-seven learned papers even though he never held a position higher than that of biology teacher in a St. Louis, Missouri high school.

All born since the turn of the century, the men enumerated in the following list have achieved distinction in different scientific fields: Harold E. Finley (cytology and the physiology of protozoa), Samuel M. Nabrit (embryology), Lloyd A. Hall (cereal chemistry and protein hydrolysates), Warren E. Henry (cyrogenics, thermodynamics and semi-conductors), Julius H. Taylor (electrical properties of semi-conductors and high pressure physics), Hubert M. Thaxton (theoretical physics and information theory), David H. Blackwell and Joseph A. Pierce (statistics and the study of probability) and Wade Ellis (abstract algebra and electromagnetic theory).

The list could be extended by noting such men as J. Ernest Wilkins, Jr. who earned a Ph. D. degree in mathematics from the University of Chicago at the age of nineteen; or Dr. Robert P. Barnes of Howard University whose students, according to one authority, at one point were publishing more articles in the *Journal of the American Chemical Society* than all of the chemistry professors in all of the Negro colleges combined; or Dr. Lloyd E. Ferguson, also of Howard University, who authored a chemistry text which has been used by many colleges in the country.

It is perhaps in the field of general medicine that a combination of inventiveness, scientific research and community service may be seen most clearly. Dr. Louis T. Wright, a pioneer in the use of the antibiotic aureomycin on human beings, was a vigorous opponent of discrimination in the medical profession. Dr. William A. Hinton, a long-time member of the Harvard Medical School faculty, developed what is known as the "Hinton Test" for syphilis. He once headed the Wasserman Laboratory of the Massachusetts Department of Health. Dr. Peter Marshall Murray, a specialist in gynecology, became the first Negro member of the House of Delegates of the American Medical Association. Julian Lewis, armed with both an M.D. and a Ph.D., for a time was on the faculty of the University of Chicago and, later, a professional pathologist with client-hospitals in the Chicago area.

The caliber of men now in medicine may be seen in the examples listed below. Dr. Nathaniel O. Calloway is a widely recognized specialist in internal medicine, the author of many scientific papers, a community leader and hospital administrator. W. Montague Cobb, an outstanding anatomist at Howard University, has been a vice-president of the American Academy of Science and president of the American Association of Physical Anthropologists. Asa G. Yancey is director of surgery at the Hughes Spalding Pavilion of the Grady Memorial Hospital in Atlanta, Georgia. Dr. Leonidas H. Berry holds a professorship of gastroenterology at Chicago's Cook County Hospital.

The above paragraphs merely outline, in an extremely brief compass, the variety and scope of the Negro's participation in the development of certain phases of industry, science and medicine.

Herman R. Branson. "The Negro Scientist," in *The Negro in Science* (Julius H. Taylor, editor), Baltimore, 1955, pp. 1-9; Benjamin Brawley. *A Short History of the American Negro*, New York, 1931, pp. 226-229; W. Montague Cobb. "A New Dawn in Medicine," *Ebony*, September, 1963, pp. 166-171.

Norbert Rillieux (1806-1894)

SLAVE, SCIENTIST

N. Rillieux | Evaporating Pan.

Nº 4,879   Patented Dec. 10, 1846

As a freedman, Norbert Rillieux did not want to leave New Orleans. He was born there a slave and, after studying and teaching in France, returned to Louisiana to become the most famous engineer in the state. When he was assigned to reorganize a sugar refining plant, a fine house, complete with servants, was set aside for his exclusive use. He was one of the most important men in the state, yet he could not take part in its affairs unless he was invited. Rillieux accepted this until he was required to carry a pass. In 1854 he decided to leave Louisiana forever.

Norbert Rillieux was an important man wherever sugar was manufactured. Until 1846 the transformation of sugar cane juice into sugar was accomplished by a primitive method called the "Jamaica Train", a slow, costly process.

Before Rillieux, two other scientists, Howard and DeGrand, had developed vacuum pans and condensing coils which imperfectly utilized heat in evaporating the liquid portion of the sugar cane juice. " . . . it remained for Rillieux, by a stroke of genius, to enclose the condensing coils in a vacuum chamber and to employ the vapor from this first condensing chamber for evaporating the juice in a second chamber under higher vacuum."

The process developed by Rillieux greatly reduced the production cost and provided a superior quality of sugar. Sugar manufacturers immediately hailed the process as a revolution in the manufacturing of sugar. In the years that followed, the Rillieux process was adopted in Cuba and Mexico. Other industries having the problem of liquid reduction adopted the process.

Norbert's intelligence was recognized at an early age by his father who was master of the plantation on which his mother was a slave. He was sent to Paris to be educated and at the age of twenty-four, Norbert became an instructor at L'Ecole Centrale. He published several papers on the steam engine and steam economy.

When Rillieux left Louisiana in 1854 and returned to France, he tried to interest the Europeans in his sugar processing, but found them lukewarm and finally gave up trying. He secured a scholarship and worked with the Champollions deciphering hieroglyphics. For ten years he was engaged in this work. Eventually his special process was adopted in Europe, and with renewed interest he turned again to invention. This time he applied his process to the sugar beet, and cut production costs in half.

George Meade. "A Negro Scientist of Slavery Days," *Negro History Bulletin*, April, 1957, pp. 159-164.

Jan Ernst Matzeliger (1852-1889)

INVENTOR AND BUSINESSMAN

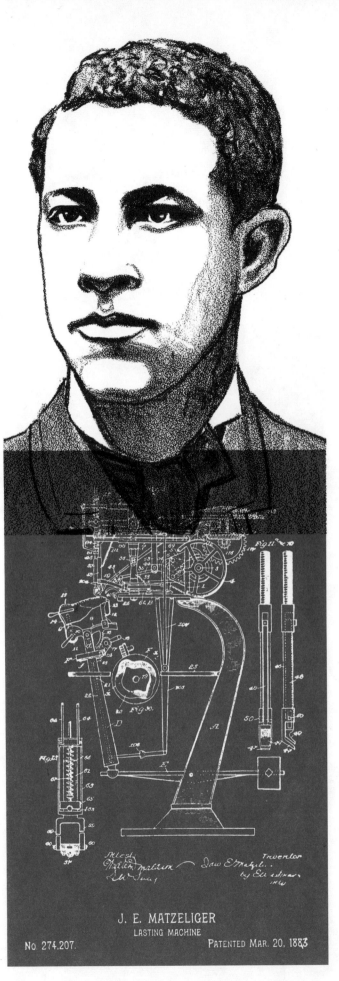

J. E. MATZELIGER
LASTING MACHINE

No. 274,207.   PATENTED MAR. 20, 1883.

When young, slim, rather handsome Jan Ernst Matzeliger arrived in Lynn, Massachusetts in 1876, he could barely speak a word of English. No one knew him; he was poor and friendless, having been for two years a sailor. When he died thirteen years later, his name was known not only in Massachusetts, but wherever inventors gathered. During the years left to him, he laid the foundation of the shoe industry in the United States and made Lynn, Massachusetts the shoe capital of the world.

Before Matzeliger, hundreds of inventors and thousands of dollars had been spent in an effort to make a complete shoe by machinery. Inventors such as Thompson, McKay and Copeland had developed crude shoe making machines but the final problem of shaping the upper leather over the last and attaching this leather to the bottom of the shoe stymied them. The "hand-lasters," as they were called, performed this crucial and final step. They were the aristocrats of the shoe industry and, in effect, had control of the shoe manufacturing industry. They were highly paid and tempermental but no matter how fast the other portions of the shoe were completed, they could turn out only forty to fifty pairs each per day.

Matzeliger heard of the problem. Already extremely competent with mechanical things, such a challenge suited him perfectly. As he worked in shoe factories around Lynn and Boston, he heard it said many times that it was impossible to last shoes by machines; the job simply could not be done. In secret he started experimenting, first with a crude wooden machine, then with a model made out of scrap iron. For ten years he worked, steadily and patiently, with no encouragement. Indeed, when the news of his tinkering finally reached the public, there were jeers of derision. Matzeliger only smiled and continued working.

Meanwhile, after being denied membership in several churches, he finally joined a young adult group which made his days less lonely. Little did he hear of his Dutch father or Surinamese mother in his native Dutch Guiana. There is no record of his courting or marrying. Yet when he was working on his invention, acquaintances and friends would drop in to chat and perhaps smile condescendingly.

Finally in 1882, Matzeliger felt he had perfected his machine to solve the impossible problem. When he applied for a patent and sent his diagrams to Washington, patent reviewers could not even understand them. They were so complicated that a man was dispatched from Washington to Lynn, Massachusetts to see the model itself. On March 20, 1883, patent number 274,207 was granted to Jan E. Matzeliger. Six years later he died of tuberculosis.

Sidney Kaplan. "Jan Ernst Matzeliger and the Making of the Shoe," *Journal of Negro History*, XL (January, 1958), pp. 8-33.

Granville T. Woods (1856-1910)

PROLIFIC INVENTOR

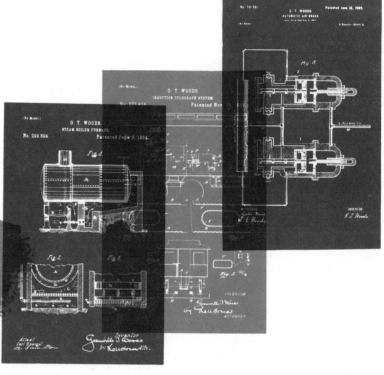

The *Catholic Tribune* (Cincinnati, Ohio) of January 14, 1886 carried an article which included this statement, "Granville T. Woods, the greatest colored inventor in the history of the race, and equal, if not superior, to any inventor in the country, is destined to revolutionize the mode of street car transit."

A little more than a year later, April 1, 1887 it said, "Mr. Woods, who is the greatest electrician in the world, still continues to add to his long list of electrical inventions."

Since the Woods' Railway Telegraph Company was located in Cincinnati at that time, the extravagance of these two statements may be partly attributed to civic pride, but they also truthfully reflect the inventive fertility of this mechanical genius. During his lifetime he earned over thirty-five patents, ranging from a steam boiler furnace (1884), and an incubator (1900) to the automatic air brake (1902). Many of his electrical inventions were sold to the American Bell Telephone Company and the General Electric Company; the Westinghouse Air Brake Company eventually obtained his air brake patent.

While he patented more than a dozen inventions for electric railways and many more for electrical control and distribution, his most noteworthy device in this area was the "Induction Telegraph", a system for communicating to and from moving trains. Accidents and collisions were causing great concern both to the public and the railways at that time and many electrical engineers were seeking improvement of the conventional telegraph as a solution. When Woods came out with his Synchronous Multiplex Railway Telegraph "for the purpose of averting accidents by keeping each train informed of the whereabouts of the one immediately ahead or following it; in communicating with stations from moving trains; and in promoting general social and commercial intercourse", he was contested by the Edison and Phelps Company which was working on a similar device. In the patent offices' case of *Woods vs. Phelps*, Woods was twice declared the inventor.

G. T. Woods was born in Columbus, Ohio, April 23, 1856, where he attended school until he was 10 and then worked in a machine shop. This basic mechanical knowledge was increased, by jobs on a Missouri railroad in 1872, in a Springfield rolling mill in 1874, and mechanical engineering training at an Eastern College in 1876. In 1878 he obtained work as an engineer on board the *Ironsides*, a British steamer, and in 1880 actually handled a steam locomotive on the D & S Railroad. In spite of his background and engineering skill he was unable to advance in these jobs. He then started his own company to market his telegraph and other inventions.

Benjamin Brawley. *A Short History of the American Negro*, New York, 1931, pp. 227-228; Henry E. Baker. "The Negro in the Field of Invention", *Journal of Negro History*, II (January, 1917), p. 32.

Garrett A. Morgan (1875-1963)

INVENTOR FOR SAFETY

The time: July 25, 1916; the place: five miles out and 228 feet below Lake Erie and the Cleveland Waterworks. An explosion in Tunnel Number Five had trapped over two dozen men. No one knew for sure whether there were any survivors. And there was only one way to tell—have someone descend into the tunnel. With great quantities of smoke, natural gases, dust and debris, it was simply impossible for anyone to go into Number Five and live. At two A.M. when all seemed hopeless, someone recalled that one Garrett Morgan had been demonstrating a gas inhalator in an effort to interest manufacturers.

Immediately, a call went out for Morgan who wasted no time in reaching the scene of the disaster. Grim-lipped men and sobbing women moved aside as Garrett and his brother Frank arrived. Quickly donning their inhalators, the two brothers, assisted by two volunteers, entered the tunnel. Down, down, down, 100 feet, 200 feet into the darkness they descended. Soon Garrett Morgan stumbled into the body of a man. Quickly gathering up this body and locating other men, Garrett's small party returned to the tunnel's elevator which whisked them to the surface. Again and again, Garrett Morgan led rescuers into Tunnel Number Five to save over a score of the workmen.

Morgan's heroic act thrust him before the public. Many manufacturers and fire departments showed keen interest in his breathing device. Morgan was requested to demonstrate his inhalator in many cities and towns. In the deep south it was necessary for Morgan to employ a white man to show off his invention. Orders began to pour into Cleveland as many municipalities purchased the Morgan inhalator. However, the orders soon stopped when the racial identity of the inventor became known.

Garrett Morgan was not discouraged. He returned to his workshop and in 1923 created a device which makes possible the orderly movement of the millions of automobiles in today's cities and towns—the automatic stop-sign. Rights to the stop sign were sold to General Electric for the sum of $40,000, a nice sum for a man who had come to Cleveland, Ohio a penniless native of Tennessee. Awarded a solid gold medal by the city of Cleveland for his heroic rescue, Garrett lived in that city until his death in 1963.

"Morgan", *Crisis*, February, 1914, p. 165; documents supplied by the inventor.

Martin R. Delaney (1812-1885)
ETHNOLOGIST

"I thank God for making me a man simply; but Delaney always thanks Him for making him a black man." Thus spoke Frederick Douglass of his old friend, Martin R. Delaney, spokesman, physician, explorer and scientist.

Martin R. Delaney was indeed proud of the Gullah and Mandingo blood which flowed in his veins. He was one of the leaders in the great debate following the passage of the Fugitive Slave Act in 1850. His pride of race was so great that he became a spokesman for those who felt that America was too inhospitable for persons of African descent. After serving as a prime mover in several conventions of free Negroes to discuss the possibility of emigrating to Africa, in 1859 Delaney led the first and only exploratory party of American-born Negroes to Africa. In the region of the Niger River, Delaney's party carried out scientific studies and made agreements with several African chiefs for the treatment of prospective emigres from America.

Trained in the natural sciences, Martin Delaney attended the International Statistical Conference meeting in London in 1860 and read a scientific paper before the Royal Geographic Society. When Lord Brougham commented favorably on Delaney's presence at the Conference, several southern delegates withdrew from it.

Even before the Fugitive Slave Law was passed, Delaney had already made a reputation as a writer and speaker on abolition and emigration. He helped Frederick Douglass to edit *The North Star* from 1847 to 1849. He received his medical and scientific training at Harvard and practiced medicine in Chicago and in Canada. When not practicing medicine, he often travelled about the country, speaking on abolition. Once in Ohio he was almost fatally beaten by a mob but continued to speak for the cause of freedom.

Delaney was a free-born native of Charleston, West Virginia but spent his youth in Pennsylvania where he was taken to be educated. It was there that he became interested in seeking solutions to the plight of the Negro in America. For a short time he published his views in his own newspaper called *The Mystery*. After gaining journalistic experience with Douglass, Delaney published two major books, *The Condition, Elevation, Emigration and Destiny of the Colored People of the United States Politically Considered* (1852) and *Principia of Ethnology: The Origins of Race and Color* (1879).

His devotion to the cause of freedom led him to seek audience with President Lincoln in 1865 to propose an army of Negroes, commanded by Negroes. Although he was not successful in persuading the President to do this, he was commissioned a major in the U. S. Colored troops, the first of his race to be so honored. He also served with the 109th Regiment.

After the war he worked with the Freedmen's Bureau for three years. Delaney later became a customs inspector in Charleston, S. C. and then a trial justice in the same city. Delaney died on January 24, 1885.

Louis Mehlinger. "The Attitude of the Free Negro Toward African Colonization", *Journal of Negro History*, I (July, 1916), pp. 276-301; *Dictionary of American Biography*, V, 1930, pp. 219-220.

Matthew A. Henson (1867-1955)

POLAR EXPLORER

When Admiral Robert E. Peary, the renowned scientist and explorer, was surveying canal sites in Nicaragua, in 1887, Matthew A. Henson was his trusty, versatile and resourceful companion. Four years later in June, 1891 when Peary set out on his expedition to Inglefield Gulf, Greenland, where he hoped to reach the North Pole by traveling the uncharted area to the north, he engaged Henson to accompany him.

On this first trip Henson was a valuable aid to Peary. He established a friendly relationship with the Eskimos, who believed him to be somehow related to them because of his brown skin. Arctic explorers, at this time depended almost solely on their legs and dog sleds. Peary's expedition was greatly aided by Henson's expert handling of the Eskimos, dogs and equipment. On the first trip Matthew went as far as Cape York, Greenland with the Admiral who pushed on to discover Independence Bay.

Henson accompanied Peary on expeditions in 1900, 1902 and 1905, when the Admiral sought to discover the magical point called the North Pole. By 1907, Peary's repeated failures caused many to consider him foolhardy. In 1908, Peary and Henson set out for what they instinctively knew would be their last venture to the top of the world. Through their long association a brotherly bond existed between them, for Henson had given Peary the sincere moral support he sorely needed. Peary, Henson and four other explorers left Cape Sheridan, Greenland in February, 1908. The going was extremely hard. Snow-blindness, frostbite and sheer physical exhaustion felled all but Henson and Peary. April 4, 1908 found them only sixty miles from their goal accompanied by four Eskimos. On April 6, Peary called a halt and painfully took a reading with his sextant. Carefully calculating to avoid any possibility of error, Peary determined the precise point of the Pole on April 7 and asked Henson to place the American flag on the spot.

Matthew A. Henson has been recognized as the indispensable man who was responsible for getting Peary to the Pole.

Matthew A. Henson. *A Negro Explorer at the North Pole*, New York, 1912; Bradley Robinson. *Dark Companion*, New York, 1947.

George Washington Carver   (1864-1943)

If an honest history of the Deep South is ever written, Dr. George Washington Carver will stand out as one of the truly great men of his time. Almost single-handedly, Dr. Carver revolutionized southern agriculture. He brought the findings of the laboratory to the land. He was a scientist, teacher, administrator and humanitarian.

From his small laboratory on the campus of Tuskegee Institute flowed hundreds of discoveries and products. From the once-neglected peanut, Dr. Carver extracted meal, instant and dry coffee, bleach, tan remover, wood filler, metal polish, paper, ink, shaving cream, rubbing oil, linoleum, synthetic rubber and plastics. From the soybean he obtained flour, breakfast food and milk. His mind laid bare over one hundred different products within the sweet potato. During World War II, he found over 500 different shades of dye to replace aniline dyes formerly imported from Germany; his work on dehydration attracted the attention of the United States government.

Dr. Carver was among the first advocates of the use of legumes to replace soil minerals depleted by cotton-growing. From *calcareous tripoli* and *siliceous tripoli* he made a universal scouring powder. Out of the Alabama clays he obtained a talcum powder. He discovered an exceptionally large deposit of *bentonite* extending from Montgomery to Mobile, Alabama. (*Bentonite* makes possible the re-use of news pulp.)

Dr. Carver always had a practical bent to his mind but it took the boll weevil to focus his wizardry on the peanut and sweet potato. In 1914 the boll weevil, marching like some dreaded scourge from Mexico eastward, threatened to dethrone king cotton on which the South depended. Dr. Carver felt that the answer to this threat lay in the South finding some sources of income other than cotton. As news of his startling discoveries in the ordinary peanut and common sweet potato circulated around the country,

"SAVIOR OF SOUTHERN AGRICULTURE"

Dr. Carver was called to Washington to report on his findings before the House Ways and Means Committee. For over one hour the gentle Doctor pulled from his bags item after item and convinced skeptical congressmen that king cotton need not continue to hold the southern region in its tyranny.

Dr. Carver's major contribution, then, was to demonstrate the use of science and scientific techniques in improving the land and diversifying the foundations of the South's economy. The peanut and the sweet potato have become major items in the south's economy.

The wizard of Tuskegee was soon known throughout the world. Scientists, inventors, promoters, governmental officials all made their way to him. Thomas A. Edison, himself the inventor of the electric light and phonograph, wanted to employ Dr. Carver. Henry Ford set up a special laboratory for him. Men from Australia, Africa, Russia and India consulted him. In 1916 he was named a Fellow of the Royal Society, London; he received the Spingarn Medal in 1923.

Dr. Carver's achievements in science have perhaps obscured the fact that he was also a competent painter. Indeed, during the early part of his life he studied art at Iowa's Simpson College. His paintings were sufficiently competent to merit recognition and display in the Columbian Exposition held in Chicago in 1893. His "Yucca, Angustifolia and Cactus" was awarded an honorable mention. One of his most charming works in still life was a cluster of peaches which is housed in the Carver Museum at Tuskegee.

Humble and devout before God and nature, Dr. Carver was eager to see others benefit from his work and the study of science. In 1938 he donated $30,000 of his life's saving to the establishment of the George Washington Carver Foundation and, shortly before his death, willed the remainder of his estate to the Foundation whose purpose is to discover uses for agricultural wastes and to develop food products from common agricultural products with the aim of creating new markets for them.

Dr. Carver was born in Diamond Grove, Missouri in 1864. At the age of thirteen he was on his own. Enduring great hardships, he worked his way through Simpson and Iowa State Colleges. Booker T. Washington called him to Tuskegee Institute in 1896. Shortly afterwards an experimental farm was set up there under Dr. Carver and the work began of re-educating farmers throughout the Tuskegee region.

The gentle, amiable and self-effacing Dr. George Washington Carver was first and foremost a research scientist whose work had immediate application. It is highly doubtful if any other individual has done as much for southern agriculture as Dr. Carver who died in 1943 and was buried next to Booker T. Washington.

Rackham Holt. *George Washington Carver*, New York, 1943; *Negro Yearbook*, 1947, Tuskegee, 1947, pp. 37-39; p. 415.

Daniel Hale Williams (1856-1931)

FIRST SUCCESSFUL HEART SURGEON

Provident Hospital - 1893

Dr. Daniel Hale Williams was raised from an unsung master of medicine to a position of national renown as one of America's greatest surgeons, by a husky, young street fighter named James Cornish. In a brawl, Cornish suffered a knife wound in an artery a fraction of an inch from the heart. Heart wounds, or even wounds in the thoracic cavity, prior to the date of this incident in 1893, were treated with sedatives and prayer, and the patient invariably died.

"Dr. Dan", as he was often called, decided to do something no other doctor had ever done: to open Cornish's chest and operate on the heart. X-rays, sulfa drugs, blood transfusion, now absolute necessities—were unknown medical tools at the time. Calling six of his colleagues on the staff of the struggling Provident Hospital in Chicago, Dr. Dan operated. The patient lived. The doctor had performed the impossible operation . . . "Sewed up his heart," headlined a Chicago paper.

From the age of twelve Daniel was on his own, working as an apprentice shoemaker, a roustabout on a lake steamer and barber, but with a constant eye on a medical career. From his birthplace in Pennsylvania, he drifted to Janesville, Illinois where he met a white physician who encouraged him to enter medicine. With the aid of friends, he finished Chicago Medical College in 1883 and opened his office on Chicago's south side. His extraordinary skill earned him a post at his alma mater as a surgeon and demonstrator in anatomy.

At this time no hospital in Chicago allowed Negro doctors to use their facilities. In 1891, against great odds and almost single-handed, Dan Williams created Provident Hospital for the use of all physicians without regard to color, thus hastening the end to operations performed on couches and kitchen tables in the crowded tenements of Chicago's south side. Dr. Dan's skill as a surgeon spread and physicians from far and near came to Provident to see the wizard of the scalpel perform.

In 1894 Dr. Williams was called to Washington to head Freedmen's Hospital, a collection of six old pre-Civil War buildings, with medical facilities equally as primitive. Dr. Dan organized Freedmen's into departments, collected a staff of twenty volunteer specialists, and created the beginning of the first nursing school for Negroes.

Desiring to resume his profession, and tiring of the pressure of administrative duties, Dr. Williams resigned from Freedmen's in 1898 and returned to Chicago where he became the first Negro to hold a post at St. Luke Hospital and Northwestern University Hospital. He also resumed his association with Provident Hospital. When he died in 1931, he bequeathed part of his estate for the advancement of Negro physicians and part to the NAACP, his major life interests.

Helen Buckler, *Dr. Dan; Pioneer American Surgeon*. Boston, 1954.

Ernest E. Just (1883-1941)
BIOLOGIST

Howard University College of Medicine

One of the most embarrassing moments in the life of Dr. Ernest E. Just occurred on the night of January 2, 1915. Accustomed to the laboratory and the passionless laws of science, the young Ernest E. Just did not want to endure the speeches and plaudits which accompany the awarding of the Spingarn Medal, given by the NAACP to the individual who has done most during the year to advance the progress of the Negro. Young Mr. Just had even written to the NAACP explaining that he was upset over being the recipient of the award for 1914. Despite his modesty and embarrassment, this accolade could not be denied him.

Dr. Just was given the award not for making speeches about the condition of the Negro in the United States or leading demonstrations of protest; rather, he was being recognized for his work as a pure scientist who was making pioneer investigations into the mysteries of egg fertilization and the study of the cell. His work was earning him the title, "Scientist's Scientist," for he was a meticulously brilliant investigator of biological phenomena relating to the structure of the cell.

A measure of his contribution to biological knowledge may be seen in the words of the late Dr. Charles Drew, himself an outstanding researcher in blood plasma preservation. Dr. Drew described Dr. Just as a "biologist of unusual skill and the greatest of our original thinkers in the field." He was seen as producing "new concepts of cell life and metabolism which will make for him a place for all time."

Dr. Just wrote two major books and over sixty scientific papers in his field. He was for many years Howard University's outstanding professor in the biological siences and received many awards and grants for his research. Scientists from all over America and Europe sought him out and studied his work. He loved Howard but from time to time he went abroad to study and confer with other scientists, researchers and investigators.

Ernest E. Just was a native of South Carolina and he worked his way from Charleston to Meriden, New Hampshire to enter Dartmouth College on a scholarship. His first two years at Dartmouth were lonely and discouraging but when his routine studies in biology introduced him to the intricacies of cellular reproduction, his entire mind caught fire and he graduated from Dartmouth magna cum laude and Phi Beta Kappa.

Mary White Ovington. *Portraits in Color*, New York, 1927; *Negro Yearbook, 1947*, Tuskegee, 1947, pp. 35-36.

Ulysses Grant Dailey
(1885-1961)

SURGEON

Named for the victor in the war between the North and South, Ulysses Grant Dailey was one of the most distinguished surgeons in America. Whenever a roster of outstanding medical men is compiled, the name of Dr. Dailey ranks high on the list.

A native of Donaldsonville, Louisiana, Dr. Dailey rose to international prominence within his profession. A graduate of Northwestern University Medical School in 1906, Dr. Dailey's name was always associated with outstanding work in the fields of anatomy and surgery. Upon graduating from Northwestern he was appointed a Demonstrator in Anatomy at his alma mater. Following this he spent four years (1908-1912) as surgical assistant to the renowned Dr. Daniel Hale Williams, the founder of Provident Hospital, Chicago.

Not content with experience as an ambulance surgeon for the city of Chicago and his work with Dr. Williams, Dr. Dailey studied abroad in London, Paris and Vienna. In 1926 he set up his own hospital and sanitarium. Over the years, his brilliant mind and nimble fingers brought him increasing fame. He became a member of many medical societies, national and international. For thirty-eight years he was associate editor of the *Journal* of the National Medical Association. In 1948-49 he served as editor-in-chief of this publication. News of his competence spread as far afield as Pakistan and he was made corresponding Editor of *The Medius* at Karachi.

In 1953, Dr. Dailey circled the world under the sponsorship of the International College of Surgeons of which he was a Founder Fellow. In 1951 and 1953, the U. S. State Department sent him as a health advisor to Pakistan and to India, Ceylon and Africa. He was named Honorary Consul to Haiti in 1954.

In the midst of all of his travel and organizational work, Dr. Dailey for over two decades was Chief Attending Surgeon, Provident Hospital, located in the heart of Chicago's teeming Southside. He also found time to write numerous technical articles in different areas of his field. His death in 1961 ended an exceptional career of unstinting service to his fellowman.

Who's Who in Colored America, 1950, p. 132 and Lucille A. Chambers, *America's Tenth Man*, New York, 1957, p. 82. *American Men of Science*, (3rd Edition), Farmingdale, New York, 1961, p. 157.

Charles Drew
(1904-1950)

PIONEER IN BLOOD PLASMA RESEARCH

One night in North Carolina a tired man fell asleep at the wheel, wrecked his car and was badly injured. For a time he lay bleeding and in a little while he died without ever regaining consciousness. The man had been a star athlete, scholar, scientist and surgeon who had already made his mark in his profession. The dead man was Dr. Charles Drew, head of Freedmen's Hospital, Washington, D.C.

Dr. Drew was not yet fifty years old, but already his contribution to medicine had saved hundreds of thousands of lives during World War II. Dr. Drew was a pioneer in blood plasma preservation. Before his time there was no efficient way to store large quantities of blood plasma for use during emergencies or for use in wartime where thousands of lives depended on the availability of blood for blood transfusions. After Dr. Drew this was no longer a problem, for he discovered ways and means of preserving blood plasma in what are commonly known as blood banks.

A native of Washington, D. C., Dr. Drew had been a letter man in track, a Mossman trophy winner in general scholarship and a Spingarn Medalist in his contributions to human welfare. Dr. Drew's entire life was spent in the pursuit of excellence whether it was on the track cinders or in the operating room or in the research laboratory. As an Amherst undergraduate, he was captain of the track team and an outstanding halfback on the football team. He received the Mossman trophy for having brought the most honor to the school over a four-year period. At Magill University in Canada, he won first prize in physiological anatomy and set track records which stood for several years.

Beginning his research into the properties of blood plasma, at Columbia University, Dr. Drew became an authority on the subject and was asked by the British to set up a plasma program for them. He later did the same thing for the United States in 1942 and won the Spingarn medal in recognition of his contributions to Negro progress. At the time of his death in 1950, Dr. Drew was chief surgeon and chief of staff at Freedmen's Hospital.

Current Biography, 1950; Negro Yearbook, 1947 Tuskegee, 1947; *Who's Who in Colored America, 1950*, pp. 163-164.

Percy Julian (1898-   )

CHEMIST

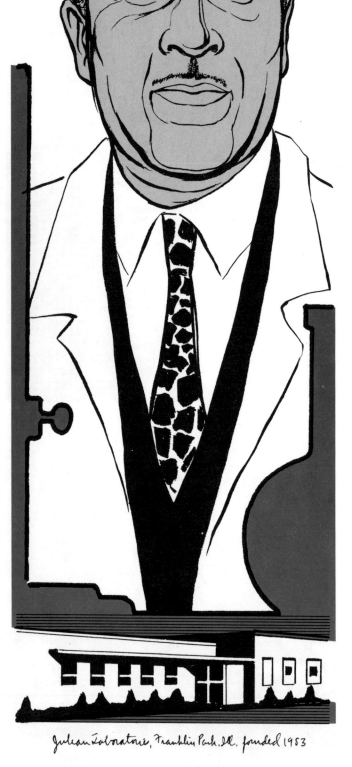

Julian Laboratories, Franklin Park, Ill. founded 1953

The citation on one of Dr. Percy Julian's nine honorary degrees sums up his career by saying in part: "Education's investment in him has been returned manyfold in the magnificence of his service to mankind." His greatest single scientific contribution helped millions suffering from the excruciating pain of arthritis.

Dr. Percy Julian is, perhaps, the most famous living Negro scientist. Just as George Washington Carver demonstrated what could be done with the ordinary peanut, Dr. Julian took the soybean, which was until his time just another bean, and extracted from it an ingredient to relieve inflammatory arthritis.

Until the late thirties, Europe had a monopoly on the production of sterols, the basis of Dr. Julian's research. These sterols were extracted from the bile of animals at a cost of several hundreds of dollars a gram. Substituting sterols from the oil of the soybean, Dr. Julian reduced the cost of sterols to less than twenty cents a gram, thus making cortisone, a sterol derivative, available to the needy at a reasonable cost.

Today (1962) Dr. Julian is a millionaire and is president of two companies bearing his name. His route to fame was not easy and, like others who have achieved it he had to toil and sacrifice. He is the son of a railway clerk. He worked his way through DePauw University at Greencastle, Indiana. For a time he lived in an attic of the fraternity house where he worked as a waiter. Applying himself to his studies, he graduated with Phi Beta Kappa honors and was valedictorian of his class. His mother was so impressed with his achievements as a student at DePauw that she moved the entire Julian family from Montgomery, Alabama to Greencastle so that the other children might have the same advantages of good schooling. Two of Dr. Julian's brothers are physicians and his three sisters have earned their masters degrees.

Graduating from DePauw in 1920, Percy Julian spent several years teaching at Fisk, and Howard Universities and West Virginia State College. He attended Harvard and then took his doctorate at the University of Vienna. For a number of years he taught at DePauw and later went on to head the soybean Research Department of the Glidden Company and form his own company which was devoted mainly to the production of sterol. When he totaled up Julian Laboratories' earnings for the first year, he found a net profit of $71.70. The next year however, he counted a profit of $97,000. In 1961 his company merged with the huge Smith, Kline and French Pharmaceutical Company in an arrangement which paid Dr. Julian several millions of dollars.

Living at this time (1963) in the exclusive residential section of Oak Park, Illinois, a prosperous suburb of Chicago which first rejected him as a resident, he and his family have become full members of the community.

Richard Bardolph. *The Negro Vanguard*, New York, 1961, pp. 428-433; *Ebony*, XIII (January, 1958). pp. 51-56.

Theodore K. Lawless (1892-   )

DERMATOLOGIST-PHILANTHROPIST

Lawless Chapel, Dillard University, N.O., Louisiana

In 1963, as they had been doing for many years, people line the sidewalk running past an old mansion in the heart of Chicago's black metropolis. Slowly they move forward, up the steps and into the waiting-room of a doctor. The doctor hears their complaints in accents representing every social strata and section in America. Often the accent is French, German or Italian. Sometimes the patients speak in halting English, for they may not be Americans at all, but citizens of another country who are present solely because of Dr. Theodore K. Lawless, the man who sees and listens to them all.

Known wherever dermatologists gather, Dr. Lawless is one of the world's leading skin specialists. His career stretches back over a period of forty years. Born in Thibodeaux, Louisiana in 1892, Dr. Lawless achieved eminence in his chosen field by hard work, superb training and outstanding intellect. He was educated at Talledega College in Alabama, the University of Kansas, Columbia, Harvard; he received the M.D. degree from Northwestern University in Evanston, Illinois. He has done special work in Vienna, Freiburg and Paris. Dr. Lawless has made signal contributions in the scientific treatment of syphilis and leprosy. From 1924 to 1941 Dr. Lawless taught at the Northwestern University School of Medicine. For many years he has been Senior Attending Physician at Provident Hospital, seven blocks from his office.

Although Dr. Lawless is a millionaire, he works as hard as ever and sees an average of one hundred patients daily. He once declared that "I am happiest when I work and so I work as much as I can." The distinguished dermatologist is as prodigal with his earnings as he is with his skill. As an example of his liberality, Dillard University in New Orleans, Louisiana has a $700,000 apartment building which was secured through his efforts in 1956. A chapel on the Dillard campus bears his name. Several other colleges attended by Negroes have benefited from his largess. His philanthrophy, however, is not restricted to his race. In the state of Israel at the Beilinson Hospital Center stands a $500,000 dermatology clinic, erected mainly through the efforts of Dr. Lawless. The clinic bears his name.

On May 16, 1963 civic leaders, the mayor of Chicago and the governor of the state of Illinois attended a testimonial dinner in his honor. As early as 1929 he won the Harmon Award for outstanding achievement in medicine; in 1954 the NAACP gave him the Spingarn medal. Dr. Lawless has served on numerous boards and committees in the areas of education and health. Neither his great wealth, his international reputation nor his many honors keep him from treating the rich and the poor with the same care and devotion he showed when he was unknown and obscure.

Who's Who in Colored America, 1950, p. 332; *Chicago Sun-Times*. June 2, 1963, p. 54.

Lunsford Lane, abolitionist and successful tobacco dealer

John B. Russwurm, Editor of "Freedom's Journal"

According to the economist Abram L. Harris, Negro enterprise and achievement in the economic sphere has been hampered by low wages, difficulties in securing credit, occupational restrictions, proscriptions against owning certain types of property, a lack of educational and cultural opportunities and a general reluctance of the wider society to help promote the economic well-being of the Negro. Despite these very real handicaps, the historical records are replete with the name of individual Negro entreprenuers whose achievements should not go unmentioned.

As early as 1769 an ex-slave known as Emmanuel operated one of the most successful ale houses in Rhode Island, and upon his death left an estate worth $2,500. Paul Cuffe was enormously successful in his shipping and trading ventures and upon his death left an estate of considerable size. James Forten, the owner of one of the largest sail-lofts on the east coast, left an estate valued at $100,000 when he died in 1842. The widow of Richard Allen, founder of the African Methodist Episcopal Church, was the beneficiary of an estate worth $25,000 in the 1830's.

As indicated by the following example, Negroes in the South and West were not without some economic success

during the years before freedom. Lunsford Lane was a leading tobacco dealer in North Carolina. He was so successful that his jealous white competitors forced him out of the state. Henry Boyd, a Kentucky-born cabinet-maker owned property appraised at $26,000 in 1859. Thomy Lafon of New Orleans, Louisiana, and Stephen Smith each left estates worth nearly $500,000. James Garrett in Detroit, Michigan and John Jones in Chicago, Illinois each were grossing $1,000 weekly as tailors.

In the years following emancipation, most southern Negroes stayed in the South and put their old skills to work in carpentry, cabinet-making, iron-working and of course, agriculture. In Mississippi, for example, the Montgomerys—Benjamin and Isiah T.—leased the farm of their former master in 1865 and gathered on it forty-six former slaves. Within two years they were able to sell 520 bales of cotton. Young Isiah T. Montgomery signed notes to buy the farm outright in 1867 when he was not yet twenty-one years old. In less than a decade, the Montgomerys and their paid workers were in third place among the ranking cotton producers in the state of Mississippi.

In the South the wealth of free Negroes was valued at $25,000,000 in 1863. At the same time free Negroes in the North and West are believed to have possessed property and other goods amounting to $50,000,000. In most cases, this wealth consisted of real estate, although there were many instances of small businesses owned and operated by Negroes.

Significant capital accumulation by Negroes started during the Civil War when the federal government created military and later freedmen's banks to hold the pay of soldiers and laborers in the Union armies. The first such military bank was set up in New Orleans in 1864. Subsequently, other branches were opened in different parts of the South. These various units were incorporated in the Freedmen's Savings and Trust Company on March 3, 1865 when Lincoln also authorized the creation of the Freedmen's Bureau.

The first bank organized and managed entirely by Negroes was the "Savings Bank of the Grand Fountain United Order of True Reformers." This bank was organized in Richmond, Virginia in 1888. In the same year the Capital Savings Bank was opened in Washington, D.C.

Having Been Faithful Over a Few Talents

S.B. Fuller, President of Fuller Products Company and other business enterprises

By 1900 scores of Negroes organized and operated burial-aid societies, banks, newspapers, shirt factories, carpet factories, dry-goods stores, small cotton mills, and many other types of enterprises. Some Negroes established cooperative enterprises. The most notable of them were the Bay Shore Hotel Company in Hampton, Virginia, the Southern Stove Hollow-Ware and Foundry Company in Chattanooga, Tennessee and the South View Cemetery Association of Jacksonville, Florida.

While most of the general business enterprises mentioned above have long since disappeared or have been succeeded by similar ones, banking, insurance and journalism continue to dominate the world of the Negro big-business man. The Citizens Trust Company of Atlanta, the only Negro bank holding membership in the federal reserve system, has assets of $13,000,000. The Mutual Federal Savings and Loan Association of Atlanta and the Broadway Federal Savings and Loan Association of Los Angeles each have assets in excess of $10,000,000. Other financial institutions which count their assets in millions of dollars are the Trans-Bay Savings and Loan Association of San Francisco, California; the Mechanics and Farmers Bank of Durham and Raleigh, North Carolina; the Industrial Bank of Washington, D.C.; the Citizens Savings Bank and Trust Company of Nashville, Tennessee; the Citizen Southern Bank and Trust Company of Philadelphia, Pennsylvania, and the Mutual Federal Savings and Loan Association of Atlanta, Georgia.

The leading insurance company is the North Carolina Mutual Life Insurance Company which has assets of $82,000,000. The Atlanta Life Insurance Company is the second largest with assets of $58,000,000. Other outstanding life insurance companies are the Supreme Life Insurance Company of America, in Chicago, Illinois, the Golden State Mutual Life Insurance Company of Los Angeles, California, the Great Lakes Mutual Life Insurance Company of Detroit, Michigan and the Afro-American Life Insurance Company of Jacksonville, Florida.

The long shadow of John B. Russwurm's *Freedom's Journal* (1827), the first Negro newspaper published in America, falls on scores of newspapers directed toward a predominantly Negro audience. The *Atlanta Daily World* and the *Chicago Defender* are the only Negro-owned papers which are published on a daily basis. The *Pittsburgh Courier*,

Frank L. Gillespie, founder of Supreme Life Insurance Company of America

the *Chicago Courier*, the *New York Age*, the *Amsterdam News*, the *Norfolk Journal and Guide*, the *St. Louis Argus* are considered by many critics to be the best-edited Negro newspapers in the country. The only Negro news service, the Associated Negro Press founded by the brilliant Claude A. Barnett, supplements the general news carried by scores of Negro newspapers throughout the nation.

Several companies in the cosmetics industry have achieved national prominence. Probably the largest and best-known of them are the Fuller Company of Chicago, Illinois, which is named for its founder, the dynamic S. B. Fuller. Others are the Murray's Superior Products Company of Chicago, the Madame C. J. Walker Manufacturing Company of Indianapolis, Indiana, the Apex News and Hair Company of Atlantic City, New Jersey and the Rose Morgan House of Beauty of New York City.

The business enterprises listed above are the happy exceptions to the relative scarcity of large-scale business organizations owned and operated by Negroes. The men and women who founded and developed them were a shrewd and hardy breed, competing against the odds of a restrictive society and environment.

Abram Harris. *The Negro as Capitalist*, Philadelphia, 1936; Joseph A. Pierce. *Negro Business and Business Education*, New York, 1947; Saunders Redding. *The Lonesome Road*, New York, 1958, pp. 93-100, 105-120.

William Leidesdorff (1810-1848)

MANEUVERING MILLIONAIRE

Born at St. Croix in the Danish Virgin Island, Leidesdorff was the son of a Danish planter and an African mother, Anna Marie Sparks. He was sent to New Orleans to work in the office of his two brothers in the cotton business. Both brothers died and Leidesdorff came into considerable wealth. He left New Orleans for California in 1841 because, legend has it, of an unhappy love affair and landed in California, captain of a 160-ton schooner, the *Julia Ann*.

At this time California was in the middle of a three-way power struggle between Mexico, who owned it, and the United States and Great Britain, who coveted it. Leidesdorff threaded his way through this political maze by first securing from Mexico, in 1843, a land grant of two 300-foot lots on the corner of Clay and Kearney streets. Upon these lots he built a store and a home where he entertained American social and political big-wigs. Soon afterwards, he was appointed American Consul in California. With the Mexican land grants in mind, he became a naturalized Mexican citizen in 1844, and promptly acquired from the Mexican government 35,000 acres of ranch land on the bank of the American River. This strategy was rewarded when in 1845 he was appointed American sub-consul at Yerba Buena. In 1846 the last Mexican mayor of San Francisco gave him the corner of what is now Leidesdorff and California streets. Upon this Mexican-given property he built a warehouse which he leased to the U. S. Government.

The power struggle for California came to a head in July, 1846. Leidesdorff was given a proclamation of the take-over of the city by Captain Montgomery of the U. S. Marines. This proclamation had to be translated into Spanish for the benefit of the Mexican citizens who could not understand English. The Marines landed and raised their flag on a pole just vacated by the Mexican flag which had been given to Leidesdorff for safe keeping. Two months later Leidesdorff held a ball at his home for the "conquerors." A week later he was named treasurer by the city council of which he was a member.

Before his fabulous career ended he bought a steamship from the Russian-American Fur Company, and also staged the first formal horse race in California history. On May 18, 1848, he died at the age of thirty-eight, leaving an estate of $1,500,000.

Ebony Magazine, November, 1958, Johnson Publishing Co.

In the downtown section of cosmopolitan, multi-racial San Francisco, there is a short street named Leidesdorff, which few know is named after a crafty, multi-racial individual, William Alexander Leidesdorff. Leidesdorff was a ship captain, trader, Mexican citizen, American diplomat, merchant, city treasurer of San Francisco, owner of several city blocks in what is now downtown San Francisco and owner of 35,000 acres of land near Sutters Mill, the birthplace of the California gold rush.

John Jones (1816-1879)

BUSINESSMAN CRUSADER

Jones Commercial School of Chicago is known to business men throughout the United States, because from its doors come some of the best-trained secretarial help in the nation. However, few know that the school was named after John Jones, a Negro from North Carolina who donated to Chicago the land on which the school now stands.

John Jones was born of free parents in 1816 and became the first Negro tailor in Chicago. He built an excellent business catering to the aristocracy of the Gold Coast. By the time he was twenty-five he had constructed a four-story office building at 119 So. Dearborn Street. His business prospered and he was soon considered one of the city's more substantial citizens.

Chicago, like many other northern cities during the first half of the 19th century, had a special set of laws defining the rights of free Negroes and setting them apart from the remainder of the citizenry. A fighter, as well as a business man, Jones refused to bow to the dictates of the "Black Laws" as they were called. He took to the streets with a petition to have them stricken from the books. He approached friends and strangers alike, asking them to sign in support of his fight for full civil rights. His efforts were finally rewarded in 1865 when the notorious "Black Laws" were repealed.

Jones built up a large following during his business career and crusading. He was encouraged to enter politics where he made a remarkable showing. In 1874 he was named a County Commissioner. He later became a powerful man in Chicago politics and used his influence to wipe out the practice of segregation in Chicago public schools. He was the first Negro appointed to the Chicago Board of Education.

Although Jones spent much of his time in politics and business, before the Civil War, he set up his palatial home as a station on the Underground Railroad. Many a night fugitive slaves, in fear and trembling, knocked at his door, and were received with open arms and aided toward their destination.

Jones was so admired among Chicagoans that when he celebrated his thirtieth year as a resident in 1875, most of the leading social and business personalities of both races were present.

Jones School, Plymouth Court at Harrison Street, Chicago

Edward T. Clayton, "Four Chicago Pioneers", *Negro Digest* Vol. VIII, September, 1950, p. 91. Bessie L. Pierce, "A History of Chicago", vol. 3, New York, 1957, p. 48.

Madame C. J. Walker
(1869-1919)

COSMETICS MANUFACTURER

While America has produced hundreds of millionaires, few ex-washerwomen are numbered among their ranks. One of the first American women of any race or rank to become a millionaire through her own efforts was Sarah Breedlove Walker.

Orphaned in her native Louisiana at six, married to one C. J. Walker at fourteen and widowed at twenty, Madame C. J. Walker invented a new method of straightening hair. Before her time, Negro women who wanted to de-kink their hair had to place it on a flat surface and press it with a flat iron. In 1905 Madame Walker invented her hair softener and a special straightening comb. For millions of women these inventions were a godsend. Overnight she found herself in business, with assistants, agents, schools and, eventually, a manufacturing company. Before her death in 1919 Madame Walker could count over 2,000 agents selling an ever-expanding line of Walker products and demonstrating the "Walker System" of treating hair.

A former laundress, Madame Walker proved herself a competent businesswoman. She organized her agents into clubs, trained operatives for her system, allocated franchises and provided the cosmetics and equipment required. Her payroll was over $200,000 annually. She donated large sums to charity and to educational institutions. She even founded an academy for girls in West Africa and bequeathed $100,000 to it.

Madame Walker constantly made headlines, both with her business and her social activities. In New York at Irvington-on-the-Hudson, she built Villa Lewaro, a $250,000 mansion. She furnished it with a gold-plated piano, a $60,000 pipe organ, Hepplewhite furniture, Persian rugs and many huge oil paintings. A "who's who" of Negro America marched through her doors. Through it all, Madame Walker remained a pleasant, kindly person genuinely interested in those less fortunate than herself.

Madame Walker's ingenuity and ability laid the foundation of the cosmetics industry among Negroes and spurred the interest in beauty among colored women.

Dictionary of American Biography, XIX, 1936; Roi Ottley. *New World A-Coming*, New York, 1943, pp. 172-173.

Maggie L. Walker
(1867-1934)

BANKER, ORGANIZER

"If the state of Virginia had done no more in fifty years with the funds spent on the education of Negroes than to educate Mrs. Walker, the state would have been amply repaid for its outlay and effort." Thus spoke the governor of Virginia in 1924 when the city of Richmond was paying tribute to the foresight and genius of Maggie L. Walker.

Mrs. Walker was being honored at the time for her contribution to Richmond's economic and civic progress. Her contributions could be seen in the huge structure which housed the St. Luke Bank and Trust Company, the national headquarters of the Independent Order of St. Luke and an insurance concern, all of which she headed. Newspaper readers could follow the course of her progress in the *St. Luke Herald*, another of her enterprises.

She was the prime mover in the establishment of a home for delinquent Negro girls in Richmond, having organized 1400 women into a council which paid the first $5,000 to purchase the land for the institution. Richmond could also boast of a community center in 1924, mainly because Mrs. Walker spurred an inter-racial group of women to build one.

When Maggie Walker became secretary for the Order of St. Luke in 1889, she accepted a salary of $8.00 a month and continued to teach school for her living. The Order had 3,408 members but no funds of any consequence, no property of value and virtually no staff. Yet dues paying members expected coverage for sickness and a decent burial. By 1924 Mrs. Walker had built the Order's membership to over 100,000, increased its headquarters staff to fifty-five full-time employees working in a $100,000 building constructed with funds advanced by the Order. Throughout Virginia and the surrounding states, 145 field workers provided excellent service to the members of the Order of St. Luke.

Maggie Walker, who grew up in dire poverty, was a native of Virginia. She managed to finish high school and became a teacher. Her contemporaries described her as having enough energy for a dozen women. She remained charming and pleasant throughout the hustle and bustle of her business and civic life.

Benjamin Brawley, *Negro Builders and Heroes*, Chapel Hill, North Carolina 1937, pp. 267-272.

Jesse Binga (1865-1950)
BANKER—FINANCIER

Binga before and after the collapse of his financial empire

Cleverly purchasing property on the southern fringe of the Negro area, Binga's own little real estate business prospered to the extent that he could count over 300 units of real estate and collect rent from nearly 1200 apartments. Following the southern exodus, Binga opened a new real estate office on the southwest corner of Chicago's 36th Place and State Street. He opened the Binga State Bank in 1908 in the same building. The then busy 35th and State Street intersection was his real goal and over the years he was able to buy most of the land in that block. The block, naturally, was called the "Binga Block."

Binga became known as the financial wizard of the southside. He was a power in the Negro community and had earned the respect of a number of white financiers and bankers. He moved into a white neighborhood over the protests of its residents, determined to enjoy his right to live where he was able.

The Binga financial and real estate empire prospered during the booming twenties. At the height of his success, Binga could count deposits of nearly one and a half million dollars. But as the signs of the coming depression caused more and more people to seek loans from his banks, the empire began to totter. Jesse Binga found it hard to say no to impecunious depositors and businessmen. He soon found himself in dire financial difficulties. Unable to meet his many pressing obligations, Binga desperately tried to save his businesses, and in the opinion of some, overstepped the bounds of legality.

The Binga State Bank had to close its doors in May of 1932. In 1933 Jesse Binga went to prison but later received a presidential pardon. Ever the optimist, Binga was nevertheless unsuccessful in his efforts to regain the high status he had enjoyed during the balmy twenties.

Inez V. Cantey. "Jesse Binga; the Sotry of a Life", *Crisis*, XXXIV, December, 1927, Abram L. Harris. *The Negro as Capitalist*, Philadelphia, 1936.

Jesse Binga was born the day after General Robert E. Lee surrendered his sword to General Ulysses S. Grant at Appomattox. A native of Detroit, Michigan, Binga received only a high school education, and after a variety of menial jobs, decided that one day he would go into business for himself and become his own boss. He had no idea of ever owning two banks and numerous parcels of real estate.

Coming to Chicago during the World's Fair of 1895, Binga became a huckster selling wares to Negroes in Chicago's burgeoning southside. Through his peddling he came to know thousands of people, their needs, desires and aspirations. As his own small business grew, he met and married Eudora Johnson, the niece of a wealthy sportsman, known as "Mushmouth" Johnson, who had strong political connections and a private fortune of nearly a quarter million dollars. After Johnson's death, Binga's wife inherited his estate which was to be the nucleus of the Binga enterprises.

Anthony Overton (1864-1946)
BANKER, MANUFACTURER

Ex-slave, judge, manufacturer, newspaper publisher, business executive, Anthony Overton was one of the outstanding business men of his generation. In a career covering almost sixty years, Anthony Overton left an indelible mark on the history of Negro business. In recognition of his achievements in the business world, Overton was awarded the Harmon Award in 1927 and the Spingarn Medal in 1929 as the individual who contributed most to the progress of the Negro in the preceding year.

A native of Monroe, Louisiana, Overton's career began in Kansas in 1888 when he received the A. B. degree in law from the University of Kansas Law school and was admitted to the bar. In a short time, he was appointed to the municipal bench in Topeka. The call of the business world was stronger than that of the law and after a period in Oklahoma as a merchant, Overton returned to Kansas and founded the Overton-Hygienic Products Company, manufacturing and selling baking powder, flavor extracts and toiletries.

In 1911 Overton moved his business operations to Chicago and within nine years, Overton-Hygienic Products Company was in the million-dollar class. In 1922 Overton ventured into the field of banking and established the Douglass National Bank which was housed in the Overton Building at 36th and State Street. The Douglass National Bank operated for ten years and when it closed its doors in 1932, its depositors received thirty-eight cents on the dollar, the highest amount paid by any bank closing its doors. Overton next started the Victory Mutual Life Insurance Company which is still in business and operated by Anthony Overton III. Following the success of the Victory Mutual Life Insurance Company, Overton then turned to journalism and for a time published the *Chicago Bee*, a newspaper which quickly gained a large readership on Chicago's South Side.

Anthony Overton was an energetic and frugal man who did not display the customary signs of success; instead he believed in returning profits to the enterprise that created them. He had little truck with abstraction, but felt that one should "Make each day count for more than the previous day." His own career was a perfect illustration of this motto.

Richard Bardolph. *The Negro Vanguard*, New York, 1961, pp. 256, 261; Abram Harris. *The Negro as Capitalist*, Philadelphia, 1936.

Robert S. Abbott (1870-1940)
THE LONELY WARRIOR

Chicago Defender
WORLD'S GREATEST WEEKLY

DEFENDER PLATFORM May 5, 1905

"American race prejudice must be destroyed!
The opening up of all trade Unions to black
Representation in the President's Cabinet.
Engineers, firemen and conductors on all American
roads, and all jobs in government controlled
Representation in all
Government schools open
preference to foreigners
Motormen and conductors on surface, elevated
motorbus lines throughout America.
Federal legislation to abolish lynching.
Full enfranchisement of all American

CHICAGO Daily Defender

The road to real success is usually a long and hard one. Without moral support and encouragement it can also be heart-breakingly lonely. Behind the *Chicago Defender*, the only Negro daily newspaper in Chicago, with its circulation and its magnificient office at 2400 South Michigan Avenue, stands a man who trod this lonely road, Robert Sengstacke Abbott.

Without bitterness, he recalled his long battle to establish his newspaper: "My friends made fun of me . . . they thought it was foolish of me to anticipate success in a field in which so many men before me had failed . . . but I went on fighting the opposition of my adversaries and the indifference of my friends; I emerged victorious but battle-scarred."

Abbott's dream of setting up a newspaper started in his youth. A native of St. Simon Island, Georgia, Robert was enrolled at Beach Institute in Savannah and later entered Claflin University in Orangeburg, South Carolina. It was at Virginia's Hampton Institute where, on the advice of his stepfather, John J. J. Sengstacke, he learned the printing trade that was to be his career some twelve years later. In the interim, Abbott migrated to Chicago, in 1896, where he attended Kent Law School and supported himself by working in a Loop printing house. Obtaining his law degree in 1899, he wandered about the Midwest for several years before he became convinced that he could do a better job of defending his people in public print than he could in a courtroom.

He returned to Chicago and his work as itinerant job printer and set foot on the lonely road. Combining a small amount of capital with borrowed money, and equipping his landlady's dining room with a folding card-table and kitchen chair as his office, he started the *Chicago Defender* on May 5, 1905. Three-hundred copies of the 4-page, handbill-size sheets were printed on his employer's press. Abbott himself sold them for two cents a copy, going from door to door, visiting every south side barber shop, poolroom, drugstore and church.

For fifteen years the lonely warrior contended for social justice and political and economic equity. The strong editorial policy of the *Defender* pushed the newspaper's national circulation to more than a quarter million copies. The *Defender* became a thriving institution.

John H. Sengstacke, nephew of Robert S. Abbott, inherited the *Defender* upon the death of his uncle. Sengstacke, a graduate of Hampton Institute, brought to the newspaper a new perspective on the specialized type of journalism it represented, and built steadily on the foundation he inherited.

Sengstacke was not satisfied with the prospects of the weekly paper and made plans for daily publication. On February 6, 1956 the first copy, the *Daily Defender*, made its appearance, and although skeptics said it could not be done, it has prospered and grown. Abbott would be proud of the *Defender* today, and even prouder of the modern plant which houses it.

Roi Ottley. *The Lonely Warrior; the Life and Times of Robert S. Abbott*, Chicago, 1955.

Robert L. Vann (1887-1940)

PITTSBURGH COURIER FOUNDER

Robert L. Vann, as a boy, lived so far from the railroad tracks that he was ten years old before he saw his first train. His parents were tenant farmers trying to eke out a living in the backwoods of North Carolina. He had no idea that his name would appear from coast to coast each week in a nationally distributed publication or that he would be the publisher of that newspaper, the *Pittsburgh Courier*.

The *Pittsburgh Courier*, like Robert L. Vann himself sprang from a rather modest beginning. A worker in a Pittsburgh pickle factory had started a two-page sheet as a vehicle for printing his occasional verse. Vann, by this time, a struggling young lawyer, saw how eagerly Negroes read the nondescript sheet and decided to convert it into a newspaper. Gathering associates and capital, Vann published the first edition of the *Pittsburgh Courier* on March 10, 1910. At first he thought he had erred in launching a newspaper, for as a struggling young lawyer just out of the University of Pittsburgh Law School, he had precious little time to spend on profitless ventures.

The *Pittsburgh Courier* caught on and Negroes came to swear by it. Staunchly Republican in those days, the newspaper spoke for the Negro community in Pittsburgh and was brutally candid in reporting the news. Over the years the *Pittsburgh Courier* grew. Hundreds of people soon found employment at the *Courier* plant. Across the country, hundreds of vendors sold the sprightly publication, and many reporters were hired in various states. A number of well known Negro authors wrote for it, and in many homes, it was the only paper read with interest. In 1940 the *Courier* was the most widely-read Negro newspaper in America, with branches in the leading metropolitan cities.

While the paper grew, Robert L. Vann's legal career also developed. In 1917 he was made city solicitor for Pittsburgh and remained in this post for four years. In 1924, he was alternate delegate-at-large from Pennsylvania to the National Republican Convention. He also served as a Republican publicity director of the campaign which saw Calvin Coolidge enter the White House. In 1935, Robert L. Vann was appointed to a committee to revise the constitution of the State of Pennsylvania. Switching from the Republican to the Democratic party at the end of the depression, he was appointed Assistant United States Attorney General by Franklin D. Roosevelt.

Robert L. Vann died in 1940, at the beginning of World War II. However, his newspaper lives on as a tribute to his energy and enterprise.

Richard Bardolph, *The Negro Vanguard*, New York, 1961 (Paperback), pp. 192-196.

Present (1963) home office in Durham, N.C.

C. C. Spaulding (1874-1952)

"FOUNDER" OF THE NORTH CAROLINA MUTUAL LIFE INSURANCE COMPANY

John Merrick and A. M. Moore were the men who actually founded the huge North Carolina Mutual Life Insurance Company when, in 1898, they converted a burial aid association into a mutual life insurance company. But Charles Clinton Spaulding built the company into what it is today, an enterprise with more than three million dollars worth of insurance inforce.

The company was so small when Spaulding joined Merrick and Moore that it was almost left bankrupt by a forty-dollar claim. Spaulding, a quiet, earnest young man, was the company's only employee and served as bookkeeper, salesman, advertising director and custodian. For many years Spaulding travelled the highways and byways of North Carolina, developing business for his struggling company and patient partners.

A pioneer in saturation advertising, Spaulding made sure that barbershops, lodges, stores and offices had their share of matchbooks, fans, calendars, pens and paper weights. The Negro press carried advertisements of North Carolina Mutual in almost every edition. School teachers were enlisted as agents for the company, thus creating an image of confidence and respectability. Under Spaulding the company grew from ten to twenty and, finally, hundreds of agents scouring the east coast to bring a measure of security to thousands of Negroes.

In 1923 C. C. Spaulding was made president of North Carolina Mutual and remained in this office until the day of his death. The habits of hard work, dependability and thrift which Spaulding had shown in his youth were infused into the growing company. Spaulding became a national figure and his advice and counsel were sought by hundreds of citizens, public and private. Spaulding gave unstintingly of his time and energy to numerous causes.

Born in comparative poverty and one of fourteen children, Spaulding rose to national prominence. Schools, parks, and playgrounds are named after him. His story is another of the authentic success stories of our history.

The Whetstone "In Memoriam", 3rd Quarter, 1952; Richard Bardolph, *The Negro Vanguard*, New York, 1961 (Paperback), pp. 260-264.

A. G. Gaston (1892-   )

MILLIONAIRE, FREE ENTERPRISER

Growing with Birmingham!

HOME OFFICES OF..
B.T.W. BUSINESS COLLEGE · VULCAN REALTY & INVESTMENT CO.
B.T.W. INSURANCE CO. · CITIZENS FEDERAL SAVINGS & LOAN ASSN.
A.G. GASTON, President

The eminence of Arthur G. Gaston does not rest on the fact of his wealth alone, even though he is one of the few Negro millionaires in the U. S. today. Credit is due him for the way he made his money rather than its amount. Gaston is a self-made millionaire in an age when individual enterprise is a rarity. He made his millions in business ventures—slowly and legitimately. He has invested and re-invested in business projects which directly help meet the needs of his race.

His philosophy, both business and personal, that "success is founded on seeing and satisfying the needs of people" has proven to be a rewarding one in his business and an enriching one in his life. Today he is president and owner of seven different companies and corporations in Birmingham, Alabama, including an insurance company, a chain of 14 funeral homes, a business college, a realty and investment corporation, a string of motels, a housing development, a large farm, a savings and loan association, and a cemetery. His business interests alone have assets totaling more than 11 million dollars.

But there was a time when Arthur G. Gaston worked for about $3 a day. Like most Negroes of 50 years ago, Gaston's parents were poor when he was born in Demopolis, Alabama in 1892. His father died while Arthur was a boy and when his mother had to work in Birmingham as a domestic, he stayed with his grandmother. Here there was a yard with a swing which was a favorite playing place for the kids in the neighborhood. Gaston's business acumen manifested itself at this early age when he started charging admission to the yard, of buttons and pins. After he finished eighth grade (Tuggles Institute, Birmingham) and a stint in the Army he settled in Westfield, Alabama and went to work for the Tennessee Coal Iron and Steel Company for $3.10 a day.

To supplement this meager income he sold peanuts on the side and also loaned money to his less thrifty coworkers at the rate of 25 cents on the dollar. In 1921 he saw the need for a burial society and, with his father-in-law as partner and $35, he started the Booker T. Washington Burial Society which grew into the incorporated

insurance company. The need for Negro housing led to the founding of the Citizens Federal Savings and Loan Association in 1923. In order to get the typists and clerks necessary for these businesses he started the Booker T. Washington Business College which today is fully accredited and supplying graduates for positions in business and government throughout the country.

His awareness of the needs of people, particularly the needs of his own people, spurred the organization of the 11,000 member Smith and Gaston Kiddie Club in 1945 and the sponsoring of the Gaston Statewide Spelling Bee for Negro students. This is no mere indulgence in the philanthropic tradition of millionaires or the tax-write-off operation of a shrewd businessman. It is an action motivated by a belief in his people. He says, "If I ever had a conviction that the Negro wasn't capable, I would sell out. But, I'm convinced, and I want to convince others."

Ebony Magazine, Jan., 1963

John H. Johnson (1918-)

PUBLISHER WITHOUT A PEER

seeking public welfare assistance. Johnson himself plunged into his high school life at DuSable High with such gusto that he became editor of the school paper and president of the student council. He continued his education at Northwestern University and the University of Chicago, while working at the Supreme Liberty Life Insurance Company in Chicago.

Encouraged by Harry H. Pace and Earl B. Dickerson who is now president of Supreme Liberty Life, Johnson borrowed five hundred dollars with his mother's furniture as collateral and started *Negro Digest* in 1942. Readers snapped up all five thousand copies of this periodical within a week. In less than six months *Negro Digest* took up so much of his time that he had to give up his job as publicity director with the Supreme Liberty Life Insurance Company. By the end of 1943, *Negro Digest* had a monthly circulation of fifty thousand copies. This periodical was discontinued in 1951, but was revived with gratifying success a decade later.

With a circulation of eight hundred thousand copies, *Ebony* is the backbone of the Johnson Publishing Company. It carries more diversified advertising lineage than any other publication directed toward a predominantly Negro audience. Most of the advertisements in Johnson's publications picture Negro models. Indeed Johnson is in large measure responsible for the increased employment of Negro models in advertising media.

In the wake of his success with *Negro Digest* and *Ebony*, Johnson added two pocket-size magazines, *Jet* and *Hue*, to his list of publications. Circulating to more than three hundred thousand readers, *Jet* is the most successful small magazine in the nation. The enterprising publisher followed *Jet* with *Tan*, a "true confession" type magazine. In 1963 he entered the field of hard cover books with volumes by Lerone Bennett, the senior editor of *Ebony*, the late Freda DeKnight, who made the Ebony Fashion Shows a national institution and other writers encouraged and developed by the Johnson publications.

The last two decades have been rich in honors and material rewards for John H. Johnson. In his publishing ventures he has made a vital contribution to the broadening of the communications media and to the history of the Negro.

John H. Johnson has been the most successful Negro journalist since Samuel Cornish and John B. Russwurm started *Freedom's Journal,* the first Negro newspaper, in 1827. His publications—*Ebony, Jet, Negro Digest* and *Tan*—possess a combined circulation of nearly two million copies. Hundreds of employees collect, write, edit and distribute hundreds of thousands of his magazines each week and month. His organization, the Johnson Publishing Company, is only twenty years old. Johnson, its founder, president, publisher and editor, is known throughout America.

A native of Arkansas City, Arkansas, Johnson was brought to Chicago by his mother in 1937. Her occasional jobs as a domestic were not enough to prevent them from

Who's Who in Colored America, 1950, pp. 305-306; *Chicago Defender*, January 6, 1962, p. A-15; *Chicago Sun-Times*, May 19, 1963, p. 60.

VI RELIGION

A Balm in Gilead

When Negroes were first brought to America no effort was made to convert them to Christianity as the slave owners felt that a baptized Christian could not be held in bondage. Around 1700 the general attitude of whites changed. The new view was that holding a human being in slavery was not compatible with the tenets of Christianity. From this point forward, slaveowners encouraged the adoption and promotion of religion among slaves with the hope that they would be easier to control, particularly if they learned patience and humility. There was also the notion that perhaps the slaves did have souls to save.

Negroes, slave and free, were allowed to attend white churches in the North and South, provided they were kept separated from the congregation. In the Deep South slaves were allowed to start plantation churches of their own. Quite often it had to be with the specific consent of the whites or under their general supervision. While the basic content of the ministers' sermons were taken from the Bible, little effort was made to control their ideas and utterances as long as they were confined to a discussion of the Hereafter.

In the time of the American Revolution, Negro churches existed. Usually they were quite small and their ministers totally untrained. There are historical accounts of Baptist churches being organized in Aiken, South Carolina in the 1780's. George Liele, baptized in 1775, preached in Georgia while the Revolution was in progress. Thomas Paul and M. C. Clayton organized churches in the North during the early nineteenth century.

The Negro church as an institution did not develop until Richard Allen united a scattered group of Methodist churches to organize the African Methodist Episcopal Church in 1816. Shortly after this Allen's associate, Absalom Jones, organized the first Episcopal Church among Negroes, and James Varick laid the foundation of the African Methodist Episcopal Zion church. John Chavis, at a somewhat later period, developed into a prime mover in bringing the Presbyterian church to the attention of Negroes. Daniel Coker and Lott Cary were pioneer Negro missionaries to Africa.

For the most part these ministers were without formal training in religion and theology. They were natural leaders and, with due allowance for their being "called" to the ministry, the Negro church at that time was the one relatively open path to leadership. John Chavis, for example, illustrates the possibilities confronting a talented Negro during the early nineteenth century. Born in Charleston South Carolina, Chavis was a brilliant unmixed black who was sent to Princeton University by kindly whites. In 1805 Chavis returned to his native Charleston a Presbyterian minister who preached to both Negro and white congregations within the state. He even

organized a preparatory school for white pupils. Among his "prep" students were a future U. S. senator, a governor, lawyers, doctors, and ministers. The Nat Turner insurrection in 1831 made it impossible for him to continue his ministry and his school.

These pioneer ministers were most active in the agitation for freedom in this world, although they couched the words in the accents of angels. Most of them were self-supporting as their congregations were too poor to support them. They worked with the various abolitionist societies, took part in the underground railroad movement, and were prime movers in the so-called Convention Movement. In general they were the spokesmen for the free Negroes in the North.

During the 1840's and thereafter, Negro leadership continued to emanate from the pulpit. Men such as Alexander Crummell, Henry Highland Garnet, Daniel Payne, Henry McNeal Turner, J. W. C. Pennington, and Benjamin Tucker Tanner came to the forefront of religious endeavor and race protest. The turn of the century found ministers still the major spokesmen and leaders despite the rise of worldly men such as Booker T. Washington, William Monroe Trotter, T. T. Thomas Fortune, and W. E. B. DuBois or Kelly Miller and Eugene Kinckle Jones.

While the influence of ministers declined in the twentieth century, many of them continued to remain national figures within and without the church. Among them are William Holmes Borders, Mark Miles Fisher, Howard Thurman, J. H. Jackson, Adam Clayton Powell, Jr., James H. Robinson, and Benjamin E. Mays. It is perhaps interesting to note that the more prominent ministers are known in more than one field, as in the cases of Adams Clayton Powell, Jr., who is also a U. S. Congressman, and James H. Robinson, who heads Operation Crossroads Africa. Benjamin E. Mays is an internationally-known minister and spokesman. He has been a national figure since the middle 1930's when he made the divinity school at Howard University a first-rate institution. As president of Morehouse College in Atlanta, Georgia and as a writer and orator boldly insisting on first-class citizenship for American Negroes, Dr. Benjamin E. Mays has remained familiar to many people beyond the sphere of organized religion.

The prime example of applied Christianity which goes far beyond the pulpit, of course, is the Rev. Dr. Martin Luther King who perhaps sums up the possibilities facing a Negro minister in the present age.

George A. Singleton. *Richard Allen: The Romance of African Methodism*, New York, 1952; Lewis G. Jordan. *Negro Baptist History U.S.A.*, Nashville, 1930, pp. 46-47. John Hope Franklin. *From Slavery to Freedom*, New York, 1961, pp. 224-225.

Martin de Porres (1579-1639)

A SAINTED LIFE

Priestly prejudice was not the only handicap surmounted by Brother Martin. He was the illegitimate offspring of Don Juan de Porres of Burgos, a Spanish nobleman, and Ana Velasquez, a young, freed Negro slave. His roving father returned eight years after Martin's birth on December 9, 1759 in Lima, Peru, and provided for his apprenticeship as a barber-surgeon.

At the age of eleven he took a job as servant in the Dominican priory and performed his chores with such devotion that he was called "the saint of the broom." He was later promoted to the job of the convent's almoner and became so efficient at begging that he was soon collecting an average of $2,000 a week from the rich. This was dispensed as food, clothing and medical care to the sick and the poor. Placed in charge of the Dominican's infirmary, he became known for his spectacular cures of the sick and his tireless comforting of the afflicted. In recognition of his fame and devotion, his superiors dropped the color bar to his becoming a friar. Martin, at the age of twenty-four, was vested in the full habit and took solemn vows as a Dominican brother.

His admission to brotherhood only increased his humility and desire to help others. He established an orphanage and foundling hospital and even extended his love to animals. He filled the convent with ailing stray cats and dogs which he nursed back to health. He set up a shelter in the garden for the convent mice and supplied them with scraps of food. In self-imposed austerity, he never ate meat, but fasted completely from Holy Thursday until Easter noon. Inspired by St. Dominic, he lashed himself three times nightly with a whip armed with iron hooks on the ends.

Brother Martin was venerated almost from the day of his death. In 1657 Fray Salvedor started the beatification investigation; he was beatified by Pope Gregory XVI in 1837. In 1926 Pope Pius XI opened the investigation required for sainthood after devotion to Brother Martin had spread world-wide from Peru.

Although miraculous cures—including raising the dead —had been attributed to Martin, these were not sufficiently authenticated for his canonization. The first of the two required "certified miracles" reported was the case of a girl in Paraguay who, in 1948, recovered from an "incurable" intestinal ailment. The second was reported in 1959 from Canary Islands where a boy "instantly recovered" from a gangrene-infested foot after prayers to the saint-to-be.

The official Vatican account of his sanctity notes: ". . . he made it clear that every race and nationality has the same dignity, the same equality, because we are all sons of one heavenly Father and redeemed by Christ the Lord."

"Mulatto Saint," *Time*, May 11, 1962, p. 87.

In May of 1962, the late Pope John XXIII, in a ceremony at St. Peter's Basilica in Rome, made Martin de Porres the Catholic church's first mulatto saint. In doing this, he amended a centuries-old order of the Dominican's Convent in Lima, Peru, which stipulated that "those who are begotten on the side of either one of their parents of Indian or African blood . . . may not be" received to the holy habit or profession of our order.

Augustus Tolton (1834-1897)

FIRST NEGRO PRIEST IN AMERICA

On Easter Sunday in the year 1886, a black man offered Holy Mass on the High Altar at St. Peter's Basilica in Rome, Italy. As a rule only the Pope himself offers Mass over the tomb of St. Peter in this holy of holies of the Christian world. But this was no regular occasion. Instead, it was the Church's way of honoring the first full-blooded American Negro ever to be ordained for the priesthood. Augustus Tolton, the priest, was from Quincy, Illinois and the road to Rome had not been easy.

The pomp and circumstances of St. Peter's was a stark contrast to the austere life which lay behind and before the twenty-seven year old priest who has been described as having the "vivid and striking likeness of a solid man, true as steel, without a shadow of pretension." Augustus Tolton was born in Ralls County, Missouri but had grown up in Quincy, Illinois where his mother had taken him after escaping from slavery. Before Augustus reached his teens, he was put to work in a tobacco factory where for twelve years he worked from sunrise to sunset.

Being a devout Catholic, Martha Tolton, his mother, saw that he attended mass and confession. His intelligence and piety quickly brought Augustus to the attention of the priests and bishops at St. Boniface's parish. They encouraged him in his studies and, when he was sure of his true vocation, helped to secure his admission to the College of Propaganda (De Propaganda Fide) at Rome in 1880. Brilliantly mastering the language and theological requirements, Augustus Tolton was ordained a priest on Holy Saturday, April 24, 1886.

Returning to Quincy, Illinois in the summer of 1886, the Reverend Father Augustus Tolton was made pastor of St. Joseph's Catholic Church for Negroes. St. Joseph's was an extremely small church and Father Tolton had time to tour the country. The newspapers made much of the fact that he was the first Negro priest in America, but he was more interested in service than in publicity. In 1889, a wealthy individual donated $10,000 for the establishment of St. Monica's Church for Negro Catholics in Chicago in the 2200 block of South Indiana Avenue. The doors of St. Monica opened in 1890 and for seven years Father Tolton went about his clerical duties, giving himself to his parishioners without reservation. The long years of work in his early youth, intense study and later service took their toll and the good Father Tolton died on July 10, 1897.

William J. Simmons. *Men of Mark*, Cleveland, 1887; p. 444: Albert S. Foley. *God's Men of Color: The Colored Catholic Priests of the United States*, 1854-1954; pp. 32-41.

Thomas Paul (1773-1831)

PIONEER BAPTIST ORGANIZER

Although there are records of small Baptist congregations among Negroes being organized as early as 1776 in Virginia, the movement toward separate denominations did not really get under way until the first decade of the 19th century. Thomas Paul was one of the leaders in this development. Until that time free Negroes had worshipped alongside whites; however, the conservative reaction following the American Revolution and the increased migration of free Negroes to the North made attendance at white churches an uneasy affair.

Shortly after his ordination as a minister in 1805, Thomas Paul organized a congregation of free Negroes in a church on Joy Street in Boston. Word of his oratorical ability and organizing skill spread among free Negroes in Boston and Philadelphia, and Paul became an early Billy Graham, taking the word of God to all who wanted to listen. By 1808, he was so famous that he was invited to speak to white churches in New York where Negroes were growing restless with their position as members of Baptist congregations. When Thomas Paul finished a series of sermons there, whites and Negroes agreed that it was possible for separate Negro congregations to be organized. The First Baptist Church thereupon granted letters of honorable "Dismission" to sixteen of its members, and under the leadership of Thomas Paul, organized a Baptist congregation which became known as the Abyssinian Baptist Church of New York City.

Brilliant, energetic and tireless, Paul did not end his labors with the organization of churches in the United States. With the aid of the Massachusetts Baptist Society, he spent six months in Haiti teaching and preaching to the Haitians.

Because he could not speak French, Paul was not as successful as he had been in the United States. On his return from Haiti he continued his labors in the North until his death in 1831.

"His understanding was vigorous (sic), his personal appearance interesting, and his elocution was grateful." (sic) He could spellbind thousands for hours, and when he left them, if they did not have an organized church, they organized one. This was the summation of the life of Thomas Paul, a Baptist minister who began the movement of independent Baptist churches in the United States.

Carter G. Woodson. *The History of the Negro Church;* Washington, 1922, pp. 76-77.

Lemuel Haynes (1753-1833)

PIONEER NEW ENGLAND MINISTER

One day Lemuel Haynes sat reading sermons to his blind bondmaster, the Deacon David Rose of Granville, Massachusetts. The good deacon was fond of the sermons of English revivalists, such as Watts, Whitefield, Doddridge, and Davies and took great pride in being able to distinguish one from another. On this particular day, Lemuel read an especially fine sermon and confused the deacon who inquired, "Lemuel, whose work is that which you have been reading? Is it Doddridge or Watts, or Whitefield's?" Lemuel said nothing for a while. Then, in a quiet voice, he declared, "It's Lemuel's sermon."

Deacon Rose was astounded! True, Lemuel had been to the district school a short period. True, he had shown a deep piety and was interested in the Bible. And, the bond servant had even been baptised. But—a mulatto composing first-rate sermons? This was indeed new and surprising!

Lemuel Haynes was in his early thirties at the time and had lived with the blind deacon since he was five months old. His mother was a hired girl of a neighbor of the Rose's and his father was a pure-blooded African who had long since disappeared. Lemuel saw his mother a few times before she died, but she refused to admit or indicate that he was her natural son.

When it became obvious that Lemuel was above average intelligence, neighbors of the Rose's urged him to go to Dartmouth College. Instead, he decided to study Latin under one David Farrand of Canaan, Connecticut. Later, he studied Greek under one Rev. William Bradford in order to read the Bible in its original Greek.

In 1780 after an "examination in the language, sciences and doctrines of experimental religion," Lemuel Haynes was licensed to preach. He was soon called to the Congregational meeting house at Middle Granville, Connecticut where he remained for five years. Then he was called to a larger church in Torrington, Connecticut. One of the leading citizens of Torrington did not relish the idea of a Negro preaching to an all-white congregation in the town's leading church and decided to show his displeasure by wearing his hat during the sermon. Said the man later, "He had not preached far when I thought I saw the whitest man I knew in the pulpit. I tossed my hat under the pew."

Rev. Haynes' success here led to other churches in New York, Vermont and other New England states. He was particularly in demand as a revival preacher and served white congregations who wanted him not as a curiosity but as the best man they could secure. When he died one person summed up his life by saying "His face betrayed his race and blood and his life revealed his Lord."

W. H. Morse. "Lemuel Haynes" *Journal of Negro History*, (January, 1919) pp. 24, 32

Richard Allen (1760-1831)
FOUNDER of AFRICAN METHODIST EPISCOPAL CHURCH

The African Methodist Episcopal Church has the distinction of being the oldest and largest institution among Negroes. It was founded in Philadelphia in 1787 by Richard Allen, an extraordinary organizer and minister. In the reaction which followed the end of the Revolutionary War, Negroes were discouraged from worshipping at churches with white congregations. One Sunday in November, 1787, Richard Allen and several of his friends rebelled against the increasing restrictions of segregation that were imposed upon their right to worship in St. George's, one of Philadelphia's leading Methodist churches. Richard Allen led an exodus of Negroes from the church and set about organizing a new denomination—the African Methodist Episcopal Church.

In less than two years, Richard Allen and his group had constructed a new church called "Bethel" and Philadelphia's Negroes joined it. In 1816, Richard Allen was a prime mover in calling together sixteen independent Negro Methodist congregations from different states and organizing them into one group. Richard Allen was elected as the first bishop of this new denomination and thus began a career of preaching and organizing which ended only with his death in 1831.

Richard Allen seemed to have a natural gift for organization. During the Revolutionary War, he was a slave who made enough money as a wood cutter and wagoner to buy his freedom (and that of his brother) in 1783. Converted to Christianity while yet a slave, Allen used the first years of his freedom to preach the gospel to Negroes in and around Pennsylvania. He was present at the organizing conference of the general Methodist Church in 1784. On April 12, 1787, Richard Allen and several other Negroes formed the Free African Society whose purpose was the improvement of the social and economic conditions of the free Negroes. Using this society as his foundation, Allen was able to bring together enough people to launch the African Methodist Episcopal Church which has endured to this day.

Charles H. Wesley. *Richard Allen; Apostle of Freedom*, Washington, 1935

Rt. Rev. James A. Handy. *Scraps of African Methodist Episcopal History*, A.M.E. Book Concern, Philadelphia, 1902.

Some church-goers of the late 1700's

Daniel Alexander Payne (1811-1893)

A GIANT OF THE A. M. E. CHURCH

If Richard Allen founded the African Methodist Episcopal Church, then Daniel Payne educated it, for it was he who insisted that the A. M. E. ministry have some standards of education. Long before he rose to eminence, Payne dreamed of a college where the "peace of God and the light of learning would shine." A native of Charleston, South Carolina, Daniel Payne secured the semblance of an education. When he was eighteen years old, he opened a school for free Negroes in Charleston. His student body consisted of three children and three adult slaves, each of whom paid fifty cents a month tuition. Payne could not buy books from bookstores as education of Negroes was discouraged in the state; he had to secure them by stealth and cunning. After the publication of Walker's *Appeal* in 1829 and Nat Turner's revolt two years later, the state of South Carolina became alarmed and in 1835, made it illegal for any person to operate a school for the education of Negroes.

Disappointed but not discouraged, Daniel Payne went to New York and soon made the acquaintance of Alexander Crummell and others interested in the abolition of slavery. With their help he continued his own education at a Lutheran Seminary in Gettysburg, Pennsylvania. He preached for a while in Troy, New York and then opened another school in Pennsylvania.

However, it was not until 1844, two years after he united with the African Methodist Episcopal Church in Philadelphia, that Daniel Payne really found an opportunity to combine his love of learning with religion. In that year, he was appointed chairman of a committee on education by the General A. M. E. Conference to study the best type of training a minister should have for the denomination. His studies made him familiar with the A. M. E. Church throughout the country. In 1852, he was elected a bishop.

Nine years later he was chosen to become the first Negro president of Wilberforce University in Ohio. From 1852 to 1876 Bishop Payne presided over the destiny of Wilberforce and saw many of his charges develop into the capable ministers he thought the church should have. The oldest institution of higher learning founded by Negro Americans, Wilberforce University stands today as a testimony to the pioneering spirit of the African Methodist Episcopal Church.

William J. Simmons. *Men of Mark*, Cleveland, 1887, pp. 1078-1085; Saunders Redding. *The Lonesome Road*, New York, 1958, pp. 26-29, 32-38.
Rt. Rev. James A. Handy. *Scraps of African Methodist Episcopal History*, A.M.E. Book Concern, Philadelphia, Pennsylvania, 1902.

Some church-goers of the early 1800's

83

James Augustine Healy
(1830-1900)
FIRST NEGRO CATHOLIC BISHOP

James A. Healy received the best possible training for his post of Bishop. For over a decade he was assistant to Bishop John Fritzpatrick of Boston. Bishop Fritzpatrick appointed him chancellor and "deputized him to handle most of the routine business of the diocese—the Bishop's account books, his official correspondence with other Bishops, with the sixty-one priests of the diocese, with the many seminarians in American and foreign seminaries and with the religious orders of men and women working in the diocese."

Healy had been pastor of St. James Church on Boston's south east end, amidst the teeming Irish where he performed his office during the various epidemics of typhoid, pneumonia and tuberculosis. The Boston Irish were at first reluctant to accept him but eventually overcame their reservations and "came to recognize him as a true priest all the way to his sacred finger clasp."

A native of Macon, Georgia, James Augustine Healy was sent north to be educated. He attended the Franklin Park Quaker School in Burlington, New York and Holy Cross College, Worcester, Massachusetts. In 1849 he graduated from Holy Cross with first honors in the first class to complete the course. Friends of his wealthy father enabled him to go abroad to continue his education.

Catholics of Massachusetts, Maine and New Hampshire came to revere Bishop Healy whose career was terminated by his death in 1900.

Albert S. Foley. *God's Men of Color: The Colored Catholic Priests of the United States*, 1854-1954, pp. 32-41.

James Augustine Healy, the mulatto son of a Georgia planter and his household servant, was the first Catholic Bishop of African descent in the United States. For twenty-five years, Bishop Healy presided over the diocese of Maine and New Hampshire. Under him, sixty-eight mission stations, eighteen parochial schools, and fifty church buildings were erected. The number of Catholic communicants more than doubled. The Church recognized Bishop Healy's work by making him Assistant to the Papal Throne, a rank just below that of Cardinal.

Henry Mc Neal Turner
(1833-1915)
MINISTER EXTRAORDINAIRE

The extraordinary talents of Henry McNeal Turner enabled him to become a bishop, politician, orator, philosopher and one of the most influential American Negroes of his day. The roots of these talents were not ordinary either. His maternal grandfather, David Greer, was the son of an African King who, after being brought to this country as a slave, was freed through a rarely observed British law forbiding the enslavement of royal blood. His paternal grandmother was German; however little is known of her, but his maternal grandmother was well known in his home town as "not so notable for female modesty . . . but physical resources; an athlete which men dreaded meeting in combat."

Henry Turner was born February 1, 1833 in South Carolina, the oldest child of Howard and Sarah Turner. Though born free, he suffered the hardships common to all Negroes of that time; these were aggravated by the absence of his father. As a boy, he worked in the cotton fields and apprenticed as a blacksmith. He had an intense desire for education—which was forbidden by state law.

However, with the help of some defiant white benefactors, he had learned half of the old Webster's spelling book by the time he was thirteen. When he was fifteen, he got a menial job in the office of some white lawyers who recognized his intellect and taught him to read. He not only finished the spelling book but studied the lawyers' books on history, theology and law.

He joined the Methodist Episcopal Church South in 1848 at the age of fifteen, and was licensed to preach five years later, in 1853. In 1858, he joined the A.M.E. Church. He was ordained deacon in 1860, and elder in 1862. He became the twelfth Bishop of the A.M.E. Church in 1880 at the general Conference in St. Louis. In 1863 he was appointed by President Lincoln as the first colored chaplain to the colored troops. Ten days after he mustered out in 1865, he was re-commissioned in the regular army by President Johnson and detailed to work with the Freedmen's Bureau in Georgia. In 1867 he was delegated by the National Republican Executive Committee in Washington to organize the Negro in Georgia,and served as a member of that state's constitutional convention. In 1868 he was elected to the Legislature and re-elected in 1870. President Grant made him postmaster of Macon, Georgia in 1869 at a salary of $4,000, and later, customs inspector and government detective.

He was awarded the title of Doctor of Literature by University of Pennsylvania in 1872 and the title of Doctor of Divinity by Wilberforce in 1873. As a politician he wrote a document defining the status of the Republican and Democratic parties which circulated more than four million copies. As a church man, he compiled a hymn book and wrote a catechism for the A. M. E. Church. He also authored the *Methodist Polity* which defined the duties of the church officers. He was a forceful and eloquent orator and many of his speeches and lectures were printed or noted by *Harpers Weekly* and other magazines.

Rt. Rev. James A. Handy. *Scraps of African Methodist Episcopal History*, A.M.E. Book Concern, Philadelphia, Pennsylvania, 1902.

William J. Simmons. *Men of Mark*, George M. Rewell Co., Cleveland, Ohio, 1887, pp. 805-819.

John Jasper (1812-1901)

OUTSTANDING SLAVERY-EMANCIPATION PREACHER

The last of his mother's twenty-four children, John Jasper spent his life at the center of crowds and controversy. Inspired to preach while a slave, John Jasper attracted wide attention as a Baptist minister during the 1880's with his flaming oratory, dramatic sermons and original views. Theologians, scholars and laymen debated Jasper's ideas of the universe.

A spell-binder in the days of free-wheeling oratory, John Jasper preached to throngs of entranced listeners. His most famous sermon was "The Sun Do Move." In it he argued that the earth is the center of the solar system and that the sun and other heavenly bodies revolve around it. Although Galileo, in the 17th century, had proved this view to be false, millions of people in Jasper's time still believed that the earth stood still at the center of things. Many other ministers felt the same way but few could outdo Jasper in using the Bible to "prove" this particular view of the universe.

Combining the force of a Daniel Webster with the dramatics of a Billy Sunday, for over sixty years, John Jasper preached to white and Negro congregations in Virginia, Washington, Maryland and New Jersey. Newspapers announced his sermons and his appearances were usually major events. In London, Paris and Berlin, scholars took note of his views and sayings even when they disagreed with them.

A native of Virginia, John Jasper was born during the War of 1812 and lived until the Spanish-American War was over. He was freed after Appomattox and started his career as a literal-minded believer in the Bible. Even his scientifically-inclined critics admitted his sincerity. Jasper's concrete descriptions of hell persuaded many people to join the church. A. S. Thomas, a minister who knew him well, said that, "It did seem to me sometimes that Rev. Jasper came into the world with a Bible in his heart, head and tongue."

Benjamin Brawley. *Negro Builders and Heroes*, New York, pp. 80-87; William J. Simmons. *Men of Mark*, Cleveland, 1887, pp. 1064-1076.

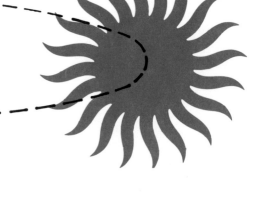

Adam Clayton Powell, Sr.
(1865-1953)

BUILDER OF AMERICA'S LARGEST NEGRO CONGREGATION

The world's largest Negro congregation is the Abyssinian Baptist Church of New York. Established by Thomas Paul and eighteen other Negroes in 1808, this church has over 15,000 members and is a major force in the total life of the Negroes of New York City. A community in itself, the Abyssinian Baptist Church is the elongated shadow of one man—Adam Clayton Powell, Sr.

Born in a one-room log cabin set on five acres of hard scrabble dirt in the backwoods of Virginia, Adam Clayton Powell, Sr. built Abyssinian Church to the point where it could care for thousands of the needy, furnish recreation for hundreds of the young and serve as the seat of power for a United States Congressman.

Powell started life in a hurry. As a seven-year old, on his first day at a rural school, he learned his alphabets, and on the second, could recite them backwards. His family, composed of sixteen brothers and sisters, could not afford to send him to school regularly. Between school sessions, Powell worked in the mines of West Virginia. Finally finishing high school, Powell decided to enter the ministry.

In 1888 he entered Wayland Academy, now Virginia Union University, and worked his way through the institution as a janitor and waiter. After graduating from Wayland Academy, he continued his education at Yale University School of Divinity. While at Yale he served as pastor of the Immanuel Baptist Church in the small Negro community in New Haven.

In 1908 Powell became pastor of the Abyssinian Baptist Church which was then located opposite the present site of the *Herald Tribune*. At this time the church had a membership of 1600 and an indebtedness of $146,354. In 1921 the church was moved to its present location and housed in a $350,000 Gothic structure of New York bluestone.

In addition to building the church, Powell was a vigorous crusader against vice and prostitution. When the Depression of 1929 reached Harlem, Powell opened soup kitchens which served thousands of meals. With his son, Powell was in the forefront of the Harlem push for job equality and for a fair share of the city's services.

After twenty-nine years, Adam Clayton Powell, Sr. retired in 1937. Abyssinian Baptist Church had 14,000 members and $400,000 in assets. Before he died in 1953, Adam Clayton Powell, Sr. had the satisfaction of seeing his church continue its growth and service in the hands of his son and heir, Adam Clayton Powell, Jr.

Ben Albert Richardson. *Great American Negroes*, New York, 1945, pp. 185-196; *Who's Who in Colored America*, 1950, pp. 422-423.

VII LEADERS and SPOKESMEN
Voices of the Multitude

In his progress down the winding road from slavery toward freedom, the American Negro has relied on leaders and spokesmen to carry the beacon of hope. Negro leaders have been the means of communicating to the nation the wishes of the inarticulate masses. Their tractics have ranged from the petitions of free Negroes during the infancy of the Republic to the moral exhortation of Frederick Douglass, from the example and opportunism of Booker T. Washington to the rage and daring of Marcus A. Garvey, from the blunt anger of W. E. B. DuBois to the cool calculation of Charles H. Houston and Walter White, and from the blazing zeal of Mary McLeod Bethune to the consuming pacificism of Martin Luther King, Jr.

Organized Negro leadership dates from the time of the American Revolution. During this early period of American history small groups of free Negroes banded together to point out the inconsistency and immorality of holding black men in bondage while fighting for political freedom from the Old World. The most active and vocal opposition to slavery, apart from the Quakers of New England, was to be found among the free Negroes of Massachusetts and Pennsylvania.

In 1780 Paul Cuffe led his people in a protest against taxation of Negro tax payers without representation. In 1788 Prince Hall petitioned the Massachusetts Legislature to end the practice of permitting free Negroes to be sold into slavery. Under the leadership of the redoubtable Absalom Jones, the free Negroes of Pennsylvania petitioned Congress for repeal of the fugitive slave act of 1793. In the city of Philadelphia, James Forten in 1813 headed opposition to plans to have all free Negroes registered with the city. At the suggestion of Hezekiah Grice, James Forten and other leaders in Philadelphia held the first of a famous series of conventions which served as forums of debate over issues facing Negroes in both the North and South.

While white abolitionists such as William Lloyd Garrison, Wendell Phillips, Arthur Tappan, James Birney, Elijah P. Lovejoy, John Brown and others were gaining public notice for their activities, several Negro leaders achieved fame as "conductors" on the underground railroad. Foremost among them were William Still, David Ruggles and Harriet Tubman. Journalists of the caliber of Samuel Cornish, John Russwurm and Charles Bennett Ray, and orators such as Sojourner Truth, Henry Highland Garnet and Theodore S. Wright publicized the views and opinions of the masses. To this list may be added the names of William Cooper Nell, Charles L. Remond, William Wells Brown and J. W. C. Pennington. Soaring above all of these was the golden voice of the leonine Frederick A. Douglass.

Following the Civil War, a new group of leaders came to the fore. Robert Smalls, Hiram Revels, Blanche K. Bruce, John R. Lynch, John Mercer Langston, Robert B. Elliott, P. S. B. Pinchback and James T. Rapier are only a few of the extremely able men who were nationally prominent during the early years of freedom. Many less well known Negroes achieved prominence in southern state and local governments. Samuel J. Lee was speaker of the South Carolina House of Representatives in 1872. A. K. Davis was lieutenant governor of Mississippi in 1873. Johnathan C. Gibbs was successively secretary of state and state superintendent of public instruction in Florida during the period of 1868-1872.

At the end of the Reconstruction era in the late 1870's the political power and influence of Negro leaders declined. While many of the older leaders such as Douglass, Langston and Lynch continued to define the issues and propose solutions to the economic and political handicaps foisted on the group, men such as Isaiah T. Montgomery, Benjamin "Pap" Singleton and Henry Adams led tens of thousands of freedmen northward to Missouri, Kansas, Indiana and other states to escape the oppressive economic and political conditions in the Deep South. By 1895 Booker T. Washington was the most famous Negro in America; however, with Ida B. Wells writing and lecturing against the evils of lynching and DuBois protesting the philosophy of accommodation to the status quo, the ground was being prepared for the birth of organizations directly devoted to the cause of racial advancement.

Excluded from the mainstream of politics, many leaders found outlets for their ambitions in organized religion. William Heard, once a minister to Liberia in the 1890's, was soon to find himself a bishop in the African Methodist Episcopal church. His influence lasted for decades. Reverdy Ransom was famous as an A. M. E. bishop and as a major figure in politics and social reform. He even ran for Congress in 1916. The masses looked to such men for leadership during what has been called the "nadir" or midnight in the long struggle for first-class citizenship.

The Afro-American League organized in 1890 by the journalist T. Thomas Fortune, the National Association for the Advancement of Colored People organized in 1909 with DuBois as its first Negro member, the Urban League organized in 1911 under George W. Haynes and Eugene Kinckle Jones, and the formation of other race relations groups marked the professionalization of the fight for freedom. Down to the middle of this century, the NAACP bore the brunt of the fight. Among its more illustrious leaders were DuBois, James Weldon Johnson and Walter White. Today this oldest of protest organizations carries on under the leadership of Roy Wilkins.

The new urgency in the civil rights movement has given rise to groups such as the Congress of Racial Equality (CORE) founded in 1942, the Southern Christian Leadership Conference (SCLC) organized by the famed Rev. Martin Luther King, Jr. in 1957 and the Student Non-Violent Coordinating Committee (SNCC) which dates from 1960. These groups and their leaders have different emphases and tactics but their objectives are in the historic tradition of Negro leadership: the achievement of a condition of freedom which would render the question of color irrelevant in American life.

Richard Bardolph. *The Negro Vanguard*, New York, 1961, p. 88; *Biographical Directory of the American Congress: 1774-1961*, Washington, D.C., 1961,

Benjamin "Pap" Singleton
(1809-1892)

WALK AND NEVER TIRE

"I started it all; I was the cause of it all," said Benjamin "Pap" Singleton to a congressional committee investigating the causes of the great "Exodus of 1879" when tens of thousands of Negroes simply packed up and moved northward from Tennessee, Texas, from South Carolina, Mississippi and Louisiana. In this great movement of Negroes were some sixty to eighty thousand men and women seeking some better place, some more tolerable clime away from the South.

"Pap" Singleton was only partly right in his statement to the Congressmen. Other causes for the migration were economic exploitation, denial of political recognition and the dreaded activity of the Ku Klux Klan. The Negro's bouyant dreams of early Reconstruction had changed to a nightmare of repression in many parts of the Deep South. "Pap" was the Pied Piper urging them away.

A native of Tennessee, "Pap" Singleton had escaped from slavery. For a time, he lived in Canada. After the Emancipation Proclamation, he returned to the South. He had been a carpenter and cabinet-maker during slavery and now supported himself through these trades. A tall, thin tawny man who could barely read, Singleton was a most persuasive talker and a compulsive promoter.

In his travels, Singleton discovered thinly populated areas in Kansas, the now-tranquil land of John Brown. While Negro intellectuals were debating the merits of emigration to Africa and South America, Singleton marched through the South advertising and preaching a haven of ease and dignity just over in Kansas. The newspapers picked up his stories and he himself produced pictures and clippings showing Negroes living where the life was easy.

In 1873 "Pap" led some three hundred Negroes to Cherokee County, Kansas to found "Singleton's Colony." Henry Adams in Louisiana and Isaiah T. Montgomery in Mississippi also headed northbound migrations from their respective states. On foot, by boat, rail and horseback, they swarmed into Kansas and Missouri and went as far north as Indiana and Illinois. Over 5,000 Negroes left South Carolina in one week; in twenty months, Kansas was inundated with over 19,000 "Exodusters" as they were called. Although these Negroes did not find an Eldorado and had to be assisted by northern philanthropy, few returned to the south.

The great exodus halted in 1881; "Pap" Singleton died in Tennessee, the state where he was born.

Roy Garvin. "Benjamin "Pap" Singleton and His Followers," *Journal of Negro History*, XXXIII (January, 1937), pp. 50-92; John G. Van Deusen. "The Exodus of 1879," *Journal of Negro History*, XXI (April, 1936, pp. 111-129).

John Hope (1864-1936)
BUILDER OF MEN

The Atlanta University System is the hub of academia for Negro America. From the portals of the colleges within the system—Morehouse, Spelman, Clark, Morris Brown and Gammon Theological Seminary—come many of the leaders and spokesmen of the Negro race. John Hope was the man most responsible for changing the separate schools into a unified system of education for thousands of young men and women. A reserved, genteel, but energetic man, John Hope's impact on the Atlanta University System was so great that twelve years after his death, when the author of this book was a student at Morehouse College, men still spoke of him as though he were yet alive.

The different colleges in the Atlanta University System were started in the aftermath of the Civil War; Morehouse and Spelman existed through the efforts of northern philanthrophy and the American Baptist Association; Clark and Morris Brown Colleges were created by the labors of the African Methodist Episcopal Church. Before the advent of John Hope these colleges got along as though their nearness to one another was merely co-incidental. After Hope, the foundation existed for a system of co-operation and mutual assistance which reserved their administrative independence but unified their academic programs so that students could benefit from what each was able to do best.

John Hope came to Morehouse College (then Atlanta Baptist Institute) as an instructor in classics in 1897, a year after W. E. B. DuBois went to Atlanta University. Georgia was not new to Hope, for he was a native of Augusta where Morehouse College was begun in 1867. Soon he became an indispensable aid to Rev. George Sale, a Canadian minister who was the President of the institution. While DuBois was turning out his volumes on the status of the Negro and feuding with Booker T. Washington, Hope was preaching the need for Negroes trained in the liberal arts.

In 1906 Hope became the first Negro President of Morehouse College and soon began to envision a co-operative center of education in Atlanta. In 1929 his dream came true when Morehouse, Spelman and Atlanta University agreed to affiliate and to work in concert for their mutual benefit. John Hope was elected President of Atlanta University and hence, head of the System.

During these years, he found time to travel in behalf of the YMCA and to serve on numerous boards, committees and commissions. Today every college within the area has benefited from John Hope's faith, foresight and vision.

Ridgely Torrence. *The Story of John Hope*, New York, 1948.

Marcus A. Garvey (1887-1940)
LOOK AWAY TO AFRICA

To some people he was a charlatan, a naive dreamer; to others a messiah. To himself, Marcus A. Garvey was the Negro's best hope of finding dignity and honor, not in America but in his original home of Africa.

Coming to America from Jamaica in 1916, Marcus Garvey found dissatisfaction, discontent and frustration among millions of Negroes pushed northward by oppressive conditions in the South during World War I. Within two months, Garvey had recruited 1500 followers for his Universal Negro Improvement Association (U.N.I.A.). Five years later he claimed upwards of one million members.

A short, stocky, dark man possessing a shrewd sense of crowd psychology, Garvey preached economic independence and the return of Negroes to Africa as the solution to being a "Negro" in the western world. In 1921 he called an international convention which attracted thousands of Negroes to New York City from twenty-five countries, and laid the foundation for a steamship company, The Black Star Line, and the Negro Factory Corporation as devices for business and industry among Negroes.

For five years Garvey led many of the discontented masses in New York, Chicago, Cleveland, Detroit and other cities. He praised everything black and was suspicious of everything white. He formed the Universal Black Cross Nurses, the Universal African Motor Corps, and the Black Flying Eagles. His newspaper, *The Negro World*, carried his views and information about the U.N.I.A. to all corners of the country.

While millions in the masses followed him without hesitation, Negro intellectuals were skeptical of him and his promises. In 1925 Garvey was imprisoned for using the United States mails to defraud in connection with the sale of stock in his Black Star line, and his dream began to fade. After serving two years in prison, he was deported from America and died in London in 1940, a lonely and penniless man.

Marcus A. Garvey captured the interest of the ordinary Negro as no other leader before or since, but his dream was based on a fatal flaw: his failure to understand that the overwhelming mass of Negroes considered America their rightful home and had no real desire to leave it. His weakness lay in thinking that the Negro, after helping to build America, would abandon it. His greatness lies in his daring to dream of a better future for Negroes somewhere on earth.

Edmund Cronon. *The Story of Marcus Garvey and the Universal Negro Improvement Association*, Madison, Wisconsin, 1955; E. U. Essien-Udom. *Black Nationalism: A Search for an Identity in America*, Chicago, 1962, pp. 36-39.

AFRICA

Oscar Depriest (1871-1951)

FIRST NEGRO CONGRESSMAN IN THE 20TH CENTURY

During the Reconstruction era when the Negro population numbered between five and six million, some twenty-two Negroes represented them in the U.S. Congress. From 1901 to 1929, despite a doubling of the number of black Americans, not a single Negro sat in the nation's highest legislative tribunal.

When Oscar DePriest took his seat on April 15, 1930, in the U.S. House of Representatives, he was the only Negro there. He was elected as a Republican to the 71st, 72nd and 73rd Congresses.

Oscar DePriest was shaped in the crucible of Chicago politics. His first public office was that of County Commissioner which he held from 1904 to 1908. In 1915 he became the first Negro member of the Chicago City Council. He also served as a member of the Illinois Commerce Commission and was a delegate to several Republican National Conventions. He was a member of the board of directors of the famed Binga State Bank.

After his election to Congress, he was constantly in demand as a speaker. He had no grandiose plans to lead 12,000,000 Negroes. He did realize that he was not only a representative of voters from Illinois' 21st Congressional District, but also a symbol of the Negro in politics. He urged his many audiences to study political organization to learn their rights under the federal constitution, and to see campaign activity as a public duty.

Oscar DePriest was a native of Florence, Alabama but spent his youth in Salina, Kansas. He went to Chicago, Illinois in 1889. DePriest's early interest in politics can be traced back to his father, Alexander DePriest, who knew and admired James T. Rapier, who represented Alabama in Congress in the days of Reconstruction. The elder DePriest learned to study people and politics while a drayman; Oscar DePriest learned them through his successful career as a real estate entepreneur. Through his long life he maintained a keen interest in politics and in the progress of the Negro. His success in business and politics did not change him, he insisted to his dying day in 1951 that "I am of the common herd."

Harold F. Gosnell. *Negro Politicians*, Chicago, 1935, pp. 163-195.
Who's Who in Colored America, 1950, p. 151.

Arthur Mitchell (1883-   )

U. S. CONGRESSMAN FROM ILLINOIS

When Arthur Mitchell walked sixty-five miles from his home in Chambers County, Alabama to become Booker T. Washington's office boy, he had no idea that he would become the second Negro to sit in the United States House of Representatives in the 20th century. He was educated at Tuskegee, Columbia and Harvard. Emulating his one-time employer, Mitchell founded and was president of the Armstrong Agricultural School in Butler, Alabama.

He read law in the office of a Washington, D.C. attorney and was admitted to the bar in 1927. For a time he practiced law and handled real estate. He moved to Chicago in 1929 and entered politics, first as a Republican and later as a Democrat. He was the first Negro ever to address a National Democratic Convention. In the hungry politics of the thirties, Mitchell was elected to succeed Oscar DePriest.

From January 3, 1935 to January 3, 1943, Arthur Mitchell was the only Negro in Congress. He was not a spectacular crusader for civil rights but in his way served well the voters of Illinois' First Congressional District.

Perhaps his most significant achievement was not in Congress, but before the United States Supreme Court in his suit against the Pullman Company. Although a Congressman, Arthur Mitchell was denied the use of Pullman tickets for a compartment on a train. Many Negroes had been denied the use of travel facilities purchased and paid for. Until Mitchell, a common practice was to shunt Negro holders of such tickets to the Jim-Crow car. However, the Congressman took his case to the United States Supreme Court and won. The suit has been termed "a milestone in the history of minority rights."

When his third term expired in 1943, Arthur Mitchell became a gentleman farmer in St. Petersburg, Virginia.

Biographical Directory of the American Congress, 1774-1961, Washington, D. C., 1961, p. 1339; Bardolph, Richard, *The Negro Vanguard*, New York, 1961 (Paperback), pp. 197-198.

J. Finley Wilson (1881-1952)

RENOWNED FRATERNAL LEADER

J. Finley Wilson once described himself as a former "bellboy, newsboy, bootblack, porter, hotel waiter, cowboy, miner, newspaper reporter, newspaper editor and publisher, and president of the Negro Newspaper Association." However, for twenty years, he was known to millions as the Grand Exalted Ruler of the Improved Benevolent and Protective Order of Elks of the World. (IBPOE).

The IBPOE was started in 1897 when Arthur J. Riggs in Cincinnati, Ohio and B. F. Howard in Covington, Kentucky organized Elk lodges in their respective states. The social and fraternal organization showed a moderate rate of growth and by 1921 claimed a membership of 36,306. With the election of J. Finley Wilson as Exalted Grand Ruler, the IBPOE took on new life. During his first year in office he travelled over 50,000 miles and the Elk membership rose to 51,491. Wilson could count eighty-five new lodges when he made his first annual report.

Under Wilson's leadership, the Elks' scholarship program was launched in 1925 and the famed Elks Oratorical Contest in 1927. The Elks initiated the first systematic health survey among Negroes. During the war years the organization assisted in drives for Allied War Relief funds, contributed books to servicemen in its Victory Book Campaign, initiated campaigns for buying defense bonds and stamps and sold over $2,000,000 worth in New York City alone.

J. Finley Wilson was forever on the move, promoting the causes and programs of his beloved order. Each year some city would see the small, dynamic, and somewhat flamboyant Exalted Grand Ruler leading a long and colorful parade of fellow lodgemen. Few men in public life he did not know. He came to exercise great influence in Republican party platform drafting and patronage politics. When Wilson died in 1952 the IBPOE had net assets of $450,000, including $181,390 in cash, and could look back on scores of young people who had benefited from its scholarship and oratorical contests.

A native of Tennessee, Wilson left home at the age of thirteen. He wandered west and worked with Buffalo Bill in Colorado and Arizona. (He joined the IBPOE while in Colorado). At Salt Lake City, Utah, he edited a newspaper called the *Plaindealer*. In the east he was a reporter for the Baltimore Times, edited the *Washington Eagle*, and worked on the *New York Age* with T. Thomas Fortune.

The entire course of Wilson's life is summed up in his favorite saying: "Forward!"

Charles H. Wesley. *History of the Improved Benevolent and Protective Order of Elks of the World:* 1898-1954, Washington, D. C., 1955. *Who's Who in Colored America*, 1950, p. 565.

Mary Church Terrell (1863-1954)

CHAMPION OF WOMEN'S RIGHTS

Mary Church Terrell was born in 1863, the year of the Emancipation Proclamation. Her entire life was devoted to the fight for equality. A writer, lecturer, organizer, and demonstrator, Mrs. Terrell was active in the successful campaign to secure women the right to vote. She was instrumental in the campaign to desegregate the restaurants in the nation's capital.

Her achievements were numerous. In 1895 she was appointed to the District of Columbia school board; in 1896 she became one of the charter members of the National Association of Colored Women. In 1909 she joined the NAACP, then less than a year old. In 1913-14 she helped to organize the Delta Sigma Theta sorority and twenty-six years later wrote its famous creed, setting up a code of conduct for Negro women. She was also active in politics, campaigning and speaking out against discrimination and segregation. In World War I, she worked with the War Camp Community Service, an organization which, among other things, aided in the demobilization of Negro servicemen.

Mary Church Terrell was a United States delegate to several international conferences. In London she met the famous writer, H. G. Wells and other luminaries. At the International Council of Women in Berlin, she delivered her address in three languages—English, French, and German—to the amazement of the assembled delegates. Her theme was the same: equal rights for women and the Negro wherever they may be found.

A strikingly handsome woman, Mary Church was born to wealth and ease. She was a "rare combination of the high intellectual in close understanding with the mass." A native of Memphis, Tennessee, she was the daughter of Robert Church, an ex-slave of extremely high business skill who amassed a fortune in real estate before the turn of the century. Unwilling to have his daughter face discrimination in Tennessee, Robert Church sent Mary to Ohio where she attended private and public schools, and later, Oberlin College from which she was graduated in 1884 with a major in the classics.

By her own choice, Mary Church Terrell made her home in Washington in the 1890's, at that time a heavily segregated city. Except for public transportation, Washington remained segregated until 1953. In that year, at the age of eighty-nine, Mrs. Terrell won the biggest and toughest battle in her life-long struggle against racial intolerance. She headed a committee of distinguished citizens to demand enforcement of a seventy-five year old law banning discrimination of "respectable persons" from restaurants. With several other Negroes she went to a number of restaurants and was refused service. A suit was filed and the resulting test case went to the United Supreme Court which held that the old law was still valid. Shortly thereafter, the walls of segregation began to crumble in hotels, theaters and other places hitherto off-limits to Negroes.

Mary Church Terrell died in Annapolis, Maryland in 1954, a few months after hearing the United States Supreme Court declare that segregation itself was unconstitutional.

Mary Church Terrell. *A Colored Woman in a White World*. Washington, 1940.

Mary McLeod Bethune (1875-1955)
COTTON PICKER, EDUCATOR, WHITE HOUSE ADVISOR

Bethune-Cookman College

Mary McLeod Bethune ranks high among the great women of America. Her life story is one of an ennobling rise from a field hand picking cotton to the position of confidante and friend of Franklin D. and Eleanor Roosevelt. The last of seventeen children born to South Carolina sharecroppers, Mary Bethune lifted herself from the cotton fields to the White House as an advisor to the President of the United States. Almost single-handedly she built Bethune-Cookman College.

Mary McLeod Bethune rose by no golden stair or silver spoon, but by sheer courage, faith and perseverance. She was the only one of the McLeods born this side of slavery. She had a burning desire for an education and used the three-month school term between planting and harvesting to good advantage, so that when a seamstress in Colorado offered to pay the cost of educating one Negro girl at Scotia Seminary in Concord, North Carolina, Mary was selected. Graduating from this institution in 1893, Mary McLeod journeyed to Chicago where she enrolled in Moody Bible Institute with the idea of becoming a missionary to Africa. Instead, she returned to the Deep South to teach at Haines Institute in Augusta, Georgia.

It was in Georgia that she reached the real turning point in her life. She heard of railroads being constructed on the east coast of Florida. Mary Bethune immediately thought of the hundreds of Negro railroad laborers' children clustered in many squalid section settlements, destined to grow up without any sort of education. With only $1.50, nerve and determination, she set out to build a school for them.

In her own words, she summed up her effort to build the school: "I rang doorbells . . . , I wrote articles for whoever would print them, distributed leaflets, rode interminable miles of dusty roads on my old bicycle, invaded churches, clubs, lodges, chambers of commerce." Slowly the school rose from old crates, boxes and odd rooms of old houses near the Daytona Beach city dump. The student body grew from an enrollment of five little girls to a co-ed institution numbering its pupils in the hundreds. By 1923 when Bethune College merged with Cookman Institute, it had an enrollment of 600 students and 32 teachers; its property was worth well-over half a million dollars. Today, Bethune-Cookman graduates number in the thousands.

By 1935 Mary McLeod Bethune was nationally known. That year she received the NAACP's Spingarn medal as a symbol of distinguished achievement. The following year Franklin D. Roosevelt appointed her director of Negro Affairs Division of the National Youth Administration. She became a familiar figure at the White House as Roosevelt came to demand her wisdom and insight.

Edward R. Embree. *13 Against the Odds*, New York, 1946, pp. 9-24.

A. Philip Randolph (1889-   )
IN UNION—STRENGTH

Train, Chair Car, Coach Porters and Attendants

A. Philip Randolph is the elder statesman of Negro labor leaders. For almost forty years he has been in the thick of the fight for improved working conditions and higher wages for all laborers. He has been particularly vigorous in his opposition to racial discrimination within the labor movement.

In 1925 Randolph organized the Brotherhood of Sleeping Car Porters, the strongest labor group among Negroes. With the Pullman car porters as a foundation, A. Philip Randolph rose to the topmost hierarchy of the labor movement to become the only Negro vice-president of the AFL-CIO. He is the founder and organizer of the Negro American Labor Council. During World War II he was the prime mover in the celebrated "March on Washington" movement which prodded the United States government into banning discrimination in the industries having government contracts. He was one of the most effective lobbyists for the establishment of a permanent fair employment practices committee.

The basic character of the man may be seen in the bitter struggle to organize porters and maids working on trains during the late twenties and early thirties. Railroad management fought Randolph and his union every step of the way. Nonetheless Randolph never compromised his principles or the goals of the Brotherhood. The union survived every onslaught of management and became a potent force in American labor generally.

A native of Crescent City, Florida, A. Philip Randolph had no specific desire to develop into a spokesman for labor and the Negro. He fancied himself a writer and, with Chandler Owens, edited the *Messenger*, a rather outspoken magazine of comment and opinion. He also wrote for *Opportunity* magazine, the journal of the Urban League.

In addition to his writing, Randolph has gained wide acclaim with his oratory. His speeches reflect the influence of frequent readings of Shakespeare and other prose masters. Because of his vocal opposition to World War I he was imprisoned. But upon his release, he threw himself into the fight for the underdog. Still the president of the Brotherhood of Sleeping Car Porters, Randolph often shakes the entire house of labor with his unflinching demands that Negroes be allowed a full share of the fruits of labor and of the American economy. For many years Randolph's influence has been felt far beyond the ranks of organized labor. At the age of seventy-four, he was one of the organizers and leaders of the famous 1963 March on Washington.

Edwin Embree. *13 Against the Odds.* New York, 1946, pp. 211-230
Brailsford R. Brazeal. *The Brotherhood of Sleeping Car Porters,* New York, 1946

Walter Francis White (1896-1955)

A GUIDE TO THE PROMISED LAND

Completely out of breath, the blue-eyed, pink-skinned Negro with reddish hair flopped down in his seat. The conductor was passing through the train collecting tickets from passengers coming aboard at the little depot in Arkansas. As he neared the slender blue-eyed man still gasping for breath, he said "Mister, you're leaving town just as the fun is about to start. They're after a yaller nigger down here passing as white."

The "Yaller nigger" referred to was Walter Francis White, special investigator of lynchings for the National Association for the Advancement of Colored People. This was Walter White, destined to become the leader of the Negro's oldest and largest civil rights organization. This was Walter White beginning a long fight against lynching, discrimination and segregation.

Walter White, a native of Atlanta, Georgia could have slipped across the color "line" and vanished into white anonymity. Instead, he chose to remain identified with America's most oppressed minority. His abilities doubtless would have earned him security, ease and respect beyond the color curtain. But he, like his father before him, was a fighter and a strong believer in simple justice.

For almost a generation, the voice of the NAACP was his voice. Under White's direction, this organization fought forcefully for equality in voting rights, turned the eyes of America to the real evil and horror of lynching, and moved against segregation and discrimination in travel and education. During the era of Walter White, NAACP critics felt that the NAACP was moving too fast on too many fronts, that White wielded too much power over the organization for his and the organization's own good. But he felt that America had much too far to go for his organization to move slowly.

Perhaps he had a special interest in moving the organization rapidly. Perhaps he could not forget that his father, whom he revered, died from neglect in a Georgia hospital while the doctors argued over whether or not he was Negro. Perhaps he could never forget the night a rampaging mob of racists tried to burn down his father's home in Atlanta, Georgia while he and his father waited inside with drawn guns. In any event, Walter White moved himself and the NAACP as though the world was aflame. The tutelage of men such as Charles Houston, James Weldon Johnson and W. E. B. DuBois was too strong for him to ignore.

Walter White was also an urbane man, equally at home at the White House or a Harlem tenement. The fight for freedom was one that consumed his every waking hour. In matters racial his theme was always "Now is the time."

Edwin R. Embree. *13 Against the Odds*, New York, 1946, pp. 71-95; *Who's Who in Colored America*, 7th Edition, 1950, p. 550.

Colonel Charles Young
(1864-1922)

FIRST NEGRO OF DISTINCTION
AT WEST POINT

Colonel Charles Young was the first Negro graduate of West Point to achieve distinction in the military. Henry O. Flipper was the first Negro to finish that institution in 1877 but was separated from the service in 1881. He had a distinguished career as a civilian engineer in Latin America.

Colonel Charles Young entered West Point in 1884; he completed his studies there in 1889. The young lieutenant then began a career of active service that was to take him to Mexico, Haiti, Liberia and to Cuba where he rode with "Teddy" Roosevelt and his Rough Riders in the famous charge up San Juan Hill in Cuba.

Colonel Young was not only a good soldier, but also a gentleman and a scholar. He was proficient in several languages, including Latin, Greek, German, French, Spanish and Italian. The Colonel owned a magnificent library with volumes in these languages. He was a writer of pageants and poetry; he played the piano and violin and composed music for both instruments. While teaching military science and tactics at Wilberforce University in Ohio, his home was a gathering place for such men as Paul Laurence Dunbar and W. E. B. DuBois.

However, his career was that of a soldier and it was in this connection that he achieved his greatest fame. Soldiers are trained to fight. With the outbreak of World War I, Colonel Young expected to be given an active assignment overseas. The Negro press clamored for him to be given a command. Military doctors examined the Colonel only to announce that his health was too poor at that time for active duty.

Angered by this Colonel Young mounted his favorite horse at Chillicothe and rode the five hundred miles back to Washington, D.C. as proof of his fitness for service. Instead of retiring the Colonel for "reasons of health," he was assigned to train Negro troops at Fort Grant, Illinois. Later he was sent to Liberia as Military attache in Monrovia. Shortly after his arrival in Africa, the Colonel died in Lagos, Nigeria in 1922. He was returned to America to be buried in the Vahalla of heroes—Arlington National Cemetery.

Wesley Brown. "Eleven Men of West Point," *Negro History Bulletin*, XIX (April, 1956), pp. 147-157; Bernie Young Mitchell Wells, "A Verstile Relative of Mine: Colonel Charles Young," in Herman Dreer, *American Literature by Negro Authors*, New York, 1950, pp. 179-184.

Benjamin O. Davis, Sr.
(1877-   )

FIRST NEGRO GENERAL
IN THE U. S. ARMY

For ten years he remained a Colonel until the pressures of World War II forced his promotion to Brigadier-General. During the long years since joining the regular Army, Davis had served in the Philippines, had been Military Attache at Monrovia, Liberia. Stateside, he had been an instructor in the Ohio National Guard, professor of military science and tactics at Wilberforce in Ohio and later at Tuskegee Institute. He was also an instructor and commander of the 369th Infantry, New York National Guard. New York National Guard.

After 1940, Brigadier General Benjamin O. Davis, Sr., served as a special advisor and co-ordinator in the European Theatre of Operations. He rendered extremely valuable service in the desegregation of the military establishment. From 1945 to 1947 he was Assistant to the Inspector-General of the Army. In 1947 General Davis was appointed Special Assistant to the Secretary of the Army.

After fifty years of outstanding service to his country, Brigadier General Benjamin O. Davis, Sr. retired in 1948. He could count among his military decorations medals for service in the Philippines, the Spanish-American War, and along the Mexican Border; he could point to service medals of two world wars, including the Bronze Star, the French Croix de Guerre with palm and the Distinguished Service Medal. At the time of writing (1963) the old soldier was still alive, having set a mark for length of service with distinction.

Although Negroes have served in the United States Armed Forces since the war for independence, it was not until 1940 that any had earned the rank of General. In that year Colonel Benjamin Oliver Davis, Sr. was named a Brigadier General in the Regular Army.

His career began in 1898. Because of his skill and ability, he was promoted to the rank of First Lieutenant in the 9th United States volunteers shortly after he was graduated from Howard University. Mustered out of the volunteers in 1899, he re-enlisted in the Regular Army that same year. By 1901 he had moved up to the rank of Second-Lieutenant in the Cavalry.

Step by step he mounted the military ladder. In 1905 he was a First Lieutenant; in 1915, a Captain; in 1917, a Major (temporary); in 1918-20, a Lieutenant-Colonel; and in 1930, a full Colonel.

Who's Who in Colored America, 1950, p. 139; Lee. Nichols *Breakthrough on the Color Front*, New York, 1954, pp. 28-41.

Benjamin O. Davis, Jr.
(1912-   )

LEADER ALOFT

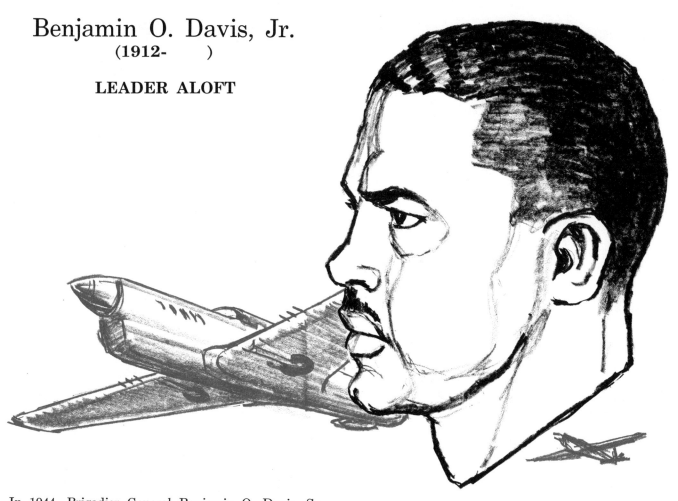

In 1944, Brigadier General Benjamin O. Davis, Sr. pinned the Distinguished Flying Cross to the chest of one Colonel B. O. Davis, Jr., who had led the 332nd Pursuit Squadron, a Negro group, on a successful bombing raid against a German installation located deep in occupied France. This was more than a ceremony of decoration, it was a father saying to his only son, "Well done."

For B. O. Davis, Jr., this was also a particularly sweet moment—a moment of realization and culmination, the realization of who and what he was, and the culmination of his father's, as well as his own struggles to prove the worth of the Negro as a "fighting man."

There was a time when B. O. Davis, Jr. did not know what to make of himself—when he was first appointed to West Point he was not particularly elated. He was well aware of the fact that it took his father over thirty years to attain the rank of Colonel. Young Davis' indifference was so great that he failed his first West Point examination. But after 1932 when he finally entered West Point, this indifference was replaced by a purposefulness born of the awareness that he had to succeed, because failure would be interpreted by many as a failure of his race.

Born in 1912 and traveling about the country with his soldier-father, young Davis was well prepared for a career in the military. He also possessed the necessary physical and mental equipment; he was 6'2" tall and had a sharp mind. In school, his main academic interest was mathematics and he was president of his class. His grades at the University of Chicago and Northwestern were above average.

This same mental and physical equipment stood him in good stead at a time when he was the only Negro student at West Point. During his first year and intermittently thereafter, he was subjected to the silent treatment. He overcame this hostility and became the first Negro to be graduated from West Point in forty-seven years. But he was under this same type of pressure at Tuskegee Air Base where he took his flying training, and, later, when he led the 99th Fighter Squadron, 332nd Fighter Group in the European theater during World War II. Here Davis earned the Distinguished Flying Cross and Silver Star for personal bravery, and his group won a Presidential Unit Citation.

After the war he became the first Negro to command an Air Base. During the Korean War he headed a Fighter Branch at Air Force headquarters in the Pentagon. Since then, he has not only risen to the rank of Major General, but as deputy chief of staff for operations to the USAFE, he became one of the top four officers responsible for maintaining combat-ready units for the possible defense of the West. No other Negro has been entrusted with such heavy responsibility.

Who's Who in Colored America, 1950, p. 139; Lee Nichols, *Breakthrough on the Color Front*, New York, 1950, pp. 47-50.

Charles H. Houston
William H. Hastie
James B. Parsons

LAWYERS AND JUDGES

In a nation of law, the American Negro, for the most part, has been an "outcast, asylumed 'neath these skies." Yet he had maintained faith in the ideals of democracy and has relied upon the law as one of the avenues to a fuller role in the democratic experiment. Where existing law has been directed toward his repression and degradation, the Negro has tried to bring about new laws more in keeping with the fulfillment of the American dream.

Ever since Macon B. Allen was admitted to the bar in the state of Maine in 1854, Negro lawyers have played an important role in the fight for equality. Of the twenty-two Negroes who sat in the U. S. Congress during the Reconstruction era, six were lawyers. Among the most brilliant of them was Robert B. Elliott who had one of the finest law libraries in the South. John Mercer Langston was an ex-Dean of the Howard University Law School when he took his seat in the U. S. House of Representatives in 1889. Johnathan J. Wright was an Associate Justice of the State Supreme Court of South Carolina from 1870 to 1877.

However, not until the twentieth century did the Negro lawyer come into his own. The best brains and talents of the legal profession were directed toward securing of the constitutional rights of Negroes. For decades the Negro's top legal talent was focused on Howard University in Washington, D.C. From Howard either as students or teachers have emerged some of the giants in the history of Negro lawyers: William Hart, James Cobb, Herman E. Moore, William Hastie and Charles H. Houston, to name only a few. Other lawyers such as Howard's present Law Dean, Spottswood Robinson, Raymond and Sadie T. Alexander of Philadelphia, A. T. Walden of Atlanta, Robert Ming of Chicago, Henry J. Richardson, Jr. of Indianapolis, Indiana, Perry Howard of Washington, D.C., Arthur Shores of Birmingham, Alabama and scores of other brilliant lawyers have served the Negro and the nation with valor and distinction.

A closer view of some of the lawyers in the history of civil rights litigation will perhaps give some indication of the quality of the men before the bar and on the bench.

Charles Hamilton Houston (1895-1950) has been credited with laying the legal strategy for the justly famous case of *Brown v. Board of Education* in which the U. S. Supreme Court in 1954 declared segregation itself to be unconstitutional. Working with the NAACP he "set the pattern for *fundamental* attacks on barriers to equal justice, in place of the former practice of meeting emergencies and opportunities as they arose." His was the strategic thinking behind the brilliant series of cases on restrictive covenants, discrimination in education and in labor as well as in interstate travel.

HOUSTON

In the course of his work at Howard University from 1924 until his death in 1950, Charles H. Houston raised the Howard Law School to unrivalled superiority in the area of civil rights law. Houston's own formal training was obtained at the Harvard University Law School from which he was graduated in 1922. Earlier he had graduated from Amherst with a brilliant record.

Charles Houston attracted many able men to the Howard Law School. Outstanding among them are William Hastie and Thurgood Marshall. When William Hastie was appointed U. S. District Judge for the Virgin Islands in 1937, he became the first Negro ever appointed to the Federal Bench. He had been a law partner of Houston, and followed him to Howard in 1930. Hastie too could claim Amherst and Harvard as his alma maters.

In 1939, William Hastie became Dean of the Howard Law School. A year later he took a leave of absence to serve as Civilian Aide to the Secretary of War (now Defense). All policy questions regarding Negro servicemen were to be referred to him. While Hastie was in this post only two years, he made heroic efforts to accelerate the integration of the armed forces. In 1944 he was appointed Governor of the Virgin Islands. Since 1949, he has been

HASTIE   PARSONS

on the appellate bench of the U. S. Circuit Court of Appeals, Third Circuit.

Since the early days of Hastie and his successor in the Virgin Islands, Herman E. Moore, many outstanding lawyers have become judges in different states. Most promising among the new generation of Negro judges is James Benson Parsons, who was appointed to the U. S. District Court for the Northern District of Illinois in 1961, just twelve years after he was admitted to the bar. An example of lawyers giving effective service in their states is the instance of attorney Henry J. Richardson, Jr. of Indiana. A stalwart fighter against the Indiana Ku Klux Klan, Richardson won a seat in the Indiana state legislature in 1932. His first act in the legislature in 1933 was to successfully introduce legislation outlawing the Klan and prohibiting the wearing of masks by marchers. As chief counsel of Indiana's NAACP, Richardson won the first case at the Federal level on housing desegregation in 1953.

The field of law has not been the exclusive preserve of men. A number of brilliant women have made outstanding reputations as lawyers and jurists. With her famous husband, Sadie T. Alexander became a veteran of many

legal battles in Philadelphia. Edith Sampson, formerly a practicing attorney and United Nations delegate, later became a judge with the Cook County Municipal Court. Constance Baker Motley was associate counsel of the NAACP Legal Defense Fund. In 1964 she was elected to the New York State Senate. Jewel Stratford Lafontant, of Chicago was the first Negro woman United States Assistant District Attorney. Juanita Stout of Pennsylvania became a judge in the city of Philadelphia. After a distinguished career as an attorney, Marjorie Lawson went to work with the Juvenile Court in Washington, D.C.

Negro lawyers and Judges, men who argue and decide, are thus an extremely important group. They have been makers not only of Negro history but also of American history. Neither their profession nor their successes have come easy. Theirs has been the task of weaving the final patterns of equal justice for all citizens into the incomplete fabric of American law.

Saunders Redding. *The Lonesome Road*, New York, 1958, pp. 319-320; Langston Hughes. *Fight for Freedom: The Story of the NAACP*, New York, 1962, Berkley Medallion Edition, p. 69; Richard Bardolph. *The Negro Vanguard*, New York, 1962, Vintage Edition, pp. 254-255.

Thurgood Marshall (1908-   )

"MR. CIVIL RIGHTS"

Every American owes something of a debt to Thurgood Marshall, former Chief Legal counsel of the NAACP, and now Federal Judge, Fifth Circuit, New York. Perhaps the greatest constitutional lawyer of this century and certainly the most widely known legal mind in America, Thurgood Marshall earned for himself the title "Mr. Civil Rights." For twenty-four years, as legal counsel for the NAACP, Marshall exerted "an influence as a mover and shaker of American society that few of his white contemporaries in the profession could match."

Thurgood Marshall master-minded or laid the basis of legal cases firmly establishing the right of Negroes to serve on juries and to vote in Democratic primaries in the South, to travel from state to state free of jim-crow, to be free of restrictive covenants denying them the equal right to the use and purchase of property, and the right to a public education without discrimination and segregation.

As the NAACP's lawyer, he won thirty-two out of thirty-five cases taken by him before the United States Supreme Court. During his career as a lawyer, Marshall won the respect of his opponents by his careful, precise, and objective arguments. Warm and friendly, a man's man among intimates, he was the most feared antagonists of the best legal brains the South could buy. As his reputation grew, Marshall received lucrative offers from some of the nation's leading law firms to pay him several times more than the NAACP, but he felt it his duty to remain in the thick of the battle to make America what it ought to be. As a Federal Judge, it is expected that he will apply to his work the same fairness and brilliance that characterized him as a lawyer. He once said, "My commitments have always been to justice for all people regardless of race, creed or color."

Hard work and a sense of humor with dignity carried him through Lincoln University where he waited tables and hopped bells, and through Howard University Law School which he helped to make the legal arsenal for all civil rights suits in recent decades.

After finishing Howard with honors, Marshall returned to his native Baltimore, Maryland where he made a modest living. It was here that he "learned what rights were." His clients were poor, usually victims of dispossession, eviction, police brutality and the like. He handled many cases, knowing full well there would be no fee. Soon he was known in Maryland as the "little man's lawyer." All of his life since has been dedicated to the defense of the "little man," for the United States Constitution was designed for the least as well as the greatest Americans. If John Marshall, the United States Supreme Court's first Chief Justice, made the court into a going concern, then one hundred and seventy-five years later, one Thurgood Marshall had a great hand in guiding the court nearer to where the Founding Fathers wanted it to go.

Current Biography, 1944.
Richard Bardolph, *The Negro Vanguard*, pp. 433-439.
Saunders Redding, *The Lonesome Road*, pp. 314-329.

Ralph J. Bunche (1904–)

DIPLOMAT, U. N. MEDIATOR

Dr. Ralph Johnson Bunche's forty-odd honorary degrees and one Nobel Prize are eloquent testimony to the contributions he has made to America and to world peace. High school class valedictorian at Los Angeles' Jefferson High School; Magna Cum Laud graduate of the University of California; winner of the Tappan Prize at Harvard University for the best doctoral dissertation in the social sciences in 1934; post-doctoral study at Northwestern University, the London School of Economics and the University of Capetown, Johannesburg, South Africa: such is the academic background of one of America's most honored Negroes.

After a career at Howard University which paralleled his academic advancement, Dr. Bunche was named chairman of Howard's Political Science Department in 1937, and a year later he joined the Swedish economist, Gunnar Myrdal, to begin the comprehensive study of the American Negro, published in 1945 as *An American Dilemma*.

By 1942 Dr. Bunche was at work in the Office of Strategic Services as a research analyst of material relating to Africa. By 1946 he had advanced to the position of Associate Chief of the State Department's Dependent Areas section. Already a foreign affairs adviser of growing reputation, Dr. Bunche left the State Department for the Trusteeship Division of the United Nations. In quick succession, he was head of the United Nation's Trusteeship Department and personal representative of the United Nation's Secretary-General in the extremely dangerous Arab-Israeli dis-

pute. Following the assassination of the United Nation's Palestine Mediator in 1947, Dr. Bunche was named Acting Mediator and achieved a historic settlement of the Palestine question.

In 1949, Dr. Bunche was awarded the Springarn medal. In 1950 he received the Nobel Prize for Peace. Other honors and offers came to him, including a professorship at Harvard University, the presidency of the City College of New York and the post of Assistant Secretary of State. However, Dr. Bunche has remained with the United Nations and is now its Under Secretary-General. He went to the Congo in 1960 as the United Nation's special representative during the height of the turmoil there.

The achievements of Dr. Bunche are based on an extraordinary personal ability and hard work. His father was a poor Detroit barber; his mother an amateur musician. Both parents died before Bunche reached his teens and he found himself living in California with his grandmother and several aunts. When he won an athletic scholarship to the University of California, he paid his other expenses by working as a campus janitor. Friends and neighbors raised money for his living expenses for one year after he won a tuition scholarship to Harvard. From this point onward, Ralph Johnson Bunche depended on nothing but his brains to carry him the rest of the way.

Current Biography, 1948, pp. 77-79.
Who's Who in Colored America, 1950, pp. 74-75.
Who's Who, 1962-63, p. 427.

Martin Luther King, Jr. (1929-1968)

THE NON-VIOLENT CRUSADER

Some people have called Martin Luther King the "jet-age Ghandi." Others have called him a "crusader without violence." The Reverend Dr. Martin Luther King has been described as an idealist as well as a realist. In a sense all of these descriptions are accurate. Thrust into the international spotlight at the age of twenty-seven, Rev. King is regarded in 1963 as the enduring symbol of the Negro "revolt."

Rev. King's broad public career and the Negro "revolt" began about the same time. Mrs. Rosa Parks, an Alabama seamstress, refused to yield her bus seat to a white male in accordance with the laws and customs of the state of Alabama as they existed on December 1, 1955. When Mrs. Parks was hauled away to jail, the long-standing grievances of the Negroes of Montgomery, Alabama were thrown into unbearable relief. Within five days after the arrest of Mrs. Parks, the Negroes organized the Montgomery Improvement Association (MIA) and elected the Reverend Martin Luther King president.

Thus began a struggle between the blacks and whites of the city of Montgomery, a city deep in the heart of the late Confederacy. The Negroes, under the leadership of the MIA and Martin Luther King, simply decided not to ride the buses of the Montgomery City Lines, a southern branch of the National City Lines with headquarters in Chicago, Illinois. The boycott was almost immediately one hundred per cent effective. A car pool of three hundred vehicles transported Negroes to and from their jobs. Neither protests by whites nor threats, nor petty harassment hurt the new-found pride of Montgomery's black citizens. United as never before the Negroes stayed off the buses for 381 days.

Rev. King and some seventy of his followers were arrested and convicted for "illegally boycotting" the buses. Rev. King declared that his only offense was in seeking to "instill in my people a sense of dignity and self-respect." The convictions were appealed and eventually overturned. The higher court held that the segregation laws of the city of Montgomery and the state of Alabama were unconstitutional. The city of Montgomery officially declared an end to segregation on the city buses on December 20, 1956. When the buses resumed their rounds unsegregated, Rev. King was among the first to ride them.

During the long contest with the officialdom of Montgomery, Rev. King preached the gospel of love and non-violence. There was no violence from the Negroes of Montgomery. On the day the bus desegregation order reached the city, Rev. King declared that "violence must not come from any of us, for if we become victimized with violent intents, we will have walked in vain, and twelve months of glorious dignity will be transformed into an eve of gloomy catastrophe." The only violence accompanying the desegregation of the buses came from disgruntled whites who bombed churches and assaulted Negro bus riders.

Shortly after the buses were integrated, Rev. King and a group of Atlanta ministers created the Southern Christian Leadership Conference (SCLC). The SCLC had broader goals than the MIA at the time it was formed. Today the Reverend Dr. King spends most of his time and energy travelling the length and breadth of the country explaining the goals of the SCLC and raising funds for the support of its work.

Dr. King continued his style of direct involvement in the fight against racial segregation. Arrested more than a dozen times for taking part in civil rights protest demonstrations, Rev. King harbored no bitterness toward his jailers nor toward those who supported the jailers. While by no means naive in the ways of the world, Rev. King developed a deep faith in the power of love and non-violence in social relations. One of his favorite admonitions to his followers is this: "Let no man drag you so low as to hate." This modern Mahatma's thinking is a mixture of old-fashioned Christianity, the social gospel of Walter Rauschenbusch, the "Satyagraha" or love-force of Ghandi's philosophy, interwoven with influences from Hegel to Reinhold Niebuhr.

The Reverend Dr. Martin Luther King is an even-tempered, deceptively brilliant young leader. Born in Atlanta, Georgia with the name Michael Lewis King, Jr., he comes from a line of old-fashioned Georgia ministers.

His maternal grandfather, the Rev. A. D. Williams, helped to secure the first high school in Atlanta for Negro pupils. The Reverend M. L. King, Sr., a stern, highly-astute man of the cloth, is distinguished in his own right, both as a minister and as a crusader for justice. He was a leader in the fight for the equalization of salaries for Negro teachers in Georgia.

The young Michael Lewis King adopted the name Martin Luther when his father told him about the great Protestant Reformation figure of the same name. Although a great admirer of the courageous Martin Luther, the young Martin Luther King was at first indifferent to the ministry as a vocation. After attending the local Booker T. Washington High School, he entered Morehouse College in Atlanta. Under the influence of its famed president, Dr. Benjamin E. Mays, King changed his mind about the ministry and was ordained by his father in 1947. He was graduated from Morehouse College in 1948 and enrolled for graduate study in the Crozer Theological Seminary in Chester, Pennsylvania. King was one of six Negroes in a student body of one hundred.

Rev. King received the bachelor of divinity degree from Crozer in 1951. He was awarded the Pearl Plafkner prize for outstanding scholarship and was elected president of the Crozer student body. King continued his studies at Boston University and was awarded the doctor of Philosophy degree in 1955.

Two years before receiving his doctorate, he married attractive Coretta Scott, a native of Marion, Alabama, who was studying at the New England Conservatory of Music. As he approached the end of his formal education, Reverend King was uncertain about returning to the South. But the lure of the South and his love for many southern people and places proved too strong. He finally accepted a call to the pastorate of the Dexter Avenue Baptist Church in Montgomery, Alabama on September 1, 1954.

Martin Luther King, Jr. *Stride Toward Freedom*, New York, 1958; L. D. Reddick. *Crusader Without Violence*, New York, 1959; *Current Biography*, 1957, pp. 299-300; Louis Lomax. *The Negro Revolt*, New York, 1962, pp. 81-100.

VIII EDUCATION

They Carried The Lamp

The American Negro has always possessed a deep faith in the power of education to bring about a change in his status and in the quality of his personal life. He has believed that education is the key to many of the fetters that bind him. In the days of slavery this was also believed by his masters who made it a crime for him to learn to read and to write.

In the North among free Negroes the hunger for education was manifested in schools, such as the African Free School, which was opened in New York by the Manumission Society in 1787. In 1798 a school for Negro pupils was set up in Boston, Massachusetts in the home of a prominent Negro, Primus Hall. When the city of Boston refused to support a school for Negro students, the Negro community of Boston organized a school and paid two Harvard men to teach them. Under the impetus of the Quakers in Philadelphia, schools were provided for Negroes as early as 1774. Small schools were set up in Virginia at the beginning of the nineteenth century.

As the nineteenth century progressed, more free Negroes attended institutions of learning. By 1820 the African Free School, for example, had over five hundred students. Scores of Negroes attended the famous Oneida Institute, Oneida County, New York during this period.

The intensity of the Negro's desire for education may be seen in the case of the great educator of the Methodist ministry, Daniel Payne. In 1829 Payne opened a school in his native Charleston, South Carolina with three freeborn children and three adult slaves. His school building was a room provided by one Caesar Wright, a prosperous free Negro. Payne had to purchase books surreptiously from peddlers as no bookstores would sell them to him. After the Nat Turner uprising, a wave of repression hit the South. In 1835 Daniel Payne was forced to close his little school which by this time had sixty students.

John Chavis, another native of Charleston, had been teaching whites by day and Negroes by night. He, too, had to close his school in the city of Charleston. Up in Canterbury, Connecticut during the same general period, Prudence Crandall was taken to court for violating a state law forbidding non-residents to study in Connecticut schools when she attempted to admit Negro girls.

None of these events suppressed the desire of Negroes to secure an education. Church and abolitionist groups continued to run great risks to bring the lamp of learning to the Negro. A Negro woman opened a private school in New Orleans, Louisiana in 1835. Philadelphia had thirteen private schools for Negroes by 1838. The Methodist

Episcopal Church purchased 120 acres of land in Green County, Ohio in 1847 and created the basis for Wilberforce University.

In the wake of the Civil War, schools sprang up throughout the South. During this period, in the words, of Booker T. Washington, "It was a whole race trying to go to school." Northern missionary and church organizations sent teaching personnel and money to aid in the education of four million ex-slaves. Howard, Fisk, and Atlanta Universities, Hampton and Tuskegee Institutes, Clark, Morehouse, Morris Brown and Spelman Colleges got their start in the Reconstruction era.

It is commonly thought that Negroes did little to aid in the development of education in these dawning years of freedom. In many cases, Negroes raised large amounts of cash for elementary school education in particular. In Baltimore, Maryland, for example, Nancy Addison left $15,000 and Louis Bode left $30,000 for the benefit of young Negro students. In the area of higher education Negroes were no less philanthropic. Daniel Payne donated several thousand dollars to Wilberforce University. One Mary Shaw bequeathed $38,000 to Tuskegee Institute.

Although John B. Russwurm was the first Negro to graduate from a college (Bowdoin, class of 1829), Negroes did not come into prominence in education until the twentieth century. By 1900 there were nearly one hundred colleges, or institutions bearing that title. The more important of them, such as Fisk, Hampton, Howard University, were headed by white presidents.

The great debate between Booker T. Washington and W. E. B. DuBois over the type of education best-calculated to secure the Negro's entry into the wider society indicated a growing desire by the Negro to control the destiny and content of his education. The appointment of William Scarborough as president of Wilberforce in 1908, of Modecai Johnson as president of Howard in 1926, of John Hope as president of Atlanta University in 1936, and Charles S. Johnson as president of Fisk University in 1946 pointed to a basic shift in the control of education among Negroes.

Today education continues to be one of the major avenues by which the Negro hopes to help America live up to its ideals. Throughout the nations are thousands of competent teachers dedicated to this task.

Leon Litwack. *North of Slavery*, Chicago, 1961; Willard Range. *The Rise and Progress of Negro Colleges in Georgia: 1865-1949*, Athens, Georgia, 1951; Ridgely Torrence. *The Story of John Hope*, New York, 1948, pp. 312-367; Gunnar Mvrdal. *An American Dilemma* (vol. II), New York, 1944, pp. 887-903.

William Scarborough
(1852-1926)

LECTURER, SCHOLAR, LINGUIST

A lecturer, linguist and college president, William Saunders Scarborough was a member of that unusual band of ex-slaves who achieved eminence in freedom. Like many of his contemporaries, Scarborough early showed a desire to learn and secured his basic education by stealthy reading, with the help of sympathetic white playmates and adults. Although he became a minister at an early age, he did not devote himself solely to the pulpit but concentrated on the Greek classics. Extremely proficient with languages, he was elected to the American Philological Association in 1882, the American Spelling Reform Association in 1883, the Modern Language Association and the American Social Science Association in 1884 and 1885 respectively.

Scarborough was born on February 16, 1852 in Macon, Georgia and began school at the age of six. At the age of ten he could read and write, and during the Civil War, was able to forge passes for his fellow slaves and to read the war news to men at the shoemaker's shop where he worked part-time. At the age of twelve, he began the study of music; at fifteen he entered the Lewis High School and completed the course in two years. He then attended Atlanta University and later Oberlin College,

earning the B. A. degree from the latter institution in 1875, and the M.A. degree in 1878. He managed to get to Africa and attended Liberia College, completing his studies there in 1882 with the LL. D. degree.

Even before receiving his M. A. degree, Scarborough had taught Latin, Greek and mathematics at his former high school. In 1881 he authored a Greek textbook which was published by A. B. Barnes Company, New York and received high cirical acclaim in academic circles. In 1886 Scarborough wrote *Birds of Aristophanes*. With an early grounding in Greek and Latin, Scarborough became an able student of Slavonic languages, Sanskrit and even Hebrew. He read papers before a number of scholarly societies, including the American Philological Association.

After a short period as president of a small denominational college in Columbia, South Carolina, Scarborough joined the faculty of Wilberforce University in Ohio and in 1908 became president of the institution. He rendered outstanding service as an administrator during this time, and finally retired at the age of sixty-eight in 1920.

William J. Simmons. *Men of Mark*, Cleveland, 1887, pp. 410-418; *Dictionary of American Biography*, XVI, 1935.

Booker T. Washington (1856-1915)

When the Board of Commissioners of Tuskegee Normal Institute asked General Samuel C. Armstrong of Hampton Institute for a principal to head their institution, they wanted a white man. Instead, Booker T. Washington was selected, and he searched the map in vain for the location of Tuskegee. When he arrived at Tuskegee in June of 1881, the institute consisted of a rickety church and a small shanty, plus thirty-one students from the nearby farms.

Two men were responsible for the creation of the institute: Lewis Adams, a successful Negro farmer and W. F. Foster, a local white politician who was trying to win votes among the Negroes of Macon County, Alabama. Foster had obtained an annual appropriation of $2,000 and a few acres of land for the school.

On July 4, 1881, Booker T. Washington opened the doors of the school. Physical survival was the main problem confronting the principal and his young charges. Food had to be grown and buildings erected, for the two dilapidated structures were totally insufficient. With a directness typical of him, Washington led the way in felling trees, clearing the land, digging wells for water and constructing buildings to house the new school.

A natural politician, Washington cultivated the good will of whites and Negroes in Macon County. He explained that Tuskegee was to be an industrial training school, not a liberal arts college. All of the students were to work to pay their way and to run the school. His gospel of self-help appealed to many people. The student body increased and permanent buildings replaced temporary shelters and shanties. By 1900 over forty buildings dotted the clearing that was Tuskegee, erected mainly by student labor and paid for by northern philanthropy.

Booker Washington spoke to numerous audiences in the North and seemed to offer a solution to the nagging problems of the freedmen. His industrial school was turning out graduates who were successful farmers, carpenters and bricklayers; these were sober, hard-working citizens who minded their own business. His name was known throughout the South.

In 1895 Booker T. Washington was invited to speak at the Atlanta Exposition. This was the first such invitation extended to a Negro leader in the deep South. Much speculation developed over what he was going to say. Washington himself realized that this was a special occasion and took great pains in composing his speech.

Birthplace replica at Rocky Mount, Va.

THE LENGTHENED SHADOW

On September 18, Booker T. Washington, on the same platform with Georgia's governor and other dignitaries, rose to make his speech. James Creel, a noted correspondent for the New York *World*, described Washington as he appeared that day: "There was a remarkable figure; tall, bony, straight as a Sioux chief, high forehead, straight nose, heavy jaws, and strong, determined mouth, with big white teeth, piercing eyes and a commanding manner. . . ."

In his speech Washington apoligized for the "errors" his race had made in beginning "at the top instead of at the bottom"; in seeking seats in state legislatures rather than developing skills in industry and real estate, in pursuing politics rather than cultivating truck gardens. He urged the southern Negro to "Cast down your bucket where you are" in agriculture, mechanics, commerce, domestic service and the like. He said that "The wisest among my race understand that the agitation of questions of social equality is the extremest folly," and he felt that "in all things that are social we can be as separate as the fingers, yet one as the hand in all things essential for mutual progress."

The white audience went wild; the governor shook his hand publicly. The nation's press heralded his speech as the greatest utterance of an American Negro. Overnight Washington was a national figure with more speaking engagements than he could possibly handle. Philanthropists pressed money upon his Institute.

At this time Tuskegee had eight hundred students, a staff of fifty-five, $200,000 worth of buildings and one-hundred sixty-five graduates taking the Tuskegee idea throughout the South. After the speech, enrollment increased: Dorothy Hall, Douglas Hall, Institute Chapel, and other buildings rose on the wings of Northern cash.

Washington himself helped to institutionalize Northern philanthropy. In 1907 he helped set up the Anna T. Jeanes Foundation for Negro rural schools; in 1910 he was host to the formative meetings of the General Education Board fund; in 1911 he cooperated in the establishment of the Phelp-Stokes Fund and the Carnegie Foundation. Two years later he participated in the development of the Rosenwald Fund idea.

By 1915 Tuskegee had over sixty buildings and an endowment of nearly three million dollars. Both the school and the man were internationally famous. Washington never slackened the tempo of his work. He suffered a fatal heart attack on November 14, 1915.

Debate over his racial adjustment philosophy continues to this day; however, there was never any question of his role and place in the building of Tuskegee Institute.

Booker T. Washington, *Up From Slavery*, New York, (Bantam Pathfinder Edition), 1963; Samuel R. Spencer, Jr., *Booker T. Washington and the Negro's Place in American Life*, Boston, 1955.

...at the time he founded Tuskegee

William Edward Burghart DuBois (1868-1963)

SCHOLAR, SPOKESMAN, WRITER

Few scholars in American history become national legends in their own time. For over fifty years, W. E. B. DuBois has been regarded as the dean of Negro intellectuals. The sheer brilliance of his scholarship and the vigor of his pen have made him known throughout the nation. *Who's Who in America* has listed DuBois in its pages every year since it was first published in 1898. DuBois was a pioneer social scientist; he authored one of the standard books on the reconstruction era. He also conducted the first studies of the Negro in Philadelphia and Atlanta.

DuBois was the founder and first editor of *Crisis* magazine. Years later while a professor at Atlanta University, he founded *Phylon*, a noted quarterly devoted to the Negro in America.

Perhaps his greatest fame came not from his scholarly work but from his debate at the turn of the century with Booker T. Washington over the type of education needed by the Negro in America. Washington, of course, stressed vocational education whereas DuBois insisted on training in the liberal arts and the humanities. After the death of Booker T. Washington, W. E. B. DuBois became the one generally recognized spokesman for the Negro.

In 1905 he launched the Niagara movement, advocating the immediate ending of racial discrimination and segregation. He was one of the founders of the NAACP in 1908. In 1919 DuBois initiated the first of several early Pan-African Congresses in Paris with the hope of focussing world opinion on the conditions and status of black men everywhere. Setting forth his views in books, articles, poems and speeches, DuBois has never ceased his fight against racial and economic exploitation.

Proud, aristocratic, confident, DuBois was the son of a wandering father and a mother who had to take in washing and boarders to support him in his native Great Barrington, Massachusetts. His obvious mental ability won for him scholarships to Fisk and Harvard universities and the University of Berlin. His life has been long and eventful. His uncompromising views of fifty years ago, that the Negro is entitled to develop all of his faculties and talents to the utmost, make him yet a pioneer and a prophet.

At the time of his death on August 28, 1963, DuBois was a citizen of Ghana. He had been hard at work on a mammoth compendium of African history and culture entitled *Encyclopedia Africana*.

Frances L. S. Broderick. *DuBois: Negro Leader in a Time of Crisis*, Stanford, 1959; Elbert L. Tatum. *The Changed Political Thought of the Negro, 1915-1940*, Chicago, 1942.

Alain L. Locke (1886-1954)

RHODES SCHOLAR, PHILOSOPHER

The Nobel Prize is to the world of intellectual achievement what the Rhodes Scholarship is to the world of academic preparation. Both prizes stand for the highest excellence. The Rhodes Scholarships are based on intellectual ability, moral character and the potentialities for significant achievement in later life.

Only three Negroes have been selected for the Rhodes Scholarships since they were created by Cecil Rhodes in 1899. Two Negroes — John E. Wideman of Pittsburgh, Pennsylvania and Joseph Stanley Sanders of Los Angeles —were chosen in 1962, fifty-five years after Alain LeRoy Locke was selected.

A native of Philadelphia, Alain Locke went to Oxford as a Rhodes Scholar in 1907. After three years he left Oxford for the University of Berlin. Upon his return to America from Germany in 1912, Locke joined the faculty of Howard University that same year, and became a full professor of philosophy in 1917, a year before he received his Ph.D. from Harvard University.

In the area of philosophy, Locke's writings have been regarded as "original contributions in a highly controversial field." His philosophical works include *The Problem of Classification in the Theory of Value* and *Values and Imperatives in American Philosophy: Today and Tomorrow.*

Dr. Locke's intellectual influence spread far beyond his academic specialty. In 1925 he edited a collection of significant literature by young Negro authors in an epochal volume called *The New Negro.* During the Negro Renaissance (sometimes called the "Harlem Renaissance") Locke became the leading intellectual spokesman for the remarkable upsurge of creativity among Negroes in literature, art and drama.

In 1933 he published *The Negro in America*; in 1936, *The Negro and His Music.* The next year he wrote *Negro Art: Past and Present* and in 1941 published *The Negro in Art.* For a number of years he wrote annual reviews of the developments in literature by Negro authors. He encouraged many promising young writers and artists.

Many awards and honors came to Dr. Locke. He was the first Negro to be elected president of the National Council of Adult Education. He was an exchange professor to Haiti in 1943 and a visiting professor at several universities, including Fisk and the University of Wisconsin.

So busy was Dr. Locke in encouraging others, his own masterwork *The Negro in American Culture* was completed by Margaret Just Butcher after his death. Alain Locke lived up to every expectation of the donor of the Rhodes Scholarships.

Who's Who in Colored America, 1950, pp. 342-343; *Negro Yearbook, 1947*, pp. 411-412; Margaret Just Butcher, *The Negro In American Culture.*

Carter G. Woodson (1875-1950)

FATHER OF NEGRO HISTORY

William Cooper Nell, William Still, William Wells Brown, George Washington Williams and W. E. B. DuBois wrote books on various aspects of the history of the Negro. Despite their pioneering efforts, however, systematic treatment of Negro history was not begun until 1915 when Carter G. Woodson, an ex-coal miner and school teacher, organized the Association for the Study of Negro Life and History. Over the years the still-thriving Association has published many important volumes in this field. Today most educational institutions are conscious of the Negro's past. Many of them are developing study programs to fill this neglected gap in the education of most Americans.

Woodson himself set the pace for research in this area. Among his books are *The Education of the Negro Prior to 1861, A Century of Negro Migration, The Negro in Our History, Negro Makers of History, The Story of The Negro Retold, The Mind of the Negro as Reflected in Letters Written During the Crisis of 1800-1861, Negro Orators and Their Orations* and *The History of the Negro Church.*

In the year 1916, Dr. Woodson started the *Journal of Negro History*, a scholarly repository of research which is used by students throughout the world. He initiated the observance of Negro History Week in 1926. Eleven years later the Association began the publication of *The Negro History Bulletin*, a more popular vehicle for disseminating the findings of scholars and researchers.

Carter G. Woodson was born in Canton, Virginia in 1875. Having little opportunity or money to attend school, he was twenty-two years old when he completed high school. During this period Woodson supported himself by working as a coal miner. He continued his education at Berea College in Kentucky and at the University of Chicago. He terminated his formal studies with a Doctor of Philosophy degree from Harvard in 1912. Three years later he organized the Association for the Study of Negro Life and History. Dr. Woodson firmly believed that "the achievements of the Negro properly set forth will crown him as a factor in early human progress and a maker of modern civilization." His life and work are eloquent testimony to that belief.

Who's Who in Colored America, 1950; p. 572; John Hope Franklin, "The Place of Carter G. Woodson in American Historiography," *The Negro History Bulletin,* May, 1950, pp. 174-176.

Charles S. Johnson (1893-1956)

EDUCATOR, SOCIAL SCIENTIST

Jubilee Hall, Fisk University, Nashville, Tenn.

While the field of sociology has attracted hundreds of Negro scholars, none of them has ever achieved the eminence of Charles Spurgeon Johnson. In volume after volume of social research, Charles S. Johnson revealed to the world the status and strivings of the Negro on the farms and in the cities. Any serious study of the Negro in America must include his work.

The very titles of his books give some indication of his interests: *The Negro in Chicago* (1922); *The Negro in American Civilization* (1930); *Negro Housing* (1932); *Economic Status of the Negro* (1933); *Shadow of the Plantation* (1934); *Collapse of Cotton Tenancy* (1934); *Growing Up in the Black Belt* (1941) and *Into the Mainstream* (1947).

In 1946 Charles Johnson was named president of Fisk University in Nashville, Tennessee. He was the first Negro to head this institution since it was founded in 1865. Before and after his elevation from his directorship of the able Social Science Department at Fisk University, Johnson helped this institution to remain a leader in the scientific study of race relations in America.

Dr. Johnson's training in social science research may be traced back to his student days at the University of Chicago when he witnessed the Chicago race riot of 1919. The Chicago Urban League selected him to head an investigation of the social forces causing the riot. For six years (1923-29) he was associate Executive Director of the Chicago Commission on Human Relations. In 1928 he was appointed to the faculty of Fisk University and remained with this institution the balance of his life.

His knowledge and experience were sought at several White House Conferences on youth. He was a consultant to, and a member of, many commissions, including those devoted to educational problems in Japan, and with the United Nations.

A native of Bristol, Virginia, Dr. Johnson received his formal education at Virginia Union University and the University of Chicago from which he received the Ph.B. in 1928. As a youth shining shoes in Bristol, he developed the detachment, the curiosity and the concern about people which characterized all of his scientific work. His death in 1956 created a void in the study of race relations in America.

Who's Who in Colored America, 1950, pp. 302-320.
Edward Embree, *Thirteen Against the Odds*, New York, 1956.

Mordecai Johnson (1890-)

ORATOR, EDUCATOR

Before assuming the presidency of Howard University in 1926 Mordecai, Johnson had been a successful Baptist minister in Charleston, West Virginia. Prior to this he had taught economics and history at his alma mater, Morehouse College (class of 1911). He had also served as student secretary with the national office of the Young Men's Christian Association.

Born in Columbus, Tennessee, Mordecai Johnson was an only child. His father, a minister and laborer, was a rather stern man who worked at a mill six days a week, twelve hours a day for forty years. His mother cushioned the sternness of the father and encouraged him in his education.

Johnson's oratorical ability won for him acclaim even while in high school and was quite evident at Morehouse and Harvard where in 1922 he attracted national attention with a commencement speech entitled "The Faith of the American Negro." Mordecai Johnson earned his A. B. degree from Morehouse in 1911, the Master of Sacred Theology degree from Harvard in 1923, and the Doctor of Divinity degree from Gammon Theological Seminary in 1928.

Dr. Johnson was active in numerous religious and governmental bodies, including a presidential commission for the study and review of conditions in Haiti and the Virgin Islands. He was a member of the Advisory Council of the National Youth Administration and a member of the National Advisory Council on Education. In addition to many honorary degrees, Dr. Johnson is one of the few Negroes who have won the Spingarn Medal (1929) as having done the most to contribute to the progress of the Negro during the previous year.

Who's Who in Colored America, 1950, p. 307.
Richard Bardolph. *The Negro Vanguard*, New York, 1961 (Paperback), pp. 168-169.

For over thirty years, Mordecai Johnson was one of the most renowned university presidents in America. As president of Howard University in Washington, D.C. he became a near-legendary figure in his own lifetime. Under Dr. Johnson, Howard University, founded in 1867 in an abandoned dance-hall and beer saloon, changed from a cluster of second-rate departments to nationally-approved units of distinction. The University's school of law is preeminent in the area of civil rights.

When Mordecai Johnson came to the University at the age of thirty-six, many people questioned his ability. When he retired thirty years later, he was acknowledged as *the* great president of the school. The faculty had tripled; salaries had doubled. Congressional appropriations which support the school, had increased to $6,000,000 annually. Freedmen's Hospital was turning out half of the Negro physicians in the country. The University's physical plant was valued at $34,000,000

IX LITERATURE

Tellers of Troubled Tales

The growth of an important body of literature in Negro America is very recent. In centuries past, however, individual Negroes made notable contributions to the literature of their respective adopted cultures. James E. J. Captien in Holland, Juan Latino in Spain, Alexander Pushkin in Russia and Alexander Dumas, *pere* in France were men of color whose writing skill brought them to public notice.

While Jupiter Hammon and Phillis Wheatley wrote poems of some merit in the eighteenth century, the birth of a real literary tradition dates from around 1853, when William Wells Brown wrote *Clotel, or The President's Daughter*, a story of the hardships of a mulatto family. This novel went through several editions. Brown's book was published during the period when the slave narrative was in vogue.

In the eighteen nineties, a number of Negro authors wrote novels and poems which attracted small audiences. For the most part these were works of protest and propaganda. Frances Ellen Harper wrote *Iola, or Shadows Uplifted*, in 1892. In 1896 McHenry Jones published *Heart of Gold*. In 1900 Pauline Hopkins tried to portray the life of free Negroes in the North and South in her *Contending Forces*. Beginning in 1896, Sutton E. Griggs wrote, published, and distributed a number of novels devoted to themes of miscegenation, Negro leadership and southern politics. His novels such as *Imperium in Imperio, Unfettered* and *The Hindered Hand* received a rather wide distribution among literate Negroes.

These early writers were neophytes in letters. Charles Waddell Chesnutt was perhaps the first Negro writer to give serious consideration to the artistic requirements of the short story and the novel. National magazines were publishing his short stories as early as 1887. In subsequent years he published several novels, all of which were artistically superior to those of his contemporaries. He was the first Negro writer to rise above the double standard of literary criticism then applied to Negro authors. Charles Waddell Chestnutt's work was judged alongside the best of general American fiction.

Between 1903 and 1923 only W. E. B. DuBois and James Weldon Johnson commanded a national audience. In 1903 DuBois published his influential collection of essays *The Souls of Black Folk*. In 1912 James Weldon Johnson produced his *Autobiography · of an Ex-Coloured Man* and saw the publication of *Fifty Years and Other Poems* five years later. In the year 1922 Claude McKay burst into print with his *Harlem Shadows*. Countee Cullen carried Negro poetry to a peak which was probably unsurpassed during this period. James Weldon Johnson brought a classical elegance to Negro poetry in his *God's Trombones* which continues to move readers. Between the publication of Cullen and Johnson's work during this period, poetry lovers were introduced to Langston Hughes, perhaps the most prolific and durable of all the writers of the "Negro Renaissance." *The Weary Blues*, a precursor of several collections of Hughes' poems, came off the press in 1925.

A casual reading of the lists of books written by Negroes during this period might suggest that poetry was the only medium of literary expression open to Negroes. A closer view, however, reveals important writers of prose. Jean Toomer's *Cane*, Walter White's *The Fire in the Flint*, Wallace Thurman's *The Blacker the Berry*, Eric Walrond's *Tropic Death* and Rudolph Fisher's *The Walls of Jericho* were published between 1923 and 1929. Alain Locke, the intellectual guide and interpreter of the era, attempted to explain the background and significance of the Negro Renaissance in his famous preface to *The New Negro*, an anthology of prose and poetry by Negro authors.

Langston Hughes opened the decade of the thirties with an excellent first novel entitled *Not Without Laughter*. George Schuyler wrote *Black No More* and the prolific Arna Bontemps penned *God Sends Sunday* in 1931. Jessie Redmond Fauset, perhaps the leading woman author of the "Negro Renaissance" wrote *The Chinaberry Tree* in the same year. George W. Lee, George Henderson, Waters Turpin and William Attaway were among the newer writers in this period. Zora Neal Hurston, a prolific but strangely neglected author, published *Jonah's Gourd Vine* in 1934. In 1937 Hurston wrote *Their Eyes Were Watching God*. Two years later her *Moses, Man of the Mountain* appeared. This was followed by *Seraph on the Suwannee* in the year 1948. By this time poetry-lovers were acquanted with the work of Melvin B. Tolson, Owen Dodson, Sterling Brown and Gwendolyn Brooks.

The publication in 1940 of Richard Wright's *Native Son* is often considered the beginning of the present stage of the evolution of the Negro's literary tradition. He was perhaps the first Negro writer of fiction to have reached hundreds of thousands of readers of all races both in America and abroad. Willard Motley with *Knock on Any Door*, Chester Himes with *If He Hollers Let Him Go*, Ann Petry with *The Street* preceded Ralph Ellison who received the National Book Award in 1952 for *Invisible Man*. A year later James Baldwin exploded on the literary scene with *Go Tell It on The Mountain*. Ellison and Baldwin catapulted to the front ranks of American literature and developed a huge following.

Hugh Gloster accurately described the "Negro Renaissance" of the twenties and forecast the tenor of subsequent writing by Negro authors when he declared that their work was "disdainful of supplication, unhibited by defeatism, unapologetic in protest and assertive in demands for justice." James Baldwin may have been speaking for the scores of excellent Negro writers when, in his *Notes of a Native Son*, he wrote "I want to be an honest man and a good writer."

Hugh M. Gloster. *Negro Voices in American Fiction*, Chapel Hill, 1948; Herman Dreer. *American Literature by Negro Authors*, New York, 1950.

Phillis Wheatley (1753-1784)

A DUSKY SAPPHO

Mrs. Wheatley had a lot of time on her hands and immediately began to teach the new slave girl. She named her Phillis and became very fond of her. Within a few months, little Phillis could speak and write English as though she had been reared in Boston all of her life. After seven or eight years, Phillis was reading the classic romantic poets, such as Horace and Virgil. She eventually read Alexander Pope who had died ten years before she was born in Senegal. His verses so impressed her that she mastered his poetic style and unconsciously used it in most of her own poems.

When thirteen years old, Phillis Wheatley wrote "To the University of Cambridge in New England." When she translated a poem from the Latin of Ovid, her admirers in Boston were so astounded that they had the poem published. In 1768 she wrote "To the King's Most Excellent Majesty" and a year later "On the Death of Rev. Dr. Sewall." These were followed by other occasional poems.

By 1773 Phillis Wheatley had turned out enough poems to have a collection of them published in London under the title *Poems on Various Subjects*. In 1772 she composed "A Farewell to America: To Mrs. S. W." who freed her in the same year and helped her secure passage to England. On both sides of the Atlantic, her poems won widespread admiration. The abolitionists pointed to her skill as proof that the Negro should be freed. A former Lord Mayor of London presented her with a copy of the great John Milton's *Paradise Lost*.

After she returned to America, she sent a letter and a poem to George Washington in 1775 who replied and invited her to visit him. After the death of her former masters, Phillis Wheatley married a handsome Negro, John Peters, and bore him several children, the last of which caused her death in childbirth in 1784.

Vernon Loggins, *The Negro Author*, New York, 1931, pp. 17-29; *Dictionary of American Biography*, vol. XX, 1936, pp. 36-37.

One day in 1761 John Wheatley wandered up and down the stalls and auction blocks of the Boston, Massachusetts slave market. He wanted to buy a female slave as a companion for his wife. Already he had looked over several possibilities but was not pleased. Then his eye fell upon a dark little girl with delicate features and an inborn sense of dignity. After having the slave-dealer place her on the auction block, he decided that the eight-year old slave was just what Mrs. Wheatley wanted even though the child was a little frail. With the same casualness he showed in buying a bolt of cloth for his prospering tailoring business, John Wheatley made his purchase. He then led the little girl home to his wife.

Alexander Pushkin (1799-1837)

RUSSIA'S GREATEST POET

Russia's greatest poet, Alexander Sergeyevich Pushkin, was the grandson of Abram Hannibal, the transplanted African who achieved greatness in the armies of the Czars. Pushkin's poetry is still widely loved and read in Russia and, despite the passing years, holds front rank in the land of Tolstoy and Dostoevski.

Pushkin's physical appearance does not fit the common ideas of how a poet should look. He had a short muscular frame, a head of thick, dark, curly hair, a flat nose, thick lips and a swarthy complexion. Only his intensely brilliant eyes suggested the poet within.

For his early education Pushkin was sent to Tsarkoe Selo near St. Petersburg in 1811. He left this school in 1818 and joined the Russian foreign ministry as a clerk. His early poems "Ode to Freedom" and "Noel" were thought to be critical of the government of Czar Alexander I, and he was sent to the south of Russia to Ekaterinoslav. Here, he wrote "Ruslan and Ludmila," epic of six parts, containing 3,000 lines.

After two years in Ekaterinoslav, Pushkin was then transferred to the small village of Kishinev in the Caucasus. Here he began his "Eugenie Onegin" under the influence of Lord Byron's work and after three years in Kishnev, he was shifted to Odessa, where he wrote the "Bakchisarai Fountain." In 1824, he was discharged from the government's service and returned to his mother's native village of Mikhailvskoe.

Poetry became his life. In 1825 Pushkin finished "Boris Godunov," and in 1832, "Eugenie Onegin." Both later became operas of the same title. Already behind him were his *The Captive of the Caucasus*, a novel and "Ode to Napoleon," plus "The Gypsies." In his "The Bronze Horseman," Pushkin expressed his concern with the rights of the individual as opposed to those of the state. His novel *The Captain's Daughter* was to influence greatly subsequent novels in Russian literature.

Alexander Pushkin was far from the brooding poet. He had a fiery temperament; his considerable charm saw him through many love affairs and dashing escapades. He married a beautiful but frivolous woman, Nathalie Goncharova, whose cousin engaged him in a fatal duel over her. Stilled by death at the age of thirty-eight, Pushkin still speaks to the world through his impassioned poetry.

Samuel H. Cross and Ernest J. Simmons. *Alexander Pushkin, 1799-1837: His Life and Literary Heritage*, New York, 1937.

Alexander Dumas
(1802-1870)

TIME DOES NOT DIM

Dumas' famous "Three Musketeers"

Sooner or later every boy and girl learns of *The Three Musketeers* and *The Count of Monte Cristo*, romantic sagas of an earlier day. Few of them get to know of Alexander Dumas, their author.

Born Alexander Davy de la Pailleterie, Alexander Dumas wrote over two hundred volumes of plays and historical romances. He was the son of a General Dumas, a Haitian-born general and the natural son of Antoine Davy Pailleterie and Marie Cessette Dumas, a black woman of Haiti.

Paris became accustomed to Dumas' "great height, his strong and squarely-built figure, his perpetually smiling face, his large head crowned with curly grey locks, . . . his deep chest and his firm step." He reminded them of a "good tempered Hercules."

The young Dumas was born at Villers-Cotterets in comparative poverty and obtained a smattering of education from a local priest. As an unknown and unproduced playwright, he made his way to Paris in 1827. While supporting himself as a clerk, he and a friend, Adolphe de Leuven, began writing vaudeville sketches and plays. Dumas first won recognition as a playwright in *Henry III et SaCour* (1829), a play which has been described as the first great triumph of Romantic drama.

With the Duke of Orleans as his patron, Dumas began turning out one play after another. In fifteen years, he wrote more than forty of them. *Anthony, Richard Darlington* and *Mademoiselle de Belle-Isle* were among his more prominent efforts.

In 1839 Dumas began writing historical novels with the intention of reviewing the history of France in them. In 1844 appeared the world famous *Three Musketeers* (8 volumes); in 1845 *Vingt ans Apres* (10 volumes). Readers in England as well as in France followed the adventures of the musketeers—Porthas, Aramis and Athos.

Keeping several works in progress at the same time, Dumas completed the *Count of Monte Cristo* (12 volumes) in 1845 and *La Reine Margot* in 1845. Other historical romances and plays flowed from his pen and all of Paris turned to his writings. A corp of assistants worked on outlines which Dumas then used and transformed into literature peculiarly his own.

Dumas even started a newspaper, *Le Mouquetaire*; for four years he wrote most of the copy that appeared in it each day. In addition, he travelled in Italy and Russia. Thousands of francs poured in and he spent them on a prodigious scale. Dumas constructed his own theatre for the performance of his plays and maintained a splendid residence. He was a most regal host.

A great favorite with the ladies, Dumas had one natural son, Alexander Dumas, fils, who became a distinguished author in his own right.

Beatrice Flemming and Marion Pryde. *Distinguished Negroes Abroad*, Washington, 1946, pp. 81-82.

Charles Waddell Chesnutt
(1858-1932)

FICTION'S
"PIONEER OF THE COLOR LINE"

Charles Waddell Chesnutt was the first American Negro to approach the short story and the novel as a professional artist fully aware of their artistic requirements. In four novels, Chesnutt dealt with the themes of mob violence and miscegenation. His work was distinguished by its impartial and unsparing portrayal of southern Negroes and whites and by his pioneering concern with color distinctions among Negroes.

In his *The House Behind the Cedars* (1900), Chesnutt handles the problems involved in racial "passing." In *The Marrow of Tradition* (1901), he wrote of the blurring of the color "lines" and the problems of the culturally superior Negro in the South. Chesnutt's last novel, *The Colonel's Dream* (1905) was a candid treatment of the South in which a Confederate Colonel's ideas of social reform are thwarted by the bigotry of a small North Carolina town.

Although born in Cleveland, Ohio in 1858, Chesnutt was carried by his family to North Carolina when he was quite young. Fair enough to pass for white, he was a bookkeeper in a white saloon when he was fourteen years old. He attended the local public schools for Negroes near Fayetteville, North Carolina but spent a good deal of time in the libraries of prominent whites, reading everything on which he could lay his hands. Chesnutt was made the principal of the State Normal (high) School for Negroes at Fayetteville when he was only twenty-two.

Chesnutt spent some time studying stenography, not knowing that later this would be the major source of his income. Leaving Carolina in 1883, Chesnutt headed for New York where he worked as a stenographer for Dow Jones, a commercial reporting firm, and from there he went to Cleveland, Ohio where he spent the remainder of his life.

In Cleveland, Chesnutt became a commercial and legal stenographer. His fiction began appearing in the Cleveland newspapers and the famous *Puck* magazine. By reading law, in 1887 Chesnutt passed the Ohio bar examination with the highest scores recorded for that period. However, he never practiced law, for his legal stenography business was more lucrative.

From 1905 until his death in 1932 Chesnutt wrote no fiction but contributed many essays and articles to various newspapers and magazines. In 1927 he was awarded the Spingarn Medal for contribution to literature.

Helen M. Chestnutt. *Charles Waddell Chestnutt: Pioneer of the Color Line*, Herman Dreer. *American Literature by Negro Authors*, New York, 1950, pp. 229-230.

Paul Laurence Dunbar
(1872-1906)

THE PEOPLE'S POET

Be proud my Race, in mind and soul;
Thy name is writ on Glory's scroll
*   In Characters of fire.*
High 'mid the clouds of Fame's bright sky
Thy banners' blazoned folds now fly,
*   And truth shall lift them higher.*

Dunbar was equally capable of
*   Little brown baby wif' spa'klin eyes,*
*   Who's pappy's darlin' an' who's pappy's child?*
*   Who is it all de day never once tires*
*   Fu' to be cross, er once loses dat smile?*

It was for his poems in dialect that Paul Laurence Dunbar became famous, although he longed to be recognized for his work in conventional English. In the dialect poems of *Majors and Minors* (1895) and *Lyrics of Lowly Life* (1896) Dunbar captured the humor and gentleness of the lives of Negroes in the rural South. He was primarily a gentle poet who did not try to shock his predominantly white reading audience. Nevertheless Dunbar's deeper feelings would often show up in disquieting poems such as "We Wear the Mask."

Dunbar's poetic genius was evident in his high school days when he was class poet at Dayton, Ohio's Central High School. Dunbar, the only Negro in his class, was the editor of the school paper and edited the yearbook for his graduating class. Several of his early poems were published by the Wright brothers of later aviation fame when they experimented with printing newspapers on their homemade press.

Upon finishing high school, the best job Dunbar could find was that of an elevator operator at a local hotel. William Dean Howells, then the reigning critic in American letters, discovered Dunbar in 1893. From this point on Dunbar's career as as poet took a turn for the better. He became one of Dayton's better known native sons. His first two volumes sold out rather rapidly and in 1896 the best poems in them were published in *Lyrics of Lowly Life*.

Dunbar also tried his hand at fiction. He wrote three collections of short stories and four novels, including a passably good novel entitled *The Uncalled*. Paul Laurence Dunbar turned out the bulk of his work in just ten years. It is suspected that the strain of such heavy production underminded his health and weakened him for a fatal siege of pneumonia in 1906.

Brawley Benjamin. Paul Laurence Dunbar, *Poet of His People*, Hdapel Hill, 1936; Virginia Cunningham. *Paul Laurence Dunbar and His Song*, New York, 1947; Robert A. Bone. *The Negro Novel in America*, 1958, pp. 38-43.

Shortly after his first collection of poems *Oak and Ivy* had been published, Paul Laurence Dunbar was invited to address the West End Club of Toledo, Ohio. Dunbar walked into the club's meeting room just as one Dr. Chapman finished reading a paper denouncing the Negro and doubting his basic intelligence. When the good doctor had finished, Dunbar was called upon to recite. He said, "I shall give you one poem which I had not intended reciting when I first came in." In measured and stately tones, the twenty-one year old poet gave his "Ode to Ethiopia," putting extra stress on the lines

Claude McKay
(1889-1948)

"HOME TO HARLEM"

If we must die, let it not be like hogs
Hunted and penned in an inglorious spot,
While round us bark the mad and hungry dogs,
Making their mock at our accursed lot.
If we must die, O let us nobly die, . . .

Thus commented Claude McKay on the race riots of 1919. Claude McKay was perhaps the most blunt and outspoken of the "Harlem Renaissance" poets and novelists as can be seen in the above lines from his famous protest poem "If We Must Die." In his prose McKay celebrated the joyful and the primitive in preference to the sedate and sanctimonious. Some critics felt that he placed the lusty, easy-going virtues of an island paradise above the stern, cheerless inclinations of an industrial civilization, even if he did declare that:

"I love this cultured hell that tests my youth . . ."

A native of Jamaica, McKay came to America to attend Tuskegee Institute in 1912. After a few months he left for the University of Kansas where he remained for two years. Then, with the help of a timely inheritance, McKay cut short his formal education and headed for New York to pursue his interests among kindred souls in Bohemian circles. Supporting body and soul with a variety of odd jobs, McKay continued his writing which had started in Jamaica with the publication of his first book of verse *Songs of Jamaica* (1911).

In 1919 McKay was living abroad; in 1920 he published his second collection of verse *Spring in New Hampshire*. Back in America by 1922, McKay saw the publication of *Harlem Shadows*, still another collection of verse. *Harlem Shadows* made his reputation as a writer of poetry. Six years were to pass before he produced another major work. In 1928 McKay wrote *Home to Harlem*, the first of three thematically related novels. This was followed by *Banjo* (1929) which was set in Paris and then in 1933, he produced *Banana Bottom* with Jamaica as the setting.

Claude McKay lived in many parts of the world, including Paris, Morocco, Marseilles and Russia. He was well-versed in the intellectual discourse of his time. He enjoyed living among the masses and felt that despite his artistic achievements, he was always a part of them.

In his later years when he no longer wrote, he joined the Catholic Youth Organization in Chicago. KcKay retained his concern for the young and the free until his death in 1948.

James Weldon Johnson, *Black Manhattan*, New York, 1930, pp. 264-266.
Herman Dreer, *American Literature by Negro Authors*, New York, 1950, pp. 36-37.

Countee Cullen
(1903-1946)

WHAT IS AFRICA TO ME?

What is Africa to me:
Copper sun or scarlet sea,
Jungle star or jungle track,
Strong bronzed men or regal black
Women from whose loins I sprang
When the birds of Eden sang?

To most readers of poetry by Negroes, these lines identify Countee Cullen, one of the leading poets of the "Negro Renaissance" of the twenties. Precocious, enormously talented, Countee Cullen was a nationally acclaimed poet at the age of twenty-one with the publication of his first book of poems, *Color*, which won the Harmond Award for high achievement in literature in 1925. Sure of his ability in poetry and despite the predominance of Negro themes in his work, Cullen wanted to be known simply as a poet rather than as a Negro poet.

In addition to *Color*, Cullen published other collections of poems under the titles of *The Ballad of the Brown Girl* (1927), *Copper Sun* (1927) and *The Black Christ and Other Poems* (1929). He also edited an anthology of poems called *Caroling Dusk* (1929). In 1932 he saw the publication of his only novel, *One Way to Heaven*.

Countee Cullen was born in New York City and reared by a Methodist minister who gave him the name Cullen. While a high school student, Cullen's poetic skill was recognized and encouraged. After completing his high school education, Cullen entered the undergraduate division of New York University. Here he distinguished himself by winning the Witter Bynner poetry prize for undergraduates in American colleges. More than a dozen campus literary journals published his work. After earning a Phi Beta Kappa key from New York University, Cullen entered Harvard and received the master of arts degree in 1926.

While Cullen wrote in the classical idiom, he was able to adapt his style to the protest motif which was present in the "Negro Renaissance," particularly in his long poem on lynching, "*The Black Christ*." An example to the classical style applied to a racial theme might be noted in the concluding lines of "Black Majesty," a poem about the Haitian revolutionists, Henri Christophe, Dessalines, and Toussaint L'Ouverture:

"Lo, I am dark, but comely," Sheba sings.
"And we were black," three shades reply, "but kings."

Countee Cullen. *The Black Christ and Other Poems*, Copyright, 1929, by Harper and Brothers, New York.

124

James Weldon Johnson
(1871-1938)

A GENTLEMAN OF LETTERS

James Weldon Johnson has been called "the only true artist among the early Negro novelists." Not only as a novelist but also as a poet, NAACP official and diplomat, Johnson left a lasting impression on the cultural and social life of the Negro in America. His famous poem "Lift Every Voice and Sing" (1900), when set to music by his talented brother, James Rosamond Johnson, became a sort of Negro national anthem during the early forties. His strikingly dramatic poem "God's Trombones" (1927) may still be heard recited from the stages of many high schools and colleges in the South. In one of Johnson's collections of verse, *St. Peter Relates an Incident* (1917) his poem "O Black and Unknown Bards" is still accepted as the best poetic explanation of the origins of the spirituals. His *Autobiography of an Ex-Colored Man* (1912) was one of the earliest accounts of a Negro exploring different levels of American society by "passing" and is still being reprinted in soft cover editions. This fictional "autobiography" was so real that Johnson felt the need to publish his own life's story in his now classic *Along This Way* (1933).

Aside from his creative work, Johnson edited the New York *Age* and ran an extremely popular column in it for ten years. He also published an anthology, *The Book of American Negro Poetry* (1922). He wrote articles for the *Nation* on the conduct of United States Marines in Haiti and helped to make the United States' occupation of that country a presidential campaign issue in 1921. His essays on the roots of the Negro's cultural contributions helped to explain the foundation of the Negro's achievements in literature and music, especially during the decade of the twenties. In *Negro Americans, What Now* (1934), he eloquently set forth his own philosophy and beliefs.

In 1916 James Weldon Johnson joined the NAACP and for many years was its Executive Secretary. Among his many achievements with this organization are: sparking the drive behind the Dyer Anti-Lynching Bill in 1921; leading the fight against the lily-white primary which made it illegal for Negroes to be denied participation in southern primary elections. Before he joined the NAACP, Johnson served as consul to Nicaragua and Venezuela.

James Weldon Johnson was a native of Florida with family roots stretching as far south as the Bahamas. He was educated at Atlanta, and in New York. He was the first Negro to pass a written examination for the bar in Florida, and after practicing law and teaching school for a few years, he moved to New York where he joined his brother in writing successful musical comedies. His last major post was that of Professor of Creative Literature at Fisk University in Nashville, Tennesse.

Robert Bone. The Negro Novel in America, New Haven, 1958, pp. 45-49.
James Weldon Johnson, Along This Way, New York (1933).
Dictionary of American Biography, XXII (1958) Supplement 2, pp. 345-346.

Richard Wright (1908-1960)

A SOUND OF THUNDER

Prior to the publication of *Native Son*, Wright's volumes of short stories, *Uncle Tom's Children*, heralded the advent of a writer to be reckoned with. *Uncle Tom's Children* had won the author a Guggenheim fellowship and a $500 prize. His earlier work had appeared in the smaller magazines, *The Daily Worker* and the radical *New Masses*. During the Depression he had toiled on the Federal Writers Project in Chicago and New York.

Born in Natchez, Mississippi, Wright wandered to Memphis, Tennessee and in 1925 found himself in Chicago where, for years, he earned his living from a variety of odd jobs. Although he had been keenly interested in writing before he reached his teens, Richard Wright's formal education ended with high school. In Chicago he was able to meet other aspiring writers and studied the techniques of bending words to his will. His experiences in Mississippi and Chicago furnished the material for his fiction; the power and fervor of his earlier work came from his truthfulness, honesty and deep social concern.

In recognition of his literary talent Richard Wright received the Spingarn medal in 1939. Over the next twenty years he was to write additional books, *The Outsider* (1953), *The Long Dream* (1958) and *Lawd, Today* (1963) were the only other novels by him. *Black Boy* (1945) was his autobiography. His remaining books were devoted to various aspects of the problem of color: *Black Power* (1954) was an account of his travels in Africa. *The Color Curtain* (1956) was his report on the Bandung Conference of 1955.

A man deeply troubled by the crudities and dilemmas of race, Wright became an expatriate and spent his last years in Paris. Wright's work was protest fiction which approached art; while other writers have approached the themes of race and personality with greater finesse and subtlety, few have surpassed Richard Wright in calling the world's attention to the consequences of exploitation of man by man on the basis of color.

The shattering sound of the clock in Richard Wright's *Native Son* was heard throughout America and echoed overseas. Wright's raw and powerful account of the life and death of "Bigger Thomas" in Chicago resounded in the conscience of America. Published in 1940, *Native Son* sold over 300,000 copies and was translated into six languages. It was a Book-of-the-Month Club choice. It was made into an equally powerful play starring Canada Lee. Overnight, Richard Wright was famous; his royalties exceeded his wildest dreams.

Edwin Embree. *Thirteen Against the Odds*, New York, 1946, pp. 25-46; Harold Isaacs. *The New World of American Negroes*, New York, 1963, pp. 247-260.

Langston Hughes (1902-1967)

A BARDIC VOICE

Langston Hughes is so prolific that he seems to be three-fourths print and one-fourth person. In reality, however, the man and his works are one. In his writing, Hughes has tried almost every conceivable form men have used to arrange their words and thoughts on paper. Poems, songs, novels, plays, biographies, histories and essays have been the vehicles employed by him to communicate with his fellowmen.

Known primarily as a poet, Hughes has published many volumes of verse. Among them are *Weary Blues, Fine Clothes to the Jew, The Dream Keeper, Dear Lovely Death, Shakespeare in Harlem, Fields of Wonder, One Way Ticket* and *Ask Your Mama*. His novels are *Not Without Laughter* and *Tambourines to Glory*. For the theatre Langston Hughes has written *Scottsboro Limited* and *Mulatto;* the later work was also staged as an opera *The Barries*. In the field of biography Hughes books include *Famous American Negroes, Famous Negro Heroes* and *Famous Negro Music Makers*. He has also written books for juveniles and lyrics for William Grant Still, Elmer Rice and Kurt Weill.

Langston Hughes is one of the most honored authors in America. He began by winning the Witter Bynner undergraduate prize for excellence in poetry for 1926. He has been a Rosenwald and Guggenheim fellow, as well as a grantee of the American Academy of Arts and letters. In 1959 he received the Anisfield-Wolfe award and in 1960 he won the Spingarn Medal for contributions to the progress of the Negro.

A native of Joplin, Missouri, Langston Hughes has lived in many parts of the world including Haiti, Mexico, France, Italy and Russia. No poet of the Ivory Tower, he has worked as a busboy, clerk, cafe bouncer and office boy with the *Journal of Negro History*. He was a part of the "Harlem Renaissance" and achieved a measure of fame during the twenties; however, he did not begin to depend on his writings for a living until 1930. Although his education ended with his undergraduate days at Columbia University, Langston Hughes has lectured at leading schools and colleges in the country.

The theme of his work has been the common man, more specifically the ordinary Negro and his pleasures, joys and sorrows. Of the hundreds of poems written by him perhaps the best-known and most durable is "The Negro Speaks of Rivers,": part of which is reproduced below:

I have known rivers:
I've known rivers ancient as the world and older than
the flow of human blood in human veins.
My soul has grown deep like the rivers.

James M. Ethridge (ed). *Contemporary Authors*, Detroit, 1962, p. 143; *Who's Who in Colored America*, 1950, p. 278; Edwin R. Embree. *Thirteen Against the Odds*, New York, 1946, pp. 117-138.

Gwendolyn Brooks
(1917-   )

PULITZER PRIZE WINNER

Book reviewers heaped praise upon her first volume of poems, *A Street in Bronzeville* (1945), which won for her the Merit Award of *Mademoiselle* magazine as the outstanding woman of the year. Her second volume *Annie Allen* (1949), brought her the Pulitzer Prize for Poetry. Her other major writings include *Bronzeville Boys and Girls* (1956) and *The Bean Eaters* (1960). She also wrote a novel, *Maude Martha*.

Miss Brooks career is studded with honors and awards. She has received two Guggenheim Fellowships with substantial stipends; the American Academy of Arts and Letters awarded her a prize of $1000. She received the prestigious Eunice Tietjeans award from *Poetry* magazine and for three consecutive years Miss Brooks won the Midwest Writers Conference Prize.

Miss Brooks was born in Topeka, Kansas, but has spent virtually all of her life in Chicago. Although she is amazingly erudite, her formal education ended at Wilson Junior College in Chicago. Married since 1936 to Henry Blakely, a Chicago businessman, Gwendolyn Brooks manages to rear two children and to write some of the finest poetry of our time.

An example of Miss Brooks' work is this description of changing neighborhoods. The title of the poem: "The Ghosts at the Quincy Club":

. . . .

> *Where velvet voices lessened, stopped, and rose*
> *Rise raucous Howdys. And a curse comes pure.*
> *Yea it comes pure and challenges again*
> *All ghost airs, graces, all daughters-of-gentlemen*
> *Moth-soft, off-sweet. Demure.*
>
> *Where Tea and Father were (each clear*
> *And lemony) are dark folk, drinking beer.*

From *The Bean Eaters*, by Gwendolyn Brooks.

She tells you that she is a "simple housewife." She dresses rather plainly. Utterly without affectation, she is almost painfully shy and unassuming. She does not stand out in a crowd. Perhaps the most distinctive feature about her is her eyes: soft, gentle, quizzical. There is absolutely nothing about her appearance to suggest that she is one of America's leading poets. Her name is Gwendolyn Brooks and she is the only Negro ever to win the Pulitzer Prize.

In *Contemporary Authors* (vol. I, 1962, p. 36) under the name of this "simple housewife" is the following description: "Career: Writer, lecturer at Universities and Colleges." Under her deceptive exterior Miss Brooks leads an intense poetic and intellectual life. She studies the techniques of her craft as well as the people, sights and sounds of Chicago's crowded Southside and creates superb poetic renditions of urban Negro life. Her brilliant and succinct book reviews indicate a close acquaintance with a rather wide range of modern literature.

X THE THEATRE

And the World's a Stage

The history of the Negro in the theatre is very old. As early as 1821, free Negroes in New York were presenting Shakespearean plays. The African Company, located at "the corner of Bleecker and Mercer streets," catered to a small community of Negro playgoers. James Hewlett, the leading member of this company, took as his special province the title roles in *Othello* and *Richard III*. With few exceptions, however, the development of the theatre among Negroes had to wait until the twentieth century.

The minstrel tradition was started by whites who burlesqued the speech and mannerisms of Negroes in the South. Negroes began to perform in minstrel shows after the Civil War and used the white minstrels as their models. In the 1890's and early 1900's, Negro blackface comedians came into vogue. Early companies of Negro minstrels, in the words of James Weldon Johnson, "provided stage training and theatrical experience which could not be acquired from any other source."

The *Creole* show, first presented in 1891, started the trend away from the pure minstrels of earlier days. This show played for five seasons in New York and was produced at the World's Fair of 1893. The year 1895 saw the presentation of *Octoroon*, a vaudeville show which had an urban setting and featured attractive females. The following year witnessed the production of *Oriental America*, the first completely Negro show to open on Broadway and the first to make a definite break away from the pure vaudeville style.

Perhaps the most outstanding personalities of this period were Bert Williams, Bob Cole and Will Marion Cook. Bert Williams began his career as a banjo-playing balladeer in California and then made for himself a spectacularly successful career as a blackface comedian in New York. He was a standout in *Abyssinia* and *Dahomey*. Bob Cole was successful as a producer, singer, dancer and librettist. Will Marion Cook was the musical genius behind many of the successful shows such as *Shoofly Regiment* and *The Red Moon*, which were produced in 1906 and 1908 respectively.

Around 1909 a series of melodramas with Negro casts was presented at the Lincoln and Lafayette theatres in New York. The Lafayette Theatre was especially active. Some of its productions were *The Servant in the House*, *On Trial* and *Within the Law*. In 1917 three one-act plays by Ridgeley Torrence—*The Rider of Dreams*, *Granny Maumee* and *Simon, the Cyrenian*—afforded Negro actors an opportunity to show their versatility in a rustic comedy, a tragedy and a historical drama.

In the year 1920 Charles Gilpin became a national star in Eugene O'Neill's *The Emperor Jones*. His superlative acting won for him an award from the Drama League of New York. The same year Paul Robeson appeared in *All God's Chillun Got Wings*. In 1927 *Porgy* was presented.

Three years later Richard B. Harrison achieved international stardom in *The Green Pastures*.

New faces and new names entered the musical world of the twenties. In 1921, Noble Sissle and Eubie Blake produced an extremely successful musical entitled *Shuffle Along*. This show ran for two years at the Sixty-third Street Theatre in New York. Josephine Baker starred in *Chocolate Dandies* in 1925. Florence Mills was introduced to a wide audience in *Shuffle Along* but found her greatest success in *Blackbirds* in 1926.

The Federal Theatre Project was started in 1937 as a governmental effort to save the performing arts. Writing in *The History of the Negro in the Theatre*, Edith Isaacs asserted that "except for the Lafayette Theatre, no American theatre project meant more to the Negro player than the Federal Theatre did." Almost nine hundred Negroes were involved in the Federal Theatre Project. New York, as usual, was the center of activity. With the Lafayette Theatre as a base, Negroes appeared in plays such as Frank Wilson's *Walk Together Children*, Rudolph Fisher's *Conjur' Man Dies* and William DuBois' *Haiti*. A particularly striking version of *Macbeth*, transposed to the tropics, created general excitement.

Cities formerly dormant felt the effects of the Federal Theatre Project. In Chicago *Swing Mikado* was so successful that it had to be sold to commercial producers. In Los Angeles, Hall Johnson's *Run Little Chillun* ran for over a year. In Seattle, Washington, the Federal Theatre group presented *Lysistrata*, *Noah*, *In Abraham's Bosom* and *Stevedore*.

Following the termination of government support in 1939, the Negro in the theatre entered a new phase. Canada Lee made "Bigger Thomas" a living being in *Native Son*, staged in 1941. A few years later Hilda Simms starred in *Anna Lucasta* which ran for a total of 956 performances. Other important plays followed. Lillian Smith's novel *Strange Fruit* was brought to the stage. *Deep Are the Roots*, *A Member of the Wedding*, *Take a Giant Step*, *Mrs. Patterson*, *Raisin in the Sun* and *Purlie Victorious*, plays produced within the last fifteen years, all show the range of treatment and subject matter possible for the Negro in the theatre.

Compared to the legitimate stage, the Negro's progress on the silver screen has been much slower. Only within the last decade have actors such as James Edwards, Woody Strode, Dorothy Dandridge, Marpessa Dawn, Sidney Poitier, Sammy Davis, Jr., and Harry Belafonte essayed roles beyond the faded Hollywood stereotypes of Negroes. However, current trends in this phase of the performing arts, like other aspects of the theatre point towards a more liberal climate which can only enhance the prospects of those gifted with talent.

Margaret Just Butcher, *The Negro in American Culture*, New York, 1956, pp. 187-206; Edith Isaacs, *The Negro in the Theatre*, New York, 1947.

Ira Aldridge (1805-1867)

BLACK TRAGEDIAN

Such was the skill that made Ira Aldridge the toast of the European continent and the leading Shakespearean actor of his era. He played *Othello* in the major cities and capitals, including Berlin, Vienna, Dresden, Frankfort-am-Main, Krakow, Amsterdam and St. Petersburg, Russia. Until Aldridge appeared, white actors, wearing black-face make-up and black gloves, played the jealous Moor. In Aldridge, at last was found the perfect Othello. However, this great actor was not limited to playing Othello. He also played Macbeth, King Lear and the leading roles in plays which had no Negro or Moorish characters.

Honors and awards came to Ira Aldridge. Dukes, Princes and Kings honored him. From the King of Prussia, he received the First Medal of the Arts and Sciences. From the Emperor of Russia, he received the Cross of Leopold. He was named a member of many high-ranking societies. His success as an actor enabled him to maintain a fashionable home near London where he received the nobility and distinguished men of arts and letters. Among his dearest friends was Alexander Dumas, the author of the *Count of Monte Cristo* and *The Three Musketeers*.

The place and precise date of his birth is uncertain. Some accounts say that Aldridge was born in Africa. Others give Belaire, Maryland as his birthplace. Various authorities list 1804 and 1805 as his birthdate. It is known that he was apprenticed as a carpenter in Maryland, and in association with immigrant Germans he picked up the German tongue. Aldridge's interest in the theatre was stimulated by Edmund Kean, himself a leading Shakespearean actor who encouraged and aided him to enter the theatre. Years later, Aldridge was to play Othello to Edmund Kean's Iago. For a long time, Aldridge performed on the continent and, briefly, in America. He married twice, first to an Englishwoman who died shortly thereafter and then, to a Swedish baroness who was with the actor when he died in Lodz, Poland in 1867.

Mildred Stock. *Ira Aldridge, the Negro Tragedian*, New York, 1959; Walter Monfried. "The Great Ira Aldridge," *Negro Digest*, March, 1963, pp. 67-70.

The ornate theatre in St. Petersburg, Russia is crowded. The cream of Russian society is present. On the stage, the powerfully-built black man playing the title role of Othello, the Moor, comes to the fateful lines where he prepares to kill Desdemona.

"It is the cause, it is the cause, my soul.
Let me not name it to you, you chaste stars."

Up leaps a young man from his seat, crying in a terrified voice. "She is innocent, Othello, she is innocent." Not moving a muscle, Ira Aldridge finishes his speech. The young man is so carried away by the actor that he has forgotten the events on the stage were merely part of a play and Aldridge and the white female pretending sleep were only actors. The next day while dining with a Prince, Aldridge learns that the excited spectator had died shortly after making his outcry. On another occasion, as Aldridge, again playing Othello, prepares to kill Desdemona, the young actress playing the part screamed in real fright. She, too, had forgotten she was in a play.

Charles Gilpin (1878-1930)

PIONEER DRAMATIC ACTOR

Gilpin as Emperor Jones

James Weldon Johnson once wrote that Charles Gilpin "by his work in *The Emperor Jones* . . . reached the highest point of achievement on the legitimate stage that had yet been attained by a Negro in America." In *The Negro in American Culture*, Margaret Just Butcher declared that "Gilpin was the first modern American Negro to establish himself as a serious actor of first quality." In writing of Charles Gilpin's portrayal of Brutus Jones, Edith Isaacs asserted that when "the play and the player met they became one."

Charles Gilpin astounded theatre-goers with his dramatic talents in a most demanding role which required him to carry O'Neil's play alone for six lengthy scenes. With Gilpin in the lead role, *The Emperor Jones* ran in New York for four years (1920-1924). In 1921 Gilpin won the coveted Spingarn Medal for his contribution to the theatre and to the progress of the Negro.

Success did not come to Charles Gilpin the easy way. When Eugene O'Neill decided to present *The Emperor Jones*, Gilpin had just finished playing the small role of Reverend William Custis in John Drinkwater's *Abraham Lincoln*. O'Neill quickly recognized him as just the man to play the island ruler in his daring drama.

Gilpin had been connected with vaudeville and the theatre since 1890 but was unable to make a steady living as an actor. Between occasional appearances in vaudeville houses and parts with touring troupes, he supported himself with employment as a printer, elevator operator, porter and as a trainer for prize-fighters. In 1911-1914 he toured with a group called the "Pan-American Octette." In 1914 he had a small role in *Old Man's Boy*. In 1916 he was organizer and manager of the Lafayette Theatre Company, one of the first Negro dramatic stock companies in New York. Behind him was experience with the Pekin Stock Company of Chicago and appearances with Bert Williams and George Walker in *Abyssinia* and with Gus Hall's *Smart Set*.

A small intense man, Charles Gilpin was a native of Virginia. After briefly attending St. Francis' Catholic School for colored children in Richmond, he took a job as a printer's devil on the *Richmond Planet*. Whenever an opportunity arose for him to perform, Gilpin forgot all else, for he lived for the stage. In 1926, two years after *The Emperor Jones* closed, Gilpin lost his voice and had to go back to running an elevator for a living. He died in 1930, and a year later was included among notable Americans in the *Dictionary of American Biography*.

Edith Isaac. *The Negro in the American Theatre*, New York, 1947, p. 63.
James Weldon Johnson. *Black Manhattan*, New York, 1930, pp. 184-185.
Dictionary of American Biography, vol. VII (1930), 314.

Bert Williams
(1878-1922)

A COMEDIAN'S COMEDIAN

The late W. C. Fields once described Bert Williams as "The funniest man I ever saw; the saddest man I ever knew." Booker T. Washington declared that "Bert Williams has done more for the race than I have. He has smiled his way into people's hearts. I have been obliged to fight." From about 1909 until his death in 1922, Bert Williams was perhaps the most famous Negro entertainer in America. He made thousands double with laughter in his portrayal of the lazy comical stage Negro speaking an outlandish dialect. His talent as a comedian made him one of the highest paid performers in America.

Many theatre-goers declared that Williams was successful because he was "himself" on the stage. He was seen as the funniest flower of the school of blackface comedians. A closer view of Bert Williams shows that his triumphs came from his talents as an actor rather than from his personal life. His stage characterizations were based on what he observed around him.

In physical appearance Williams was a six-foot tall handsome man with decidedly Caucasian features. For his portrayals he had to use the regular blackface make-up. His weird stage dialect and drawl were a marked contrast to his natural speech which was the king's English of his native Antigua in the British West Indies. The fun-loving, shiftless, ignorant buffoon, Williams played on the stage was a far cry from the quiet, rather melancholy man that was the real Egbert Austin Williams. Instead of blackface comedy the serious stage was his real interest.

Bert Williams spent his early youth on the huge plantation of his grandfather, the Danish Consul in the Indies. Both of his parents were quadroons. Williams came to the U.S. while he was still a young boy, and upon completing his high school education in California, he decided to seek his fame on the stage. He first appeared in California dives and honky tonks with a line of patter and a banjo. In 1895, he teamed up with George Walker. By 1903, Williams and Walker was so successful that they took his hit "Dahomey" to England and repeated their earlier New York triumph. In 1909 George Walker died and the following year Williams joined the Ziegfeld Follies and remained with them as the star for nearly ten years. This was followed by his appearance in *Broadway Brevities* and *Under the Bamboo Tree*.

The famous comedy team of William + Walker

Mabel Rowland (ed). *Bert Williams, Son of Laughter*, New York, 1947.

Richard B. Harrison
(1864-1935)

THE ORIGINAL "DE LAWD"

"Gangway! Gangway for de Lawd, God, Jehovah!" announced the angel Gabriel one night in 1929. And "De Lawd" in the person of Richard B. Harrsion came on the stage of the Mansfield Theatre in New York wearing a simple black suit. From this point on, Richard B. Harrison dominated and gave lasting form to Marc Connelly's "Green Pastures." His performance as "De Lawd" during the season of 1929 was regarded as among the finest of the year.

One critic was moved to say this of "Green Pastures" and Richard B. Harrison: "Call it fable or allegory or what you will; his dramatization of an idea of primitive faith was so moving in its tender simplicity that it deserves a place among the classics of life and letters where all greatness is truly simple . . . " In 1930, Richard B. Harrison was awarded the Springarn medal as the person who contributed most to the progress of the Negro during the preceding year. Several colleges awarded honorary degrees to him. "Green Pastures" toured the North and South and ran for 557 performances.

"Green Pastures" was Harrison's first and only legitimate stage role. He was over sixty-five years old when he agreed to play "De Lawd".

Before "Green Pastures," he had toured the country reciting excerpts from Shakespeare, Kipling, Poe and Paul Laurence Dunbar. He treated Negro social and Church groups to one-man versions of "Macbeth," "Julius Caesar," and "Damon and Pythias."

Born in Canada, Richard B. Harrison went to Detroit as a boy and earned his keep as a handyman, waiter, porter and railway clerk. Whenever it was possible he would climb to the gallery of theatres to see stage productions. Noting his enthusiasm for the stage, friends assisted him in getting an opportunity to study drama in Detroit. After developing his repertoire of readings and recitations, he made his debut in Canada in 1891 and then came to America where he worked with amateur groups. When he was called to the cast of "Green Pastures," he was an instructor in drama at A. and T. College, Greensboro, North Carolina.

Richard B. Harrison appeared in "Green Pastures" a total of 1,656 times and at the time his heart gave way in 1935, was at the peak of his fame. His performance in the play has been the standard by which all subsequent revivals have been measured.

"Richard B. Harrison," *The National Cyclopedia*, Vol. XXVI, 1937, p. 364. *Who's Who in Colored America*, 1928-29, p. 166.

Frank Silvera (1914-   )

AN "EVERYMAN" OF THE THEATRE

Frank Silvera has become a sort of Everyman of the acting profession. In a career stretching back over two decades, he has proved the Negro's ability to play a wide range of parts far beyond the racial stereotypes. He has portrayed Mexicans, Spaniards, Italians as well as white and black Americans. At various times Silvera has been active on the legitimate stage, screen, television and radio, giving convincing performances of any roles assigned to him.

Frank Alvin Silvera was born in Kingston, Jamaica in 1914. He was brought to America while still a child and became a naturalized citizen in 1922. His education included two years of law at Northeastern University, Boston, Massachusetts. In 1934, however, the lure of the theatre proved irresistible. In that year he appeared in Paul Green's *Potter's Field* presented at the Plymouth Theatre, Boston. The following year he performed in *Stevedore*. From 1935 to 1938 Silvera appeared in plays such as *The Trial of Dr. Beck, Macbeth* and *Emperor Jones*, all sponsored by the Federal Theatre Project. In 1939 Silvera toured with the New England Repertory Theatre.

While serving in the Navy during World War II, Silvera wrote and directed radio shows at the Great Lakes Naval Training Station. In 1945 he appeared in the Broadway production of *Anna Lucasta*. Two years later this versatile actor had a role in *John Loves Mary* which was sponsored by the Urban League.

In the hey-dey of radio, Frank Silvera performed on such shows as *Perry Mason, Up for Parole, Counterspy* and *Two Billion Strong, The U.N. Story*. On television he appeared in *Captain Video, The Big Story* and *The Untouchables*. In the movies, his most memorable roles were in *Viva Zapata* and *The Miracle of Our Lady of Fatima*.

Who's Who in Colored America, 1950, p. 469; Lucille Arcola Chambers. *America's Tenth Man*, New York, 1956, p. 191.

Canada Lee (1907-1951)

"BIGGER THOMAS"

Canada Lee is best known for his sensitive portrayal of "Bigger Thomas," the bitterly frustrated central character in the screen and stage version of Richard Wright's book, *Native Son*. Although he had never taken an acting lesson in his life, Lee earned rave notices in this role. Richard Watts, in the *New York Herald Tribune*, declared that Canada Lee was ". . . a fine actor giving one of the seasons' (1947) best performances."

Canada Lee explained his success thusly, "I've *known* guys like Bigger Thomas all my life."

Canada Lee, christened Leonard Lionel Cornelius Canegata after his West Indian grandfather, was born in Manhattan's San Juan Hill district and attended high school in Harlem. Although he started studying violin at the age of 7 and was approaching concert status, when he was 14 he ran away from home to become a jockey. After three or four years, his racing career was ended by excess weight. He drifted into boxing where he soon rose to amateur lightweight champion. In 1926 he turned pro, moved up to the welterweight division and, after winning more than 17 of 22 bouts, became a leading contender for the welterweight crown. It was during this period, 1926 to 1933, that Leonard Canegata became known as Canada Lee. But this budding career, too, was short-lived. A hard blow to the head blinded him in one eye and he had to quit the ring.

Perhaps it was performing in front of a crowd that lead him to the career where he really found his niche. After casually reading for, and winning, a role in the W.P.A. stage play, "Brother Mose," he played in "Stevedore," the Federal Theater production of "Macbeth," "Othello," and "Haiti," and obtained a small part in "Mamba's Daughters." About this time Orson Wells chose him for the Bigger Thomas role, and from here his star ascended. "Anna Lucasta," "South Pacific," "The Tempest," a screen version of "Macbeth," and William Saroyan's "Across the Board on Tomorrow Morning." His career reached its zenith when, in addition to much radio work, he was given a leading role in the Tallulah Bankhead picture, "Life Boat."

Canada Lee's life was cut short in 1951 by a fatal heart attack.

Edith Isaacs, *The Negro in the Theatre*, New York, 1947.

Ethel Waters
(1900-   )

THIRTY YEARS ON STAGE

...in the 1949 movie, "Pinky", with Jeanne Crain

Although there have been better singers and actresses than Ethel Waters, none typifies the rise from rags to riches more dramatically than she. She started life in Chester, Pa., in 1900 with two strikes against her. Her parents, Louisa Tar Anderson and John Wesley Waters were poverty-stricken, and she was born out of wedlock. There was seldom enough food for the family. There were many days when the only meals she had were supplied by the sisters of the convent school she attended as a child.

She was married at twelve years of age and went to work as a maid and laundress in a Philadelphia hotel for $4.75 a week. A few years later she could jokingly make the claim that she "went through" swanky Swarthmore College in two weeks!—as a charwoman. Some 25 years later she was making $2,000 a week as a versatile performing artist on stage and screen, and owned two apartment houses in Harlem. But the path from maid to movies was long and tortuous.

Ethel Waters had an unusual voice — high, clear, plaintive—which, in her heyday, she projected seemingly without effort. When she was 17, her singing landed her a job at the Lincoln Theater in Baltimore where she made nine dollars a week. This was followed by years of singing in honky-tonk dives and nite-clubs which led to her big break in 1923 when she substituted for Florence Mills at New York's Plantation Club and created a sensation with her unique rendition of "Dinah," "I'm Coming, Virginia," and other currently popular songs.

In 1927 she made her first stage appearance at Daly's West Sixty-Third Street Theater in a musical called "Africana." After this she earned roles in "Blackbirds," (1930), "Rhapsody in Black" (1931-32), "As Thousands Cheer" (1933), and "At Home Abroad" (1935). She gained added stature in motion pictures such as "Cabin In The Sky" — where she sang her world famous version of "Stormy Weather"— and "Pinky."

Her place as a mature and sensitive actress was assured with her starring role in the Broadway play "The Member of the Wedding," in 1950. When the play was made into a movie, millions were moved by the big-hearted warmth and strength of the house servant who was more than a servant. Ethel Waters' years on the stage have enriched all who have been privileged to see her perform.

Ethel Waters. *His Eye Is On The Sparrow*, New York, 1951.

136

Katherine Dunham
(1910-   )

WITH ROOTS IN RYTHM AND RACE

The name Katherine Dunham is synonymous with the sensuous interpretive dances of Afro-Cuban origin which her dance troupe has made famous in their tours all over the world. Although her fame has its roots in rhythm and race, it springs from the soil of contrasts. A mixed racial background underlies her channeled interest in African dance. A stern, religious upbringing forms the basis for her successful career on the stage. The freedom and ethnic sexuality of her dance belies an early parental vise which rigidly confined her conscious life.

Miss Dunham was born in Chicago, the daughter of Fanny June Taylor, a fair-skinned divorcee of French Canadian ancestry and Albert Dunham, a hard-working tailor. After the death of her mother, her father remarried and moved to Joliet, Illinois, where Katherine attended school. Here, at the age of eight she evidenced her first interest in dancing. At nine, she staged her first production when she organized a group of children to present a dance revue for a church raising project—which grossed thirty-two dollars.

In high school she excelled in athletics and music, which merged into her great interest in dancing. As a member of the Terpsichorean Club she laid the disciplined foundation for her future career with endless hours of running, leaping and arm-waving to the cadence of a gong and tom-tom. As a college student at the University of Chicago, she financed her education by giving dance lessons which included the cultures and religions of the peoples from whom the dances originated.

In 1936 she received special field training in a West Indies research project from Northwestern University. Later that year she won a Julius Rosenwald Travel Fellowship to the West Indies where for two years she studied the life of Koromantees, a tribe of blacks brought over from the Gold Coast of Africa during the colonial days. When she returned to the University of Chicago she was awarded her masters degree in anthropology for her thesis on life in the Caribbean.

In 1939 she was made a supervisor on the Writers Project of the Work Projects Administration. Here she was associated with writers Arna Bontemps and Richard Wright. She went to New York in 1940 as a dance director. Shortly afterward she appeared in "Cabin In The Sky" and "Stormy Weather." She was engaged as choreographer for "Pardon My Sarong" and "Windy City." In 1943 she was guest artist for the San Francisco Symphony Orchestra and in 1945 for the Los Angeles Symphony Orchestra. With her own Tropical Revue she made several appearances at the Hollowood bowl. Tours with her troupe took her to almost every country on the globe. She has written several books and articles for many magazines, including *Esquire* and *Mademoiselle*.

Katherine Dunham. *A Touch of Innocence*, New York, 1959.

XI MUSIC

Lift Every Voice and Sing

The story of Negro music goes back to Africa where song was a medium by which the past was recorded, the present rendered more tolerable, and the future made less insecure. Due to the bewildering number and variety of languages and dialects, the development of writing was greatly impeded in Africa. On the other hand, a tremendous oral tradition and literature took the place of the written word and acted as a reservoir for memories of the past. The custom and habit of singing and dancing as a means of historical, emotional and intellectual expression survived the awesome "Middle Passage" across the Atlantic and laid the foundation for the development of Negro music in the New World.

Although Africans came to America from many different points and tribes on the West Coast of the African mainland and spoke a variety of languages, in the Deep South they found a means of communicating with one another via the English and French of their masters. To this new speech they joined the remembered African rhythms and passed them down through the generations. In the words of Mark Miles Fisher, "with concern for the music of their masters, Negroes employed rhythmical song to provide creature comforts, to accompany menial labor, to learn facts, to sell commodities and to share religion."

From their experiences as slaves, American Negroes developed the spirituals which "rank among the classical folk expressions because of their moving simplicity of their characteristic originality and universal appeal." In his famous essay "Of the Sorrow Songs," W. E. B. DuBois called the spirituals the "music of an unhappy people, of the children of disappointment; they tell of death and suffering and unvoiced longing toward a truer world, of misty wanderings and hidden ways."

The spirituals caught the interest of the nation during the abolitionist agitation but soon died away until the Fisk Jubilee Singers took them before the world in the 1870's. While the sacred and secular songs of the Negro slaves were taking form in the Deep South, free Negroes in the North were participating in the formal music of their day. Eugene V. McCarty, an excellent singer, pianist and composer of popular music, studied at the Conservatoire Imperial in Paris in the 1840's. About the same time Sarah Sedgewick Bowers sang operatic arias in Philadelphia and New York. Elizabeth Taylor Greenfield made a name for herself as a professional singer. She earned the title "The Black Swan" with a fine voice which carried her before Queen Victoria at Buckingham Palace in 1854. Mrs. Sampson Williams, a soprano, made a successful tour of Europe in 1880 using the professional name of "Mme. Marie Selika." In the decade of the nineties Sisserietta Jones made triumphal tours as "Black Patti."

A year after the Fisk Jubilee Singers began their astounding tour of the East and Europe in 1871, the Colored Opera Company, under John Esputa, presented such works as Eichberg's "The Doctor of Alcantra." Negroes in Massachusetts formed the Boston Musical Union in 1875 and the next year Negroes in New York organized the Philharmonic Society of New York. The Samuel Coleridge-Taylor Musical Society of Washington, D.C., boasted over two hundred members in 1903 and was probably the largest Negro musical group of its era.

Scholars have traced the history of secular music among Negroes back to the sources of the spirituals. Both types of music are blends of West African and European rhythmic and harmonic forms. While the patterns of Negro secular music—the earthy blue tonality, the call-and-response, the field holler and the falsetto break—are very old, the emergence of individual musicians whose names are recorded may be dated from the turn of the century. Scott Joplin and his ragtime out of Missouri, Will Marion Cook and his syncopated musicals in New York, W. C. Handy and the blues out of Memphis and St. Louis and James Reese Europe with his promotion of the Handy music, and Ferdinand "Jelly Roll" Morton and his jazzband were important forerunners of today's secular music. Then followed Louis Armstrong with his trumpet in the thirties, Charlie Parker in the fifties and Miles Davis with Thelonius Monk in the sixties. Indeed the list is much longer; the field of jazz is so vital that it possesses a literature of its own. Started by Negroes, jazz seems to be the characteristic musical idiom of the mid-twentieth century.

Throughout the long evolution of jazz, serious music has not been neglected. Harry T. Burleigh was arranging spirituals for the concert stage during the century's first two decades. J. Rosamond Johnson, Carl Diton, Nathaniel Dett, and John R. Work also made reputations as arrangers of Negro spirituals and as composers in their own right. Following them, William Dawson as a composer and Dean Dixon as a conductor gained national recognition. As concert artists, Roland Hayes, Paul Robeson, Marian Anderson and Etta Moten Barnett, carried vocal music to new heights of technical finesse. Other artists including Lillian Evanti, Todd Duncan, Dorothy Maynor, Carol Brice, Gloria Davy, Mattiwilda Dobbs, Camilla Williams, Robert McFerrin, Leontyne Price, William Warfield, Lawrence Winters, and Grace Bumbry continued the fine tradition of superb singing in concerts, folk opera and grand opera.

W. E. B. DuBois. *The Souls of Black Folk*, Greenwich, Connecticut, 1963 (Paperback, Premier Americana edition), p. 183; Mark Miles Fisher. *Negro Slave Songs in the United States*, Ithaca, 1953, p. 1; Marshall Stearns. *The Story of Jazz*, New York, 1960 (Paperback), pp. 11-19, 183-200.

138

George P. Bridgetower
(1779-1860)

COMPOSER

At home, on May 18. Although we have not spoken, I do not hesitate for all that, to speak of the bearer, Mr. Bridgetower, as a master of his instrument, a very skillful virtuoso worthy of recommendation. Besides concertos, he plays in quarters in a most praiseworthy manner and I wish very much that you would make him better known. He has already made the acquaintance of Lobkowitz, Fries and many other distinguished admirers. I believe that it would not be unwise to bring him some evening to Theresa Schonfeld's who I know has many friends . . .

These words were written by the immortal Ludvig Van Beethoven. He was singing the praises of George Poleridge Bridgetower, one of the outstanding violinists and composers of his day. Bridgetower was at the beginning of his career and Beethoven was taken by the skill and ability the Polish-born Bridgetower demonstrated in music.

At the age of ten, Bridgetower had taken Paris by storm with his first major violin concert. This was in 1789. The next year Bridgetower repeated his success in London at the Drury Lane Theater. So great was his skill and appeal that he was sponsored by the Prince of Wales.

His parents recognized his musical ability early and did their best to develop it. He studied under the finest available teachers, for who could ask for better instructors than Haydn, Barthelmon, or Giornovichi. As a matter of fact, the many friends of the young prodigy insisted that he meet Beethoven. The great composer was not disappointed and he himself quickly joined the ranks of Bridgetower admirers. Beethoven even appeared in concert with the Abyssinian Prince, as Bridgetower was called.

In addition to playing the music of others, Bridgetower composed works of his own, the best known being the "Henry" ballad which was dedicated to the Princess Royal in London. More than forty piano-forte suites flowed from his pen.

George Bridgetower was the son of an African who had emigrated to Poland where he met and married a lady of Polish descent. His parents found little prejudice against them and lived the life of any other upper-class family. They were quick to take an interest in George and his brother, T. Bridgetower, who became a well known cellist. Often the two brothers appeared in concert together.

Not very much is known of Bridgetowers later life, although he continued to perform in various countries. At his death in 1860 at the age of 81, George Bridgetower was able to bequeath the sum of $5,000 to his sister-in-law.

Beatrice Flemming and Marion Pryde. *Distinguished Negros Abroad*, Washington, 1946, pp. 160-165.

James Bland (1854-1911)

COMPOSER

CARRY ME BACK TO OLD VIRGINNY
SONG AND CHORUS

Words and Music by
JAMES BLAND
Author of "In the morning by the bright light," &c.

Virginia, the proudest of the southern states, is perhaps the only state in the Union whose official song was written by a Negro. Whenever citizens of the Old Dominion rise to sing "Carry me Back to Old Virginia," they are also giving homage to James Bland, a Negro composer who was born free in Long Island, New York.

Other old-time favorites such as "Oh, Dem Golden Slippers," "In The Evening By The Moonlight," "Tapioca," "Pretty Little Caroline Rose," "Listen to the Silver Trumpets," and scores upon scores of other songs flowed from the pen of this untrained composer.

Contrary to popular legend, James Bland was not a white-haired ex-slave writing songs of fealty and affection for his former masters. He was a self-made professional descending from a long line of free Negroes. Having the distinction of being the first Negro employed as an examiner in the United States Patent Office, his father, Allen Bland, was a graduate of Wilberforce and Oberlin Colleges and had a degree from the Howard University law school. His mother was a native of Wilmington, Delaware.

James Bland fell in love with the banjo while in his teens. He began his career singing and playing for parties and weddings. At the age of fourteen Bland was hired to sing at a hotel in Washington, D.C. Thinking to discourage his son from a show business career, Allen Bland sent his son to Howard University. Once there, James promptly started organizing glee clubs and minstrel groups. Finishing his courses at nineteen, Bland soon took to the road as a regular professional. He appeared with such groups as Billy Kersand's minstrels and Callenders' Original Georgia Minstrels.

In 1878 while working with George Primrose, James Bland published "Carry Me Back To Old Virginia," which became an instant success. Popular singers rushed to add the song to their repertoire. Bland was in great demand for personal appearances. On the strength of his popularity in America, James Bland went to England in 1881 and found even greater professional and personal success. He gave a command performance for Queen Victoria. The leading vaudeville houses vied for his services. At one point James Bland was earning $1000 weekly. He was called the "Prince of Negro Performers."

Dispensing with blackface and burnt cork, Bland could be seen as he was: a rather handsome, debonair man with an engaging smile. He wore the finest products of English tailoring and lived on a lavish scale. After twenty years abroad, James Bland returned to America only to find that old-time minstrelry was no longer the vogue. He died in 1911, two years after Bert Williams hit the big-time as a comedian.

John J. Daly. *A Song in His Heart*, Philadelphia, 1951; Langston Hughes. *Famous Negro Music Makers*, New York, 1955, pp. 29-34; David Ewen (ed.). *Popular American Composers*, New York, 1962, pp. 30-31.

Samuel Coleridge-Taylor (1875-1912)

ENGLISH COMPOSER

On November 16, 1903 a slim, somewhat short, mulatto from England stood before the 200-voice Samuel Coleridge Taylor Society in Washington's Convention Hall and led it in a performance of *Hiawatha*, a cantata of his own composition. A cross-section of Washington society, Cabinet members, congressmen and hundreds of music lovers turned out to hear the Society and to see the composer and conductor, Samuel Coleridge-Taylor. *Hiawatha* had already been presented in England with much success before an audience of thousands in London's famed Albert Hall.

After the Washington performance, the twenty-eight year old composer was presented with a baton made of cedar from Frederick Douglass' home, an autographed picture from Theodore Roosevelt and a loving cup from Washington Negroes inscribed with the words "Well for us, O brother, that you come so far to see us."

The son of an African father from Sierra Leone and a mother from England, Samuel Coleridge-Taylor was born in London in 1875. He began to study the violin at the age of six and showed an early aptitude for composition. In 1890 he entered the violin department of the Royal Academy of Music and in his third year won a prize for composing. He graduated from this institution with honors in 1894.

The *Hiawatha* cantata was the work which catapulted him to fame. In "The Death of Hiawatha" and "Hiawatha's Wedding Feast," Coleridge-Taylor elaborated the Hiawatha theme. Nevertheless the young composer made his most distinctive contribution to music in his symphonic works based on Negro melodies of Africa and America. For the piano he wrote "African Suite," "African Dances" and "African Romances," the latter with words by Paul Laurence Dunbar whom he met and performed with in England. Among his vocal works are "The Blind Girl of Castle-Cuille" and "The Atonement" which was presented in Washington in 1906 during his second and last trip to America. Coleridge-Taylor composed a suite for the piano based on "Othello" and an interesting choral work, "A Tale of Old Japan."

Critical estimates of his work rank Coleridge-Taylor high on the lists of English composers. He made his living entirely from his work as a musician. He supported himself by public appearances and with teaching the violin at the Croyden Conservatory of Music. Music was his life. When he died in Croyden in 1912, he imagined that he was conducting his unfinished "Violin Concerto."

W. C. Berwick Sayers. *Samuel Coleridge-Taylor: Musician*, New York, 1915; Maud Cuney-Hare. *Negro Musicians and Their Music*, Washington, 1936, pp. 244-247.

Harry T. Burleigh (1866-1949)

SINGER, COMPOSER, ARRANGER

NEGRO SPIRITUALS

Arranged for Solo Voice by

H. T. BURLEIGH

Ain't Goin' to Study War No Mo'	I've Been In De Storm So Long
Balm in Gilead	I Want To Be Ready
Behold That Star	John's Gone Down On De Island
By An' By	Joshua Fit De Battle Ob Jericho
Couldn't Hear Nobody Pray	Let Us Cheer The Weary Traveler
De Blin' Man Stood on De Road An' Cried	Little David Play on Your Harp
De Gospel Train	My Lord What A Morning
Deep River	My Way's Cloudy
Didn't My Lord Deliver Daniel	Nobody Knows De Trouble I've Seen
Don't Be Weary Traveler	Oh Didn't It Rain
Don't You Weep When I'm Gone	Oh Wasn't Dat a Wide Ribber
Ev'ry Time I Feel the Spirit	Oh Peter Go Ring Dem Bells
Give Me Jesus	O Rocks Don't Fall On Me
Go Down in De Lonesome Valley	●Ride on King Jesus
Go Down Moses	Sinner Please Doan Let Dis Harves' Pass
Go Tell It On De Mountains	Sometimes I Feel Like A Motherless Child
Hard Trials	Stan' Still Jordan
Hear de Lambs a-Cryin'	Steal Away
Heav'n Heav'n	Swing Low, Sweet Chariot
He's Just De Same Today	'Tis Me O Lord
I Don't Feel No-Ways Tired	Wade In De Water
I Got A Home In A-Dat Rock	Weepin' Mary
I Know De Lord's Laid His Hands On Me	Were You There
I Stood On De Ribber Ob Jerdon	You May Bury Me in De Eas'

The small boy stood in the snow outside the Russell home for hours, hoping to hear the pianist Rafael Joseffy when he played for the drawing room packed with guests. The Russells employed his mother as a maid and Burleigh had often accompanied her to work and heard snatches of good music whenever the Russells decided to present famous artists in their Erie, Pennsylvania home. Young Harry almost forgot about the cold, the wet and the snow as he listened to the music floating out of the windows. When the music ended, Harry hurried home, late, hungry and cold.

Mrs. Burleigh told her employer that young Harry was ill of exposure whereupon Mrs. Russell gave the Erie High School lad a job as a doorman to admit the guests — and to hear and see what was going on at her parties. Thus Harry T. Burleigh became acquainted with good music and began the contacts that were to bring him fame in later years.

When not attending school or working in Erie hotels, young Burleigh trained and sang with Negro choirs and choral groups. In 1892 he won a scholarship to the National Conservatory and began his formal training in music. Here he studied under such men as Christian Fritsche, Robin Goldmark and John White. Here also he met Anton Dvorak who was teaching there at the time. He and Dvorak became good friends. Many evenings they could be found together, the Hungarian composer and the young Negro singer. Burleigh would sing spirituals for Dvorak and in turn would be permitted to copy music from the composer's manuscripts.

In 1894, over a large field of trained competitors, Burleigh won the job of baritone soloist at the ultra-rich, ultra-fashionable St. George Episcopal Church in New York. The parishioners were divided over his being employed but the majority of them supported him. In 1900 Burleigh was selected baritone soloist at Temple Emanuel in New York, one of the nation's wealthies synagogues. He kept both posts for over a quarter century. His splendid voice even took him before King Edward VII in a command performance.

Burleigh's greatest artistic ambition was the arrangement of the spirituals for use in concert hall. Today many of the old familiar spirituals presented by leading concert singers carry the notation "Arranged by Harry T. Burleigh." He also composed art songs such as "In the Wood of Finvara," "The Prayer" and "Ethiopia Saluting the Colors." His song cycles include "Down by the Sea." and "Who's Dat Yonder."

In 1917 Harry T. Burleigh was given the Spingarn Award for distinguished contributions to the progress of the Negro in music. He died in 1949.

Maud Cuney-Hare. *Negro Musicians and Their Music*, Washington, D.C., 1936, pp. 323-329.

Nathaniel Dett (1882-1943)

COMPOSER

JUBA

R. NATHANIEL DETT

Non Troppo Allegro ♩=120-144

mf *non legato*

Nathaniel Dett made significant contributions to America's musical heritage with his compositions and arrangements. Throughout his long career Dett insisted on the dignity of the Negro spiritual. His compositions encompass both racial and non-racial themes.

Especially popular are his works "Oh Holy Lord" and "Listen To The Lambs" which are performed by many choral groups throughout the country. Dett's better known compositions for the piano are "The Magnolia Suite," "The Enchantment Suite," "In the Bottoms," and the motets "Chariot Jubilee." His opera, *The Ordering of Moses*, was performed in the forties by the National Negro Opera Company and presented at Carnegie Hall in 1951. It was recorded by the Voice of America for broadcasting overseas.

In addition to his compositions and arrangements, Dett was a highly successul choral leader. Beginning with his organization of the Musical Arts Society in 1919 at Hampton Institute, Dett raised the Hampton Institute Choir to international eminence. In 1930 under his leadership the Hampton choir made a tour of seven European countries and received great critical praise. Prior to his success at Hampton, Dett had been summoned to his home town of Drummondsville, Ontario to organize and lead a 100-voice all-white choral group in the celebration of music week in 1924. Dett also developed excellent choral groups at Lane College in Jackson, Tennessee and at Lincoln Institute (now Lincoln University) in Jefferson City, Missouri.

Born in 1882, Nathaniel Dett decided on a career in music early in life. From 1901 to 1903 he attended the Oliver Willis Conservatory of Music and received the degree of bachelor of music from Oberlin College in 1908. He continued his studies at the American Conservatory of Music in Chicago, at Columbia University and the University of Pennsylvania. Dett first achieved wide notice while at Harvard where, as a student in 1920, he won the Bowdoin Prize for an essay, "The Emancipation of Negro Music," and the Francis Boott Prize for motets on a Negro motive.

Maud Cuney-Hare, *Negro Musicians and Their Music*, Washington, D.C., 1936, pp. 336-339; Margaret Just Butcher. *The Negro in American Culture*, New York, 1957 (Mentor Edition), pp. 74-75.

W. C. Handy (1873-1958)

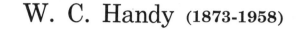

19 years old, Hampton Cornet Band, Evansville, Indiana

The story of the blues is the story of the life of W. C. Handy, often called the "father of the blues." Farm hands, washerwomen, wood cutters, railroad laborers and roustabouts for years had lightened their daily rounds with secular songs of love, of despair, of hope and longing. Unlike the spirituals, the blues are about the relationships between men and women on this earth.

W. C. Handy, in a sense, was the first to bring these secular songs to the larger world. Many other trained musicians had heard the blues and dismissed them as the rude and bawdy music of the oppressed. The music, to them was interesting but somehow too blunt and coarse to be taken seriously. W. C. Handy himself felt this way until one night while leading a group called Maharas' Band, he chanced to hear some musically illiterate country performers move an audience with the not-quite-respectable blues songs and music.

Handy, too, was moved and that very night hurried home to write the "Memphis Blues." He followed this with the "Beale Street Blues" and finally the classic "St. Louis Blues." The tremedous public response to Handy's blues soon made him an internationally known figure. Deems Taylor and Walter Damrosch, musical luminaries, led the way with their praise of him. Handy soon played his blues before high society and even royalty.

W. C. Handy was born in Florence, Alabama, in 1873. While his mother felt that his large ears indicated musical aptitude, his father strongly objected to the boy's showing any interest in the "sinful" music of the fields and streets. Handy learned the rudiments of music in the local school for Negroes in Florence. By the time he reached his teens he was arranging choral parts for church groups. He left home when he was eighteen years old and decided to strike out alone. He sang and played his way from Florence to Chicago with the Lauzetta Quartet. He then worked his way back down to St. Louis, Missouri, but found little opportunity to make a living from his music. In St. Louis Handy was so poor that he had to sleep on the levee and to depend upon his wits for food. In his wanderings Handy passed through many towns where a Negro was not welcome after sundown. He summed up these experiences in the famous line, "I hate to see the evening sun go down."

During these early days, Handy was so eager to hear good music that he once took a job as a janitor in Hender-

Weather-beaten shack where Handy was born

144

"THE FATHER OF THE BLUES"

son, Kentucky in order to hear an excellent German chorus of one hundred voices as he swept the rehearsal hall. Handy did not neglect his own music and from time to time would play with small bands and minstrel groups; the cornet and the trumpet were his favorite instruments.

By the turn of the century, Handy's fortunes had improved to the point that he was invited to Alabama A & M College to serve as director of music. He remained here for only two years and returned to the road where he could make more money and possess a freedom not usually found on college campuses.

He wrote his "Memphis Blues" in 1909, and his fame began to spread after the tune was used in a political campaign. He decided to make Memphis his headquarters and opened up the offices of the Pace and Handy Music Company. The company skyrocketed to success within a year, for among the many compositions Handy turned out for the company was the "St. Louis Blues" which was an instant success. The earlier fame of his "Memphis Blues" was such that the Handy organization could send out upwards of eighty men each night to play dance engagements in different parts of Tennessee and the surrounding areas.

The "big" song was of course the "St. Louis Blues" which was netting W. C. Handy $25,000 yearly by 1940. The composer of the blues did not stop with just the above-named tunes but wrote over sixty others. Nor was his work limited to the blues. He is the composer of "Aframerican Hymn," "Blue Destiny" (a symphonic piece) and over 150 other compositions, both sacred and secular.

In 1928 William Christopher Handy sponsored and conducted a sixty-voice chorus and a thirty-piece orchestra at Carnegie Hall in a musical history of the Negro. In this performance during the height of the "Negro Renaissance" were "Fats" Waller, J. Rosamond Johnson and other distinguished Negro musicians.

By 1930, Handy's name was a household word. The blues were regarded as a legitimate part of the country's musical heritage. In 1931 the city of Memphis, Tennessee named a park after Handy. Sixteen years later a huge theatre in Memphis bore his name. In Florence, Alabama, stands the W. C. Handy School.

W. C. Handy died in 1958, but his contributions to music live on as a part of America's musical heritage.

W. C. Handy. *The Father of the Blues*, New York, 1941: *Current Biography, 1941*, pp. 361-362.

Statue of Handy in Handy Park, Memphis, Tennessee

William Grant Still

(1895-   )

MODERN COMPOSER

The route from his native Woodville, Mississippi to the Philharmonic contained many detours and by-ways. His parents had sent him to Wilberforce to study medicine. However, his great interest was music and after three years, he withdrew from Wilberforce without taking a degree. Only in his early twenties at the time, Still became a drifter. For a short time he worked as an office boy for W. C. Handy in Tennessee and played in Handy's band. During all of his wandering, Still never lost the desire to compose.

A small inheritance enabled William Still to attend the Oberlin Conservatory of Music in Ohio. Later grants made it possible for him to go to the New England Conservatory of Music. He began the serious study of composition under George Chadwick and the famed Edgar Varese. Combining the musical heritage of Europe with his own Afro-American background, Still began to produce music for songs, ballets, symphonies and operas.

Some of his better known songs are "Breath of a Rose," "Levee Land" and the beautiful "Kaintuck." Among his ballet compositions are "Sahdji" and "La Guiablesse" which was performed in Indianapolis, Indiana. His better known symphonies are *Afro-American Symphony*, *Africa* and *Symphony in G minor*. *Blue Steel* and *Troubled Island* are among his more popular operatic compositions.

William Grant Still has received numerous awards and honors. Extended Guggenheim and Rosenwald fellowships freed him for creative activity during the early part of his formal career. He won the Harmon Award for his contributions to music in 1927. For his *Troubled Island* he was cited by the National Association for American Composers and Conductors for a distinguished contribution to American music. He has had numerous commissions from the Columbia Broadcasting Company, the New York posers and Conductors for distinguished contribution to World's Fair (1935) and several other cities for special occasions. He has received honorary degrees from a number of institution, including Wilberforce and Oberlin. His works are now a part of America's musical treasure.

Edwin R. Embree. *13 Against the Odds*, New York, 1944, pp. 197-210; Richard Bardoplh, *The Negro Vanguard*, New York, 1961 (paperback), pp. 221-222.

The night William Grant Still stood before the Los Angeles Philharmonic Orchestra in 1936 and conducted one of his own compositions marked the first time an American Negro had ever led a major orchestra in the performance of serious music. This occasion was also a high point in the life of Still who had played honky-tonks and dives in the Deep South, in Ohio and New York. The occasional "gig" (musical engagement), the catch-as-catch-can combos and bands, the orchestra pits of musical revues were all behind him.

William L. Dawson
(1898-   )

COMPOSER-ARRANGER

Taking high rank among creators of American music is William Levi Dawson, the eminent composer whose works have brought pleasure to thousands of music lovers. The beauty of his music shines through such experiences as not being allowed to take part in one of his own graduation exercises in 1927 because of his color or having to secure special permission to attend a concert featuring his work in Birmingham, Alabama, for the same reasons.

Born in Anniston, Alabama in 1898, William Dawson ran away from home to attend Tuskegee Institute. At Tuskegee he landed a job caring for the instruments of the Institute band and learned to play most of them. After finishing Tuskegee in 1921, he attended Washburn College, Topeka, Kansas, the Institute of Fine Arts, Kansas City, Missouri and later he went to Chicago, Illinois to continue his studies in composition and orchestration, At the Chicago Musical College he studied under Felix Borowski and at the American Conservatory he studied with Adolph Weidig. At the same time he earned his living playing in Windy City bands, training Negro church choirs and occasionally playing the trombone with the Chicago Civic Orchestra as its only Negro member during that time.

Among his many compositions are "I Couldn't Hear Nobody Pray," "Talk About a Child That Do Love Jesus, Here Is One." His most notable symphonic work is *Negro Folk Symphony No. 1*. Its world premiere was at Carnegie Hall under conductor Leopold Stokowski in 1934. For many years, William Dawson was director of music at Tuskegee Institute. With his compositions and arrangements, he made the Tuskegee Institute Choir one of the nation's finest. Following his retirement from active direction of the choir in 1955, Dawson was sent to Spain by the U. S. State Department to train Spanish choral groups in the singing of Negro spirituals.

Dawson has a deep and abiding love for spirituals. To their natural beauty he has added the discipline and training of the devoted professional.

Maud-Cuney-Hare. *Negro Musicians and Their Music*, Washington, 1936; *Who's Who in Colored America*, 1950, p. 145.

Two Spirituals
by WILLIAM L. DAWSON

Talk About A Child That Do Love Jesus
My Lord What A Mourning

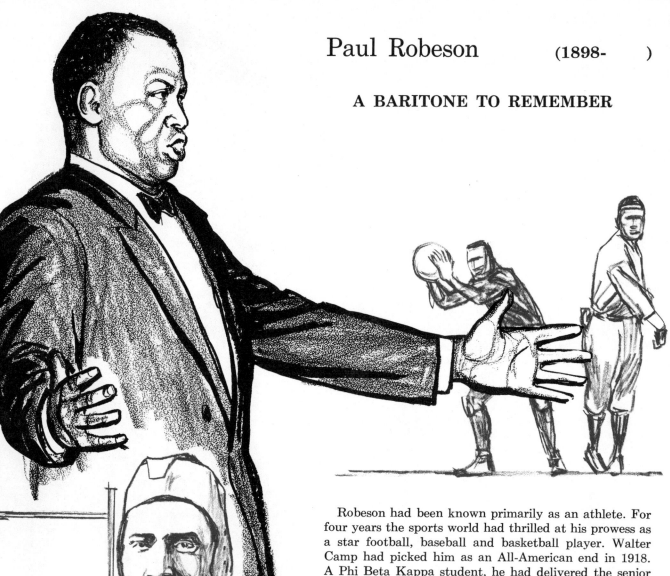

Paul Robeson (1898-   )

A BARITONE TO REMEMBER

Robeson had been known primarily as an athlete. For four years the sports world had thrilled at his prowess as a star football, baseball and basketball player. Walter Camp had picked him as an All-American end in 1918. A Phi Beta Kappa student, he had delivered the senior commencement address upon his graduation from Rutgers in 1919. After Rutgers, Robeson had gone on to the Columbia University Law School to earn a law degree by 1923.

At the suggestion of his wife Eslanda Goode, whom he had married in 1921, Robeson decided to try acting. His first part was that of a cross-bearer in a Harlem YMCA production of *Simon the Cyrenian*. After seeing him in this amateur production, Eugene O'Neill tried unsuccessfully to give him the lead role of *Emperor Jones*. In 1922 Robeson had played with Margaret Wycherly in *Voodoo*. When he later assayed the role of the porter in *Emperor Jones* his potentialities as a singer were first noticed. As an actor, he achieved wide recognition for his work in *All God's Chillun*.

After Robeson's Greenwich concert his future as a singer was assured. In 1926 he repeated his earlier triumph by singing to a full house at New York Town Hall. He then followed this with appearances in Boston, Philadelphia and Baltimore. In the same year he went abroad, repeating his American successes on a larger scale. Alternating between America and Europe, Robeson was a polished performer by 1929. On May 19, 1930 he played the role of the jealous Moor in *Othello* at London's Savoy

One night on the stage of Greenwich Village Theatre in April, 1925, during the height of the "Negro Renaissance," a huge black giant of a man, threw back his head and sang:

> Go Down Moses
> Way down in Egypt's lan'
> An' tell ol' Pharaoh
> To let——my——people—go!
> Let my people—go!

This majestic spiritual was followed by others, among them being "Sometimes I Feel Like a Motherless Child," and "Joshua Fit the Battle of Jerico." The packed hall resounded with praise and applause as the concert ended. The singer was Paul Robeson, who had never taken a singing lesson in his life.

Uta Hagen and Averell Harris co-starred with Robeson in the Theater Guild production of Othello

Theatre. Of his performance, the *London Morning Post* declared that "there has been no 'Othello' on our stage, certainly for forty years, to compare with his dignity, simplicity and true passion."

In between concert tours of Europe, Robeson appeared in O'Neill's *The Hairy Ape* and *Stevedore* (by Paul Peters and George Sklar), an important play showing the Negro's awareness of the larger economic issues of the thirties. Robeson also appeared on the screen in early productions of *Emperor Jones, Showboat, Jerico, King Solomon's Mines* and *Saunders of the River*.

On the legitimate stage Robeson is best known for his work in the American production of *Othello*, first playing the Moor in 1934 and again in 1943. In the latter production, Robeson perhaps achieved his greatest fame. He played opposite Uta Hagen's "Desdemona" and Jose Ferrer's "Iago." Critics were unrestrained in their praise. Opening on October 19, 1943, *Othello* ran for 296 performances before it closed on July 1, 1944. *The New York Sun*'s drama critic exclaimed that Paul Robeson was "the first Negro of modern times to appear in a New York production," and added that he gives a giant's stature and remarkable clarity and vitality to his role."

Robeson has been popular as a recording artist, having over 300 disks to his credit. He has studied nine languages, including Chinese and Russian. He has been able to sing to and speak with people of many different nationalities in their native tongues.

From his early youth as a poor minister's son in his native Princeton, New Jersey, Paul Robeson had a deep sympathy for the social underdog. His political views swung to favor Russia. In his admiration of that country, he sent his only son there to be educated. He himself has been to Russia many times and since the late forties, has spent much of his time there and elsewhere. Naturally his career has gone in eclipse in America. A writer once declared that it is "one of the extravagances of the theatre that Paul Robeson is not active in it." Perhaps the same could be said of a society which so embittered Robeson that he felt it necessary to leave it.

Shirley Graham. *Paul Robeson; Citizen of the World*, New York, 1946; Edwin Embree. *Thirteen Against the Odds*, New York, 1946, pp. 243-261.

Roland Hayes
(1887-   )

GOD'S OWN TENOR

Born in Georgia in 1887, Roland Hayes seemed destined for the fate of many a gifted but rudderless artist. Of his early years, the cultivated, mild-mannered Hayes has said, "It was as natural for me to sing as to breathe." By chance he was invited to hear some recordings by the great tenor Enrico Caruso and from this moment on, Roland Hayes was determined to become a professional singer.

Eventually making his way to Fisk University, it was perhaps inevitable that Hayes joined the famed Fisk Jubilee Singers. On a trip to Boston, Massachusetts as member of the Jubilee Singers, Hayes decided to give up Fisk and to secure competent training for his voice. Supporting himself with a variety of random jobs, he began the serious study of voice and by 1916 felt ready for a concert tour. He received very little encouragement, as Negro concert artists were not yet in demand. Concert managers felt that his desire to become a concert performer was noble but naive. Hayes undertook his own management and succeeded far beyond the expectations of the professionals.

After several seasons of touring in America, Hayes decided to go to Europe to enhance his professional career. Shortly after his arrival in England, he was commanded to sing before the King of England, George V. This command performance helped to secure his reputation, and for the next fifteen years the concert managers who had rejected him earlier were proudly presenting "Roland Hayes in Concert" in America as well as abroad. Once financially successful, Hayes followed a policy of low-cost admissions so that the poor of all races could hear him.

Despite many unpleasant experiences as a pioneer, Roland Hayes has never lost his belief in the essential goodness in man. He believes that social progress may take many avenues. The elevation of the hearts of men through song is one of them. When Roland Hayes received the first Amistad Award for contributing creatively to the improvement of human relations, Virgil Thomson, himself an outstanding musical composer and critic, said to him, "You do the human race honor to exist."

"Roland Hayes: A Lifetime on the Concert Stage," *Ebony*, September, 1946, pp. 42-46; McKinley Helm. *"Angel Mo' and Her Son: Roland Hayes*, Boston, 1942.

For almost half a century, Roland Hayes has taken the world for his stage and has never lacked an audience. Blessed with a superb voice, he sang his way from a window-sash factory in Chattanooga, Tennessee to the chandeliered halls of Buckingham Palace. Illiterate peasants of the Deep South and musical sophisticates of the world have been touched by the voice of the man who has been called the "greatest tenor ever born in America."

Dean Dixon
(1915-   )

CONDUCTOR INTERNATIONAL

He was born in Harlem in 1915. He speaks Swedish, French and German but he interprets the international language of classical music with a skill, insight and sensitivity which have made him one of Europe's busiest conductors. He has not had a vacation in a dozen years, for conducting has been his joy and his life. At present, the permanent conductor of the Hessian Radio Symphony in Frankfurt, Germany, Dean Dixon left America in 1949 because he could not find a regular post as a symphony conductor despite his admittedly great talents.

Before taking over the Hessian Radio Symphony in 1962, Dean Dixon had been the conductor of the Goteborg Symphony in Sweden for nearly a decade. To the Swedish orchestra he imparted a technical finesse and a melodic quality which brought it wide acclaim. He also introduced many American works to Europe, especially the compositions of William Grant Still and Gordon Parks.

Dean Dixon is known in Europe far beyond the borders of Sweden and Germany. He has conducted nearly every major symphony in Europe including those of Austria, Italy and Israel. His style of conducting is said to be restrained and controlled, possessing neither the special warmth of the Italian school or the alleged coolness of the American school.

Born of West Indian parents in New York, Dixon learned to read music and the alphabet at about the same time. When his legs were almost too short to climb the stairs, his mother would take him to Carnegie Hall. He played the violin in the DeWitt Clinton High School band and after graduation, organized an amateur interracial orchestra in the Harlem YMCA.

Dixon received very little encouragement when he decided to become a symphony conductor, especially at a time when Negro instrumentalists could not find permanent employment. Nevertheless his ability was so great that he led the New York Chamber Orchestra when he was twenty-five and still a student of conducting at the Julliard School of Music in New York.

After completing his Juilliard studies under Albert Stoessel in 1939, Dean Dixon began an uncertain career as a guest conductor, leading such groups as the New York Philharmonic Orchestra, the NBC Symphony Orchestra and the Boston Symphony. In 1948 he received the $1000 Alice M. Ditson Award as the outstanding music conductor of the year. He received several awards for his work in encouraging an interest in music among young people.

However none of the many honors and awards could take the place of a regular podium for this gifted conductor who left America nearly fifteen years ago. Dean Dixon still dreams of returning to the land of his birth, "leading my own symphony."

Arna Bontemps. *We Have Tomorrow*, Boston, 1945, pp. 46-58; *Who's Who in Colored America*, 1950, p. 157; "An American Abroad," *Time*, May 4. 1962, p. 48.

Louis "Satchmo" Armstrong
(1900-   )

THE JAZZ AMBASSADOR

When Louis Armstrong was sent to the Waif's Home for Boys for discharging a pistol in the streets of New Orleans, Louisiana, he had no idea that twenty years later he would appear before the King and Queen of England in a command performance. Then a poverty-stricken urchin of thirteen, he could play no instrument save a home-made guitar. Louis Armstrong's casual interest in music was cultivated by the bandmaster of the Waif's Home. There the round-faced youth with the wide-open eyes learned to play the cornet and bugle so well that he was leading the band before his release eighteen months later.

While supporting himself by selling newspapers and working in a dairy, Armstrong began loitering around the places where his idol Joe "King" Oliver was appearing with Kid Ory's band. "King" Oliver taught Armstrong to play the trumpet and when he left for Chicago in 1917, Louis Armstrong took his place in Ory's band. Armstrong experienced his first long journey away from New Orleans when he accompanied Kid Ory's group on a 2,000-mile cruise up and down the Mississippi in 1921-22.

In 1922 Armstrong took the Mississippi northward to Chicago to join his trumpet mentor, "King" Oliver, who was then appearing at the Royal Palm Gardens. Two years later Armstrong headed for New York and worked with Fletcher Henderson's orchestra, but returned to Chicago in 1925. In 1926 he joined Erskine Tate at the old Vendome Theater. Earl Hines, the pianist in Tate's orchestra at the time, and the boys doubled nights at the Sunset Cafe. Louis' name went up in lights—"World's Greatest Trumpeter." Following his success, he organized his own group, "Louis Armstrong and His Hot Five."

After a series of profitable engagements in Chicago, Armstrong returned to New York to a spot called Connie's Inn and had a highly successful run. He left Connie's Inn and became a star of the musical *Hot Chocolates* where he first introduced "Ain't Misbehaving."

In 1933 Armstrong made his first trip abroad and toured France, Italy, Switzerland, Norway, Holland, and England. In 1934 he appeared before England's King George VI in the first of several command performances. During most of his stay abroad the former New Orleans waif made his home at la rue de la Auvergne in Paris.

Following his return from Europe in 1936, Armstrong made his motion picture debut in *Pennies from Heaven*. In the next few years he appeared in *Everyday's a Holiday*, *Going Places*, and *Cabin in the Sky*. His recording career dates from the middle twenties, and many of his records are collectors items.

Since these early days Louis Armstrong's trumpet has been heard in many parts of the world, including Africa. His virtuosity on the trumpet and influence on early jazz earned him a secure place in the annals of popular music.

Louis Armstrong: *Satchmo: My Life in New Orleans*, New York, 1954
Louis Armstrong. *Horn of Plenty*, New York, 1947

Duke Ellington
(1899-   )
THE MAESTRO

Whenever music is discussed, by layman or professional, young or old, jazz fan or classicist, in any part of the world, the name Duke Ellington is quite likely to be mentioned. Such is the reputation and record of musical accomplishments of this maestro. He has achieved practically every musical honor imaginable, from popularity polls and hit records to sell-out, standing-room-only crowds at Carnegie Hall. His plaques and trophies, dating back to 1940, would completely fill a room. To date he has written almost 1,000 tunes, and the amazing part of his fabulous career is that it seems not to have reached its peak — his musical creativity is ever expanding, continuously growing.

The "Duke" was born Edward Kennedy Ellington in April 29, 1898, in Washington, D.C. He earned the nickname "Duke" in school for his somewhat flashy clothes: he was always "duked out." Like most truly creative people, the Duke evidenced his talent early. Although he hated to practice, he was playing the piano at seven, he composed his first piece, "The Soda Fountain Rag," at seventeen, and at eighteen was playing professionally.

At twenty-four he hit Broadway with his own band, the Washingtonians; at twenty-eight he was booked into the Cotton Club, where his nation-wide fame began; at thirty-four he played for royalty in London and toured Europe as a concert artist; at thirty-nine he gave one of the first college jazz concerts at Colgate University; at 40 he made a second triumphal European tour, giving twenty-eight performances in twenty-eight days; at forty-four he performed the first of his many concerts at Carnegie Hall; and at forty-five he added Chicago's Opera House and San Francisco's Philharmonic Hall to his list of "firsts."

National recognition of his musical superiority dates back to 1940 when he won honors in a nation-wide poll. Since then, there has hardly been a single year in which he has not won similar honors in comparable polls. He has been hailed by such outstanding names in serious music, as Lauritz Melchior, Stokowski, Reiner and Deems Taylor. He was the first living artist to sponsor a scholarship fund to the Julliard School of Music.

Ellington has evidenced creative talent, as well as interest, in serious music, also. His more ambitious musical scores include *Black, Brown and Beige*, a tone poem of the history of the American Negro; *Perfume Suite*, and his musical salute to the Negro entitled *My People*.

His popular song classics include: "Mood Indigo," "Solitude," "Black and Tan Fantasy," "Flamingo," "The A Train," "Caravan," "Sophisticated Lady," "I Got It Bad," "Perdido," and hundreds of others whose appeal, like their originator, has not been dated by the passing years.

Peter Gammond (ed.) *Duke Ellington: His Life and Music*, New York, 1958.

Marian Anderson
(1902)

THIS CENTURY'S CONTRALTO

When she stood before the famous music teacher, Giuseppe Borghetti, the church recitals, the amateur cantatas and oratorios, the timid tours south, and the tutoring of good friends were all behind her. Auditioning for a professional career, she was a stately young woman with a serene face. Her outward calm and dusky complexion seemed almost a part of the gathering twilight as she started to sing:

> Deep river; deep river
> Lord, I want to cross over
> Into camp ground. . . .

When Marion Anderson finished her audition, Mr. Borghetti sat motionless. Tears were streaming down his cheeks. Miss Anderson's church had raised money for her first year's fees and Mr. Borghetti was so impressed by her voice that he taught her an additional year without cost.

After several years of private study Miss Anderson resumed her tours of southern colleges and in 1925, she felt that she was ready for a Town Hall concert. The concert was a failure and the young, novice singer was on the brink of despair. In 1926 she sang at a Spingarn Award dinner for Roland Hayes and took a renewed interest in her own career.

In 1927 Miss Anderson entered a competition with 300 other young singers and won first prize which consisted of a contract for concert tours. This led to an appearance with the New York Philharmonic Orchestra. Finding her concert opportunities limited, Marion Anderson went to Europe in 1929 and made her continental debut in Germany. Back in America she continued her training and touring. In 1933-35 she spent two years in Europe with the aid of fellowships and sang for the crowned heads of Sweden, Norway, Denmark, and England. She also came under the management of the impresario, Sol Hurok, and the praise of Arturo Toscanini who declared that her's was a voice heard only once in a hundred years.

Within three years after her return, Marian Anderson was one of America's leading contraltos. Her recordings were a staple of the Columbia recording company. Her concerts were generally sell-outs. With Franz Rupp, Marian Anderson criss-crossed the Americas. By 1941 she was one of America's highest paid concert artists.

Her standing was so high in 1939 when the Daughter's of the American Revolution (DAR) denied her the use of Constitution Hall, a national scandal was created. Deems Taylor, Walter Damrosch, and other musical leaders expressed their disapproval of the DAR. Mrs. Eleanor Roosevelt resigned from this organization. As though in disapproval of the DAR, 75,000 people gathered before Marian Anderson on the steps of the Lincoln Memorial as she sang on Easter Sunday morning in 1943.

Marian Anderson was awarded the Spingarn Medal and the $10,000 Bok Award in 1939. Other awards and distinctions came her way. She was the first Negro to sing at the Metropolitan Opera. In 1957 she toured the Orient and in India moved tens of thousands with her music.

Without a doubt Marian Anderson, through her music and her regal behavior, has contributed greatly to the current success of other Negroes on either side of the footlights.

Marian Anderson. *My Lord, What a Morning; An Autobiography*, New York, 1956; Kosti Vehanen. *Marian Anderson; A Portrait*, New York, 1941.

XII VISUAL ART

Every Eye a Witness

Removed from his native Africa and shackled as a slave to a plow and hoe in America, the African was henceforth and forever divorced from his native artistry and culture. The creative sculpture, metalwork, weaving, and pottery of his native Africa were no longer his to pursue in the new land.

Thus, the Negro, as a group, was denied creative expression for more than a century, and it was not until the planters and merchants of the South grew rich and began to ornament their mansions and buildings that his artistic talents were employed. When given the opporunity, he proved to be a fine carpenter, cabinet maker, wood carver, blacksmith, and harness maker. In New Orleans, where he worked as a blacksmith fashioning the beautiful wrought iron grilles that decorate the balconies and balustrades of the finest homes and buildings, his artistry may be seen today. There is little doubt that the handicraft was a carryover from his ancestral Africa.

Skill in slaves was sought and encouraged among the prosperous slave holders, who recognized that a skilled slave was worth more as a worker or when sold.

Throughout the pioneer days and up to the industrial revolution in America the nation afforded little encouragement to the artists in the plastic and graphic arts. Individuals who amassed fortunes and began to acquire art, patronized the European artists. It was not until about 1870 that the American artists began to gain recognition. Before this, however, we find that Robert Duncanson, an Ohio Negro, had painted the "Blue Hole" in 1851, which is now in the collection of the Cincinnati Art Museum. Duncanson had studied in Canada, England, and Scotland. The London Art Journal in 1866 credited him with being one of the outstanding landscapists of his day. About 1870, in Providence, Rhode Island, Edward Bannister, a painter of great talent, organized the Providence Art Club in his home. This was the first American art club and he was the only Negro member. It is still that city's leading art club.

Later, around 1876, Edmonia Lewis, (Negro and Indian) who was born in Boston in 1854 of mixed parentage, came to prominence as the first Negro sculptor. Henry O. Tanner, at the turn of the century, was establishing an international reputation as a painter of religious subjects in Paris. He taught and influenced two younger painters of his day, William Harper and Edouard Scott, who became renowned after the turn of the century. A second woman sculptor, Meta Warrick Fuller, became noted for her "power and originality."

Negro artists up to this time avoided Negro subject matter in their work. Duncanson and Bannister who were landscape painters employed the style of the European masters of their day. Scott's early work showed the influence of Tanner, with whom he studied in Paris, however, during his stay in Haiti the local color of lush green foliage and rich brown skin-tones found their way into his canvases. Harper's surroundings dictated a native interpretation of his experiences into his works.

May Howard Jackson (1897) was one of the first Negro artists to break with tradition and turn to "frank and deliberate racialism." She possessed a deep feeling and love for Negro types and sculptured portraits of many important Negroes.

Before 1940 the number of professional Negro artists were few. Outstanding among these were Aaron Douglas, William Farrow, Charles Dawson, Archibald Motley, Laura Wheeler, Palmer Hayden, Hale Woodruff, Albert Smith, William H. Johnson, Lesesne Wells, Sargent Johnson, Malvin Gray Johnson, Augusta Savage, James A. Porter, Richmond Barthé, Selma Burke, James Wells, Ellis Wilson, and Charles Alston.

It would be a gross oversight not to include the creative genius of the great architect, Paul R. Williams, and the talented cartoonist, E. Simms Campbell, in the allied arts.

With the establishment of the Federal Art Projects, Works Projects Administration, America witnessed a surge of creative talent. Financed by government funds, people with artistic talent were put to work as writers, actors, musicians, and plastic and graphic artists. These projects not only encouraged talented artists, but brought about a new cultural vista in America.

Perhaps the greatest benefactors of this program were the Negro artists who were for the first time gainfully employed in the arts. In Chicago and New York, young Negro artists who had come from all over the nation to these metropolitan centers in the hope of developing their artistic talents, found the answer to their quest in the art projects. Of the two cities, Chicago produced more professional artist in all of the allied arts.

To name only a few, there were Richard Wright, Arna Bontemps, Gwendolyn Brooks, Katherine Dunham, Frank Neal, Charles Sebree, David P. Ross, Eldzier Cortor, William Carter, Charles White, Sinclair Drake, Horace Cayton, Willard Motley, and Bernard Goss.

New York and the East produced its fair share of professional artists, also. Included among these, in addition to those previously mentioned, are: Marlin Smith, Jacob Lawrence, Robert Blackburn, Donald Reid, Ernie Crichlow, Elton Fax, Ellis Wilson, Zell Ingram, Wilbert Warren, Laura Wheeling Waring, Robert Pious, Lois Mailou Jones, Wilmer Jennings, Alice Elizabeth Catlett, Allan Rohan Crite, and Frederick Flemister of Georgia.

Among the younger contemporaries who have gained recognition, there are Richard Hunt, John Aterbery, Clarence Brisco, Lawrence A. Jones, Jack Jordan, Leon Lank Leonard, Jimmie Mosely, Hayward L. Oubre, Harper T. Phillips, Gregory Ridley, Hobie Williams, Hughie Lee Smith, Geraldine McCullough, and Frank Wyley.

Alain Locke. *Negro Art: Past and Present*, Washington, D.C., 1936; Alain Locke. *The Negro in Art*, Washington, D.C. 1940; Cedric Dover. *American Negro Art* New York, 1957; James A. Porter. *Modern Negro Art*, New York, 1943.

Robert Duncanson (1821-1871)

EARLY AMERICAN ARTIST

Robert Duncanson has been called the most accomplished American Negro painter of the 1840's and 50's. His most productive years were between 1840 and 1865. A native of Cincinnati, Ohio, Duncanson was the son of a transplanted Scotsman and a Negro woman. His youth was hard and unpleasant although little or none of this is reflected in his landscapes, murals or protraits. He began sketching in his teens and before he was twenty had excited the admiration of prominent artists in and around Cincinnati.

In 1840 the Freedmen's Aid Society of Ohio collected funds to send him to Glasgow, Scotland, for formal training, where he remained for three years.

Duncanson executed many portraits of leading citizens in Cincinnati. His "William Carey" may be seen at Ohio Military Institute; his "Nicholas Longworth" hangs in the Ohio Mechanics Institute. Although Duncanson's forte was landscape painting, he was a competent muralist and painter of the American West. In 1860 the *London Art Journal* named Duncanson as one of the outstanding landscape painters in an era when such painting was in vogue.

His pictures were exhibited in the United States, England and Scotland. He often took themes from Shakespeare and Tennyson and entitled some of his works "The Trial of Shakespeare" and "The Lotus Eaters."

While abroad Duncanson met William Alfred Tennyson and enjoyed the patronage of the Earl of Essex. One of his paintings was secured for Windsor Castle. Duncanson's famous "Trial of Shakespeare" is still in Cincinnati, after having been initially presented to the Douglass Center in Toledo. Another of his paintings, "Blue Hole" is owned by the Cincinnati Art Museum. Unfortunately most of Duncanson's paintings have become lost or destroyed over the years.

Duncanson returned from his last trip abroad in 1860 and is believed to have died in a Detroit, Michigan hospital eleven years later.

James A. Porter ,*Modern Negro Art*, New York, 1943, p. 46; Alain Locke, *Negro Art: Past and Present*, Washington, 1936, pp. 18-20; *Negro Yearbook, 1947*, Tuskegee, 1947, p. 413. *Dictionary of American Artists: 1564-1860*, edited by George C. Grace and David Wallace (New Haven, Yale University Press, 1957, gives Duncanson's birth and death dates as 1817 and 1872 respectively, p. 193.

Edward M. Bannister
(1828-1901)

LANDSCAPE PAINTER

One day in 1867 Edward M. Bannister became enraged by a *New York Herald* article which flatly declared that "the Negro seems to have an appreciation of Art while being manifestly unable to produce it." He had a right to be angry, for he had been sketching since he was ten years old, had taken private instruction from Dr. William Runner, an able teacher of Art Anatomy in Boston and had studied art at Lowell Institute in Boston where he was ostracized by white artists.

Life had not been easy for Bannister. He was of mixed parentage and had been orphaned while quite young. Born in Nova Scotia, Bannister had supported himself with a variety of menial jobs: cooking on a coastal vessel, sweeping the floor in a Boston barbershop, serving as a man-of-all-work at different times. At no time did he despair of his painting and in every spare moment took out his paints and brushes. The *Herald* fired his determination to make a career as an artist.

Although he had a small reputation in Boston, Bannister moved to Providence, Rhode Island in 1870. Within six years his painting gained for him an entry in the Centennial Exhibition held in Philadelphia in 1876. His painting "Under the Oaks" took the Gold Medal. A revolt of the other entrants occurred when the judges wanted to "reconsider" the Gold Medal Award after discovering that

Bannister was a Negro. The white competitors insisted that the decision stand and Bannister walked off with the prize. "Under the Oaks" was sold for $1500 during that same year.

After the Centennial Exhibition, Bannister's reputation continued to grow and the commissions freed him from odd jobs. It is likely that he made a rather good living as a painter for one account of his life states that he could be seen sailing his yacht on Narragansett Bay and Newport Harbor studying the clouds and the sky. He produced a large number of landscapes, most of which possess a gentle arcadian quality and carry such titles as "By the Brook" and "Landscape." Today some of his work may be found in the collections of the Providence Art Club, the Rhode Island School of Design, the Howard University Art Gallery and the John Hope Collection at Atlanta University.

Edward Bannister was one of the seven charter members of the famed Providence Art Club which was incorporated in 1870. During his life he was widely recognized as one of America's more competent landscapists who happened to be Negro. He died in Providence in 1901.

Cedric Dover, *Negro American Art*, New York, 1960, pp. 26-27; Alain Locke, *The Negro in Art*, Washington, D.C., 1940, p. 130.

Henry Ossawa Tanner
(1859-1937)

PAINTER OF RELIGIOUS SUBJECTS

Sketch of detail from Tanner's "Daniel in the Lion's Den"

One day a small boy in Pittsburgh, Pennsylvania stood watching a painter at work. From pots and tubes the painter took all kinds of colors and on the easel before him a recognizable figure took shape. To the thirteen year-old boy, Henry O. Tanner, it seemed almost magical the way the dead pigments and oils were transformed into a representation of life. Inspired by the creation of the painter, Henry decided then and there that he was going to be a painter. He had no idea of the trials and tribulations facing an artist, especially a Negro artist in 1872. So Henry set out to become an artist.

He studied earnestly and his skill grew. Finally he felt confident enough to submit some of his drawings to publishers in New York, but most of his work was returned. Some drawings he never saw again. Eventually he sold a painting for $40.00, and later one brought him $80.00. Tanner grew to manhood and began to travel. He secured a position as an instructor at Clark University in Atlanta. He learned photography and between it and his art, earned a modest living. He sold one photograph for $15.00 and considered he had gotten a good price for clicking a shutter. But to his surprise, the same photo was re-sold for $250.00 in Philadelphia.

Tanner continued to develop his skill and to grow in confidence. In the 1890's the French Impressionists were creating a stir in Europe, and those who aspired to become great painters went there to study. Fired by the idea of going to Rome to study, Tanner worked hard preparing for a major exhibit in Cleveland at which he hoped to raise enough money for his trip. His show was well attended, but he sold not a single painting. His talent was recognized by Bishop and Mrs. Joseph C. Hartzell, who decided to support him by purchasing his entire collection.

Tanner sailed for Rome. The trip was to be something of a grand tour, with stops in Liverpool, London and Paris. However, he got no farther than Paris, for it was to him the perfect place to work and study. Her he met many of the great artists of the day. Benjamin Constant, the famous landscape artist, admired Tanner's work and encouraged him. After five years in the "City of Light," he had developed a technique and individual style. He had taken a special interest in religious subjects.

In 1896 his famous painting "Daniel in the Lion's Den" won him major honors. His "Resurrection of Lazarus" stunned the artistic world and was purchased by the French government. Following this, honors came one after the other. His work won the Salon Medal in 1897 and again in 1907. The Louisiana Purchase Prize was awarded him in 1904. In Philadelphia he received the Lippincott Prize in 1900. The Art Institute in Chicago awarded him the Harris Prize of $500 in 1906.

Today his paintings are regarded as a successful combination of deep religious fervor and high artistic technique, somewhat in the manner of the master painters of the Renaissance.

Benjamin Brawley, *The Negro Genius*, New York, 1940. Alain Locke, *The Negro In Art*. Washington, 1940, p. 134.

Edmonia Lewis

(1845-1890?)

PIONEER WOMAN SCULPTOR

Sketch of bust of Henry Peck

Miss Lewis first exhibited her work in Boston in 1864. At this exhibition her sculptured portrait of Colonel Robert Shaw, the martyred leader of the all-Negro Massachusetts 54th Regiment, evoked such a favorable reaction that she was able to travel to Rome to study, with the proceeds from the sale of copies of it. As her skill and fame grew, Miss Lewis exhibited her work in Chicago in 1870, in Rome in 1871 and at the Centennial Celebration in Philadelphia in 1876.

Born in Albany, New York of mixed Negro-Indian parentage, Miss Lewis was first reared by her mother's tribe, then placed in an orphanage and finally adopted by an abolitionist family. She was sent to Oberlin College in 1865. During her three years there her talent for modeling was noticed by William Lloyd Garrison who brought her to the attention of Edmund Brackett, a prominent sculptor in Boston, Massachusetts. Under his guidance, she began her career.

Resembling an East Indian in physical appearance, Miss Lewis possessed "an appealing intensity and forthrightness." In Rome she was an exotic sight, wearing mannish garb and hacking directly from marble the images she had created in her mind. Most of her adult career was spent in Italy. Sometime during her later years she returned to America. However, the vogue of neo-classicism was passing. Edmonia Lewis also passed from public notice and her last years were so obscure that art historians can only surmise that she died in 1890.

Edmonia Lewis was the first American Negro woman sculptor to achieve distinction in a field generally dominated by men. Riding the crest of the neoclassical revival in the 1870's, she attracted wide notice in artistic circles. Miss Lewis did portrait busts of a number of the prominent figures of her era, including Abraham Lincoln, Wendell Phillips, Charles Sumner and John Brown.

Miss Lewis also executed a large number of complete figures and groups. *Hagar,* depicting a biblical theme, *Hiawatha, The Marriage of Hiawatha* and *The Departure of Hiawatha* on the famous Indian legend are among her better works. Though less technically accomplished than her bust of Charles Sumner, for example, a figure group called *Forever Free* aroused the greatest general interest. This particular group shows a Negro couple, just out of slavery, becoming aware of the fact that they are no longer in bondage. (*Forever Free* was made for the Harriet Hunt Mausoleum in Cambridge, Massachusetts.) She also did a bust of William Wadsworth Longfellow for the Harvard College Library.

Cedric Dover. *American Negro Art*, New York, 1960, pp. 27-28; Alain Locke. *The Negro in Art*, Washington, D.C., 1940, pp. 133-134; Margaret Just Butcher. *The Negro in American Culture*, New York, 1957 (Mentor Edition), pp. 170-171; James A. Porter. *Modern Negro Art*, New York, 1943, pp. 57-63.

Horace Pippin
(1888-1946)

MODERN PRIMITIVE

Horace Pippin has been hailed as the greatest Negro primitive painter of this century. Some of his work has been judged the "equal of any surrealist masterpiece by Dali or De Chirico in its suggestion of typographical ruin, plastic space and the sadness of a deserted world." Completely self-taught, Pippin never took an art lesson and felt that the art of painting cannot be taught.

Born in poverty in Chester, Pennsylvania, Pippin began drawing early in life. He often wandered out to racetracks, pad in hand, to draw pictures of horses and riders. As a child he moved to Goshen, New York with his parents. His formal education ended with grammar school and he began a series of routine jobs as a hotel porter, molder, and junk dealer. His passion for art was so strong that he often sought jobs in warehouses where paintings were stored in order to touch the paint and to study the way different artists did their work.

In 1917 Pippin entered the army and served overseas until severely wounded. He received the Croix de Guerre and the Purple Heart and was discharged in 1918. Returning to America, he married in 1920 and settled down in Westchester, New York. Supported by his disability checks and his wife's earnings, Pippin could not still his desire to paint. His war wounds made it impossible for him to raise his arm above his shoulder and his first efforts at serious painting required him to place a wooden panel in his lap, draw his outlines with a hot poker and then apply the house paint he used for oils.

Not until 1931 did Pippin recover sufficiently to try his skill on canvas. His first picture was three years in the making and he labeled it "The End of the War; Starting Home." Then he executed another picture called "Shell Holes and Observation Balloon, Champagne Sector," which received very high praise.

Sketch of detail from painting "Christ"

In 1937 through the efforts of friends, Pippin had his first one-man show at the Westchester Community Art Center. By 1938 he had developed to the point that four of his paintings were exhibited at the Museum of Modern Art in a show entitled "Masters of Modern Painting." Two years later he had a one-man show in New York which was a huge success. This success was repeated in Chicago and Philadelphia. His "Cabin in the Cotton" won fourth Honorable Mention in 1944 and two years later his "Milkman of Goshen" won the J. Henry J. Scheidt Memorial Prize, one of the major awards of the Pennsylvania Academy of Fine Arts.

Current Biography, 1945, pp. 470-472; *The Americana Annual, 1947,* p. 566; James A. Porter, *Modern Negro Art,* New York, 1943, p. 149.

Malvin Gray Johnson
(1896-1934)

SYMBOLIC ABSTRACTIONIST

Sketch of detail from painting, "Self Portrait"

Although he lived only thirty-eight years, Malvin Gray Johnson ranks high in the estimate of historians of the Negro in art. In *The Negro in American Culture*, Margaret Just Butcher declared that some of his works "are among the most significant commentaries on the American Negro scene." Alain Locke felt that Johnson caught better than most artists the sardonic humor and mystical pathos in the moods of the Negro. James Porter, seeing Johnson as a maturing experimentalist, wrote that Johnson's later work was stated in "terse, pregnant patches of color."

In interpretative paintings such as "Swing Low, Sweet Chariot" and "Roll, Jordan, Roll," Johnson attempted to treat the spirituals in terms of abstract symbolism. These and similar works were regarded as technical advances in the handling of Negro thematic material. During the last years of his life, Johnson turned to genre subjects, painting a brilliant series of watercolors of urban and rural Negroes. "Dixie Madonna," "Ruby," "Brothers," "Red Road" and "Convict Labor," works from his final period, are believed to be typical of his best efforts.

Johnson's work was shown in several of the Harmon Exhibits in 1929 and the early thirties. In 1931 the Anderson Gallery displayed some of his work and in 1932, several of his paintings were hung in the Salon of America. He won the Otto H. Kahn prize for painting in 1929.

Born in 1896, Malvin Gray Johnson was a native of Greensboro, North Carolina where he grew up in dire poverty. He managed to get to New York where he studied at the New York Academy of Design. Along with many other artists, he worked on the Federal Arts Project during the depression. During the last few months of his life, he went to Brightwood, Virginia, the locale of his last and finest watercolors and paintings.

Johnson was deeply interested in the technical problems of painting. Lighting, composition and, above all, form held a deep fascination for him. This is evident in his interpretations of the spirituals, particularly where he tries to convey the awe and majesty of the nobler slave and sorrow songs. In his genre painting, Johnson even rose above form in an effort to convey the quality of the lives of his people on this earth.

Margaret Just Butcher. *The Negro in American Culture*, New York, 1957 (Mentor Edition), p. 186; Alain Locke. *Negro Art: Past and Present*, Washington, D.C. 1936, pp. 73-75; James A. Porter. "Malvin Gray Johnson, Artist," *Opportunity*, XIII, April, 1935, pp. 117-118: James A. Porter. *Modern Negro Art*, New York, 1943, pp. 122-123.

Richmond Barthé
(1901-   )

REALISTIC SCULPTOR

Sketch of bust.
"West Indian Girl"

In the plastic arts the American Negro has made significant contributions. Few sculptors rank higher, nor have achieved greater fame than Richmond Barthé whose works may be found in the collections of the museums and art galleries of the world. In America he is represented in the Metropolitan Museum of Modern Art, New York City; the Hackley Museum at Oberlin College; Pennsylvania Academy of Fine Arts; Philadelphia Museum; Atlanta University; the Art Institute of Chicago, to name a few. Barthé's works may be seen in collections in England, Germany, France, Africa, Canada, the Virgin Islands and Haiti.

Barthé has been a Rosenwald and a Guggenheim Fellow. He was a recipient of awards for interracial justice and of citations from the American Academy of Arts and Letters. In 1945, he was presented the Aubudon Artists Gold Medal, and the Haitian government commissioned him to do two special monuments in 1950.

Richmond Barthé has done both heroic and miniature sculpture, but there is general agreement that he excels in executing small works. Exquisitely graceful pieces such as "The Harmonica Player," "Shoeshine Boy," the "Boxer" or "Black Narcissus" show the sculptor at his best. His pieces such as "Mother and Son," "Black Berry Woman" and "African Boy Dancing" are likewise excellent examples of the work of this distinguished sculptor.

Born in St. Louis, Mississippi, the artist spent his early youth in New Orleans. He left school at the age of fourteen and took a job as a houseboy and handyman, and spent every available free moment drawing. After unsuccessfully trying to enter art schools in the South, he was aided and encouraged by friends of the Catholic church in getting to Chicago, where in 1924 he entered the Art Institute with the intention of becoming a painter.

He found employment at a small cafe as a busboy where he worked for four years during his study at the Institute. His paintings came to the attention of Dr. Charles Maceo Thompson, a patron of the arts and sponsor of many of the talented young Negro artists. Barthé had a flattering style as a portrait painter and Dr. Thompson was influencial in securing him many profitable commissions among the Negroes of means in the city.

At the suggestion of an instructor who recognized the direction of Barthé's greater talent, he turned to sculpture. So skilled was he that within two years, he was able to present a one-man show of his work. Within the following year, he was awarded a Rosenwald Fellowship (1931). His first commissioned work was a bust of Toussaint L 'Ouverture.

Since these early years, the artist has received many important commissions and awards, making it unnecessary for him to depend on anything other than his work as a sculptor for his livelihood. As a sculptor, a teacher and lecturer, Barthé has contributed to the advancement of the Negro and the progress of art.

James A. Porter. *Modern Negro Art*, New York, 1943, pp. 136-137; *Who's Who in Colored America*, 1950, p. 23; Richard Bardolph. *The Negro Vanguard*, 1961 (Vintage Edition), pp. 245-247.

Jacob Lawrence
(1917-   )

PAINTER:
CONTEMPORARY PRIMITIVE

Sketch in the style of Lawrence

A gouache painting by Lawrence, "Pool Player," won the $500 purchase prize at the Metropolitan Artists' Victory Show in 1942. Perhaps even more impressive than his well-known genre paintings are his brilliantly executed series of tempera panels whose titles give a clue to their subject matter: *The Life of Toussaint L'Ouverture* (forty-one panels), *The Life of Frederick Douglass* (forty panels), *The Life of Harriet Tubman* (forty panels), *The Migration of the Negro* (sixty panels) and panels on the theatre and the American Revolution. *The Migration of the Negro* won him a Rosenwald Fellowship in 1940. Some art critics feel that it is these panels which raise Lawrence's work to international stature, for they seem majestically fitting for illustrating the history of the Negro.

Jacob Lawrence was born in Atlantic City, New Jersey in 1917. The product of a broken family, he was shunted between his mother and foster parents. When his mother, a domestic, finally took him to New York to live, the two of them found living quarters near a settlement house which greatly encouraged the study of arts and crafts. Charles Alston, an able painter and a member of the settlement house staff, encouraged the boy with his early drawing and painting.

Jacob Lawrence is regarded primarily as a sophisticated primitive painter, although he studied at the Harlem Workshop and the American Artists School in New York during the thirties. His formal education was obtained in the Philadelphia and New York public schools.

With the exception of interruptions due to illness, Jacob Lawrence has devoted his adult years to expressing his version of the Negro's experience in America. Though not as prolific as he was during the thirties and forties, Lawrence is still producing exceedingly powerful work. His genre pictures and his series on historical events appear to have earned him a lasting place in American art.

Long regarded as one of the most significant painters in America, Jacob Lawrence stands high in the history of the Negro in art. His angular, seemingly two-dimensional world of ordinary Negroes doing ordinary things is familiar to all who profess to be abreast of the development of American art history. Equally well-known are Lawrence's magnificent series of panels devoted to personalities and events in Negro history.

Jacob Lawrence's paintings have been shown as far west as the Detroit Museum and as far south as Dillard and Fisk universities. He is represented in private collections and in many of the leading art galleries, including the Whitney Museum, the Phillips Memorial Gallery, the Howard University Gallery of Fine Art and the Worcester (Mass.) Art Museum.

James A. Porter. *Modern Negro Art*, New York, 1943, pp. 151-152; *Who's Who in Colored America, 1950*, p. 332.

Marion Perkins
(1908-1961)

SCULPTOR

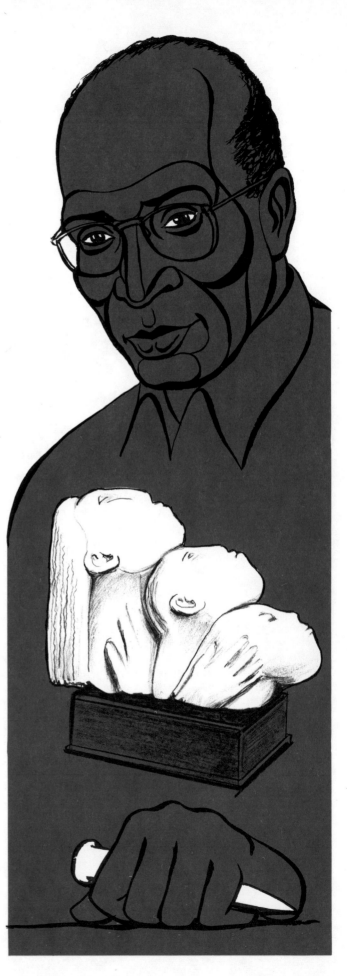

During the Depression of the thirties, Marion Perkins sold papers at a newsstand on Chicago's South Side. In his free moments at the stand he busied himself whittling on bars of soap, usually before a curious group of youngsters eagerly waiting to see just what form would evolve from his skilled fingers.

One day Peter Pollack, then director of the Community Art Center Division of the Illinois Art Project (W.P.A.), chanced upon Perkins and immediately recognized his creative talent. Pollack introduced Perkins to Si Gordon, a sculptor, who at the time was teaching at the South Side Community Art Center. Si Gordon took a special interest in Marion Perkins, and taught him to model in clay, make plaster molds and casts and eventually to chisel stone.

Perkins worked hard, as if driven by some unseen force. He labored as though he sensed that he had a limited time in which to complete his work. One might see him carting huge stones which he collected from demolished buildings, and later witness the transformation of those stones into sensitive works of art.

Working as he did, it was not long before Perkins began to earn a place for himself as a sculptor of merit. His work earned the recognition of the Rosenwald Foundation, and he received prizes and purchase awards. His "Man of Sorrow" won the Art Institute of Chicago scuplture purchase prize in 1951. Of all his achievements, he considered teaching at Jackson State Teachers College his most rewarding experience, although it was for a short time. He found that the college lacked sufficient equipment and materials to provide art education, and so he returned to Chicago and devoted his attention to securing funds and materials for the students at Jackson State.

Before Marion Perkins died on December 17, 1961, his works had been exhibited in many of the principal museums and galleries throughout the United States and Europe. He inspired his friends to the extent that they established the Marion Perkins Memorial Foundation, which has as its purpose the support of Jackson State Teachers College and other worthy schools in the area of art education.

Based on data supplied by Toussaint Perkins, son of Marion Perkins, Chicago, Ill., 1963.

Charles White
(1918-   )

MODERN PAINTER

Sketch of detail from
"There Were No Crops This Year"

As a poor boy living in the slums of Chicago's South Side, Charles had but one ambition: to become an artist. His mother's window shades were his first canvases; his first art schools were the buildings and lots surrounding him. At the age of fifteen be began exhibiting his drawings and paintings in empty stores, in churches, in vacant lots, anywhere that people would stop and look. Finally, he managed to study at the Art Institute of Chicago. When the Illinois Art Project, WPA, put artists to work in Chicago, Charles White was gainfully employed on the easel project. Here he was provided materials and complete freedom to work as he chose. He quickly won a Rosenwald Fellowship, a John Hay Whitney Fellowship and a National Institute of Arts and Letters grant. He was an artist-in-residence at Howard University.

In face of many tempting commercial offers, White has remained true to "art for art's sake." He feels that an artist, particularly, an artist who is also a Negro, has a social responsibility and that the demands of art and society are not necessarily in conflict. He says, "I look to life and to my people as the fountainhead of challenging ideas and monumental concepts. I look to the bright new world coming; as I face a blank canvas, it is with such thoughts that I, an American Negro, turn to the business at hand—Art."

Possessing the richness, power and moving simplicity of the spirituals, the graphic art and paintings of Charles White have won him the honor and recognition of being one of America's foremost modern contemporary artists. The titles of many of his works are taken directly from the spirituals: "More On Up A Little Higher," depicting a woman with her palms stretched heavenward; "Take My Mother Home," a young man with one hand raised in benediction; and another, "Mary, Don't You Weep," illustrates two women in sorrow. These and other representational works have a force, vitality and humanity absent from much of the art today.

White's work demonstrates a technical virtuosity and universality of feeling that finds a ready market for everything he produces. As of 1962 he has had fourteen one-man shows. His works may be seen in the collections of the Library of Congress, the Whitney Museum of American Art, Long Beach (California) Museum of Art, the Barnett Aden Gallery in Washington, D.C., at Atlanta University, Tuskegee Institute, Howard University and the Deutsche Akademi, Berlin, Germany. He is represented in private collections in France, England, Canada, Switzerland, Italy, Africa, India and Japan.

Janice Lovoos, *American Artist: Anniversary Issue*, June, 1962, pp. 97-102; 118-120. Hoyt W. Fuller. "Charles White, Artist," *Negro Digest*, July, 1963, pp. 40-45.

Gordon Roger Parks
(1912-   )

MASTER OF THE CAMERA

Sketch of photo from "Life" Harlem gang leader story

"A great photograph is as timeless as a great painting because it captures and records the world as we know it," wrote Gordon Roger Parks in an issue of *Photography* magazine. "Photography in itself can be as important as any pure art form, but it is immaterial whether it will ever be accepted as such, because its value will come through what it contributes to mankind rather than to the arts." Here, Parks has summed-up in a few words his concept of photography as one of the creative arts.

Born on a small farm in Ft. Scott, Kansas in 1912, Gordon Parks migrated to St. Paul, Minnesota in his teens. After leaving high school he worked as a waiter, lumberjack, piano player, band leader and semi-professional basketball player. In 1937 he chose photography as a career. He moved to Chicago where he was inspired and influenced through his association with the artists of the South Side Community Art Center. Here he was provided a darkroom in which to work, and eventually given a one-man exhibit by David P. Ross, director of the gallery. As a result of this show he won a Rosenwald Fellowship, the first awarded for photography, and went to the Farm Security Administration unit directed by Roy Stryker. After a year there, he went to work for Elmer Davis in the OWI's Overseas Division.

Parks rejoined Stryker in 1945 as a member of a seven-man photographic team which made documentaries for Standard Oil of New Jersey. In 1949 he was engaged by *Life* magazine as a staff photographer. Some of his important assignments with *Life* were stories on a Harlem gang leader, segregation in the South, crime in the United States, and on the plight of an underprivileged Brazilian boy named Flavio. He wrote and directed a documentary film on Flavio.

Gordon Parks is acclaimed one of the most versatile photographers working today," . . . he slips easily from rugged and often raw photo journalism to lush settings of fashion or the drama and emotion of the theater." The A.S.M.P. named him, "Magazine Photographer of the Year" in 1961, and he received the Newhouse Award in photography from Syracuse University. He won honors in the Art Directors show and the News Pictures of the Year competition.

As a *Life* photographer, Parks has had assignments in every part of the world. He was assigned to the European staff of *Life* and together with his wife, two sons and daughter lived in Paris for more than a year.

Parks considers himself a "week-end composer." He has written several musical compositions, including First Concerto for Piano and Orchestra, which was performed in 1953, and three piano sonatas, performed at Philadelphia in 1955. He is also a writer of note, having published one book on photography. His latest written work is a novel title *The Learning Tree*, published in the fall of 1963.

Life Magazine, 1963. *Photography* Magazine, 1963. Personal association with the Editor, 1940-1963.

E. Simms Campbell
(1908)
CARTOONIST

During the thirties and forties, the symbols of sophisticated humor included cartoons whose situations revolved around an Arabian potentate and his scantily-clad harem of tantalizing blondes, brunettes and red-heads, or the contrasting attitudes toward the fair sex of the blasé business tycoon and the baffled young newlywed. In a syndicated cartoon appearing in hundreds of newspapers, in ads for some of the nation's leading manufacterers and in *Esquire* magazine could be found drawings and illustrations signed "E. Simms Campbell."

This artist's work captivated millions, including fellow artists. Few knew that E. Simms Campbell was Elmer Simms Campbell, the most successful Negro commercial artist of that time.

Little publicity has been given the fact that Campbell has illustrated children's books and exhibited paintings of a serious nature, good enough to merit an Honorable Mention. Most readers are unaware of the fact that he attracted national attention in 1926 with his cartoon commemorating Armistice day in which he summed up the debt we all owe those who died in World War I; or his prize-winning cartoon of the tax grabbers which appeared before he was thirty years of age.

A native of St. Louis, Missouri, E. Simms Campbell attended Chicago's Englewood High School (where he was editorial cartoonist for the school paper) and the Chicago Art Institute. He broke into commercial art in his home town of St. Louis where he was told that it was a waste of time for a Negro in his youth to try to make a living in commercial art. Confident in his own ability, Campbell went to New York. With the help of other cartoonists, he began free-lancing. *Esquire* quickly spotted his talent and signed him to a long-term contract. Advertising agencies sought his talents and, in some years, he was turning out over 500 finished cartoons of high quality each year.

When the new men's magazine, *Playboy*, made its appearance in the mid 1950's, Campbell enjoyed the distinction of having his cartoons appear in competing publications.

Campbell's skill has earned him a place in *Current Biography*, *We Have Tommorrow*, *Who's Who* and other biographical works. So sophisticated is his work that the changing taste and style in journalism have failed to outdate it. In a highly competitive and specialized field of commercial art, Campbell ranks with the best. He and his wife now make their home in Switzerland. With the vigor of a beginning artist, he continues to meet the heavy demands of his syndicate and magazine contracts.

Arna Bontemps. *We Have Tomorrow*, Boston 1945, pp. 1-14.

XIII MODERN AFRICA

And They Shall Sing a New Song

In the year 1482, Christopher Columbus accompanied a Portuguese expedition to Elmina on the old Gold Coast (now Ghana). The purpose of the expedition was to build a fort for the protection of the thriving gold dust trade between the inhabitants of the area and Portuguese traders. Ten years later Columbus sailed west and found the Americas which were destined to be the final home of millions of native Africans during the next three hundred years. As early as 1443 African slaves had been introduced to Portugal and by the end of the century were carried to the Indies.

A number of factors account for the success of the slave trade. Ancient Ghana had already been razed by Sundiata Keita in 1240 A.D. Sonni Ali, the first major ruler of Songhay, was drowned in the Niger river the very year Columbus discovered America. The Ottoman Turks were in control of Egypt by 1517. In the seventeenth century Benin was weakening under the pressure of European incursions. In a final Indian summer of glory, the African states of Ashanti, Bornu, and Dahomey came into prominence during the seventeenth and eighteenth centuries. As the halcyon days of African independence and splendor were coming to an end, Europe entered the high point of its commercial and territorial exploration of Africa.

With the capture of Ceuta from the Moslems in 1415 Portugal became the first European nation to lay claim to territory south of the Sahara. In the succeeding centuries, England, France, Holland, Sweden, and Denmark also claimed parts of Africa and built forts to defend their claims. The initial European desire for trade in gold and ivory was soon replaced by a rapacious interest in black men to work the plantations and mines of the Indies and South America. The plantation system itself had been developed in the Canary Islands off the west coast of Africa and was carried by the Spaniards to the tropics of the new world.

Down to 1600 an estimated 900,000 slaves had been brought to the Americas. With the increased demand for more slave labor the number of slaves brought from Africa rose to nearly three millions for the seventeenth century, seven millions for the eighteenth century, and four millions for the nineteenth. There is no way to estimate the effect of such a drastic removal of prime human resources from the African continent.

As the slave dealers counted their enormous profits in human beings, other Europeans turned to Africa as a land where their territorial ambitions could be satisfied. The Portuguese sent their *conquistadors* to Angola around 1575. The Dutch planted a small colony at the Cape of Good Hope in South Africa in 1652 to serve as a sort of "half-way house" to India. The English succeeded the Dutch in this colony in 1795.

By the eighteenth century, Senegal was a French colony. Sierra Leone and Gambia fell to British hands before the eighteenth century came to a close. In the eighteen thirties, the French had the Algerian coast under their control. In the eighteen sixties and seventies, Belgium, under Leopold I, started laying claim to the Congo basin. With the major states of Europe scheming and intriguing in the scramble for Africa, with politicians drawing up spheres of influence on inaccurate maps, with the discovery of gold at Witwatersrand in 1886, Africa was only a pawn of international politics. Although humanitarian influences and the unprofitability of slave labor in the Americas had brought about an end to the "peculiar institution," with the exceptions of Liberia and Ethiopia, nearly all of Africa was under some form of European control by 1900.

In the meanwhile, colonial governments evolved different patterns of control over their African "possessions." In the French-controlled sectors of Africa, a system of direct rule was instituted. In British-controlled regions, indirect rule operated through native chiefs and spokesmen.

The major colonial nations had different views of their relationship with their African dominions. The effects of the different styles of rule are reflected in the development of independence movements on various parts of the continent. In British Africa eventual independence was generally at the back of the minds of the rulers. Britain had already witnessed the successful struggle of its former American colonies for independence. France, on the other hand, thought that eventually its overseas territories would become a part of metropolitan France. Portugal and Belgium felt that perpetual paternalism toward the Africans was the natural order of existence.

But change did come to Africa, if, as in some cases, only as a result of European presence. The migration of Africans to the towns to work, the use of Africans in the lower administrative jobs of the colonial powers, the influence of European ideas of nationalism and democracy, the impact of World War II on the lives of many Africans who served their colonial rulers, and the de-colonization of Britain's oriental empire stimulated the demands for African independence.

In many territories African study, social and trade associations furnished opportunities for creating political parties. The leaders profiled in this section of this book, for the most part, rose to power as a result of varying combinations of these influences. African nationalism and Pan-Africanism came to be the order of the day by the mid-twentieth century. African leaders now represent more than twenty-five republics in the assemblies of the world.

Africa's huge size—it is three times the size of the United States—alone makes it important in world politics. In addition to mere size, however, its tremendous natural and human resources and its unhappy relationship with oppression make Africa a strong ally in the struggle for freedom everywhere and for every man.

African Independence (Laurel edition), New York, 1962; Immanuel Wallerstein, *Africa: The Politics of Independence*, New York, pp. 29-119; Donald L. Wiedner. *A History of Africa: South of the Sahara*, New York, 1962, pp. 12-23, 38.

The Ethiopian tri-color — green, yellow and red — was first reported about 1894. On the present flag appears the "Conquering Lion of Judah", part of Emperor Selassie's title.

Since 1930 Lij Tafari Makonnen has been known to the world as His Imperial Majesty Haile Selassie, King of Kings of Ethiopia, Conquering Lion of Judea and the Elect of God. A short, bearded man of obvious imperial dignity, Haile Selassie sits on the oldest throne in the world. The history of his country goes back to the days of Solomon and Sheba. Ethiopia was a country with some sense of identity when most of Africa's new nations were but clusters of tribes and chieftains. Of all the kings who have ruled this ancient land, Haile Selassie is perhaps the most significant, for he has presided over the country's entrance into the world of the twentieth century.

As Lij Tafari Makonnen, he was born to power and influence. His father was Ras Makonnen, a statesman, soldier and trusted kinsman of the great Menelik II. Lij Tafari Makonnen's education is a mixture of Amharic, Coptic, Catholic and French influences. When the future emperor was ten years old his academic ability was so great that Menelik had him transferred from his native Harar province to Addis Ababa to attend the elite Menelik school in the capital.

At the age of fourteen Lij Tafari was successfully ruling a section of Harar province. In 1910 he was made provincial governor of all of Harar. During this period he continued his studies of the French language and culture which he began when he was seven years old.

Menelik II died in 1919 and his son Lij Yasu was named Emperor but proved incompetent. He was succeeded in 1917 by Zauditu, a daughter of Menelik. Lij Tafari was named adviser to her and was also made regent and heir apparent to the throne. His unusual administrative skill was then devoted to the building of hospitals and schools. He also aided many young Ethiopians in securing educations abroad. He himself travelled in Europe and learned many new ideas which he later applied to his own country.

More than anyone else, Lij Tafari Makonnen was instrumental in getting Ethiopia into the League of Nations in 1923, a move which was to have great consequences in the future. In 1924 he succeeded in abolishing the slave trade which was still practiced in Ethiopia.

As regent, Lij Tafari was able to exercise much power because Empress Zauditu, by this time, was growing feeble and left the heir apparent free to master the various factions intriguing for control of the country. In October, 1928 he was named King and after Zauditu's death, was Crowned Haile Selassie (Instrument of the Trinity) on November 2, 1930.

From the very beginning of his reign, Haile Selassie was determined to modernize his country. He established the nation's first written constitution and created an advisory parliament. Under him greater impetus was given to the building of schools and hospitals. More Ethiopians were sent abroad to study. Foreign experts were invited to aid in developing the interior of the country.

Haile Selassie (1892-   )

ETHIOPIA

In 1935 Ethiopia was attacked by Italy which was still nursing a grudge over its humiliation at Adowa in 1895. Member nations of the League of Nations did not come to the assistance of Ethiopia. Although Haile Selassie took personal command of his 1,000,000 primitively equipped soldiers, he was not able to withstand Mussolini's 250,000 troops or his airplanes, tanks and poison gas. In 1936 Haile Selassie went into exile in England, pleading his country's case. With the aid of the British, Haile Selassie drove the Italians from Ethiopian soil and returned to his people a revered hero.

An eloquent and firm believer in the principle of collective security, Haile Selassie made certain that his troops were among the first to go to Korea in 1950. Ever since the Ethiopian invasion he has been a staunch advocate of unified resistance of unlawful aggression and a reminder to the world of the risk inherent in failing to honor international agreements.

Today (1963) Haile Selassie sits in his palace at Addis Ababa, gradually admitting the winds of change to the country. In addition to his continual expansion of educational opportunities, he has vigorously promoted wider employment opportunities for the young. He has taken part in several African conferences aimed at defining the aim and roles of the newer nations on the continent.

Thomas Patrick Melady. *Profiles of African Leaders*, New York, 1961, pp. 31-45; Ronald Segal. *African Profiles*. Baltimore, 1962, pp. 136-140.

Africa

LIBERIA

South Atlantic Ocean

William V. S. Tubman
(1895-   )

LIBERIA

In 1944 William Vacanarat Shadrach Tubman became the eighteenth President of Liberia. Although Liberia was founded in 1822 as a haven for U.S. Negroes, William V. S. Tubman has had a greater impact on its fortunes than any other single individual.

When Tubman took office the affairs of the country were almost entirely in the hands of "Americo-Liberians." Many of the true natives of the country did not even have the right to vote. During his first six years as President, Tubman extended the franchise to all native Liberians; in 1947 women were permitted to vote for the first time.

Liberia is not a wealthy country but under Tubman the annual governmental budget rose from $750,000 in 1944 to $30,000,000 in 1960. The nation no longer depends on rubber for most of its revenue but has begun to develop its mineral resources in co-operation with other lands.

On the international scene, Tubman has been one of the leading exponents of a federation of African states, arguing that the new nations should follow a "formula which will be sufficiently flexible for each nation to maintain its sovereignty in its peculiar identity." More than any other African statesman, he has emphasized the natural variety of the different African states.

In physical appearance Tubman is reminiscent of an old-fashioned minister of the American South. Shrewd in intellect, flamboyant in personality, he can trace his lineage back to the state of Georgia. Born in 1895 in Maryland County, Liberia, young "Shad", as he was called, attended the local government school, Palmas Seminary and the Cuttington Collegiate and Divinity School and ended his regular education in 1913. Becoming a school teacher immediately thereafter, he also studied law during the same period. He was admitted to the bar in 1917 and had a successful practice.

Tubman rose in politics through a succession of small offices, including those of court recorder, collector of internal revenue and county attorney. When he was twenty-eight years old, he became the youngest Senator in Liberian history. Five years after this he became a lay minister and made his first trip to America to attend a Methodist conference in Kansas City.

After fourteen years as a Senator, William Tubman went to the Liberian Supreme Court as Deputy President. In 1943 he ran on the True Whig ticket and was elected to succeed Edwin Barclay as President of Liberia.

Thomas Patrick Melady. *Profiles of African Leaders*, New York, Macmillan, 1961, pp. 96-113; Ronald Segal. *African Profiles*, Balitmore, 1962, pp. 256-261.

Jomo Kenyatta
(1893-   )

KENYA

His parents named him Kamau we Ngengi; Scottish missionaries named him Johnstone Kamau; his early employers dubbed him Mucibi we Kinyata. In London he took the name of Jomo Kenyatta. In Swahili he is called *Baba We Taifa* ("The Father of Nations"). The newspapers call him "Burning Spear." The date of his birth is uncertain, probably the year 1893. One thing is definite about him: the struggle for freedom and independence in Kenya is indissolubly linked to his life and deeds.

When Jomo Kenyatta became the first African Prime Minister of Kenya in June of 1963, he passed another milestone in a road stretching back in time over a period of forty years. This short man with the leonine head, patriarchal beard and the piercing eyes stands at the head of a nation of six million people.

In 1920 Kenyatta first became active in Kenya politics. He was a member of the first African Nationalist group in Kenya, the Kikuyu Central Association, which fought for the disputed land rights of Africans. Kenyatta was mainly responsible for first stating the African's case against European appropriation and occupation of the Kenya "white" Highlands in 1929.

After making his first trip to London in 1929, Kenyatta returned in 1931 to continue his education and to write his now-classic book on Kikuyu history and customs, *Facing Mt. Kenya* in 1938. He remained in London for fifteen years. During his studies at the London School of Economics he met several of the future leaders of Africa including Kwame Nkrumah; he also met the American baritone, Paul Robeson, and once shared a flat with him. Kenyatta travelled to Russia and studied at Moscow University for a short time.

In 1945 Jomo Kenyatta published a small pamphlet, entitled *Kenya—Land of Conflict*, in which he foresaw possible African and European bloodshed if the long-standing question of land possession remained unsolved. His long stay abroad ended in 1946 and he returned to the land of his birth, Kenya. A year after his return Kenyatta was named president of the Kenya Africa Union, a political group vigorously agitating for African freedom. With oratory as flamboyant as his many names, Kenyatta succeeded in drawing many of Kenya's tribes to his Union.

By 1950 the land question erupted in the reign of terror associated with the Mau Mau underground. Thousands of Africans and hundreds of Europeans were killed. The Mau Maus were outlawed. In 1952 Kenyatta, who claimed innocence of any direct connection with the Mau Mau outburst, was convicted as being the leader of the underground and sentenced to prison for seven years. The drive for independence from Great Britain continued and finally in October, 1962 Kenyatta was unconditionally released.

Neither time nor age had robbed him of the affection and loyalty of Kenya's millions of Africans. He promises to settle the vexing question of land on a fair basis, for he sees the possibility of Europeans remaining in his beloved Kenya as equals, not superiors. Jomo Kenyatta's youthful dreams of *Uhuru* (freedom) for Kenya has indeed become almost a reality in his old age.

Ronald Segal. *African Profiles*. Baltimore, 1962, pp. 101-107.

Kwame Nkrumah
(1909-   )

GHANA

The flag of Ghana was adopted in 1957; has red stripes for fighters for independence, gold for wealth, green for forests and farms, and black star for African freedom.

Born Francis Nwia Kofie Kwame Nkrumah, he is known today as *Osagyefo* (the Redeemer) to his countrymen. The world knows him as Kwame Nkrumah. He was born in the Western Province of Ghana. Educated in America and England, he is the undisputed leader of Ghana, that bright star of African independence.

Nkrumah is the president of the first African country to emerge from the toils of colonialism. In a continent of peoples still searching for their modern identities, Nkrumah has been the major political spokesman for Pan-Africanism. Under him Ghana has contributed her good offices and resources to various pan-African movements. In 1958 Ghana was host to the first conference of independent African states as well as the first All-African peoples Conference.

Several times a prisoner for his beliefs in the independence of his beloved country, Nkrumah is the head of a nation of six million people. The son of a goldsmith of Half Assini, Nkrumah was converted to Catholicism at an early age and received his first formal training at Catholic mission schools. He was graduated from the Government Training School in 1930 and left Ghana (then the Gold Coast) in 1935 to continue his education at Linclon University (Pennsylvania) and the University of Pennsylvania. For ten years he lived in America. Of these years, he has said that they were a period of "sorrow and loneliness, poverty and hardwork." He added that he "never regretted them, because the background that they provided has helped me to formulate my philosophy of life and politics."

In 1945 Nkrumah left America for England. Already active in the African Students Organization of America and Canada, Nkrumah joined the West African Student Union. His undeniable talents were noticed by future independence leaders. When he returned to the Gold Coast in 1947, he was made General Secretary of the United Gold Coast Convention group. He found that this was in reality a minor organization and set about to build it into a major political force. The United Gold Coast Convention organization underwent a variety of changes and emerged as the Convention Peoples Party. With the Convention Peoples Party as a foundation, Nkrumah became Prime Minister in 1952 and President of the Republic of Ghana in 1960.

It is around Nkrumah's party and person that the new Ghana is taking shape. He has been the subject of various attacks because of the extreme concentration of authority within the Convention Peoples Party and himself. Whatever his personal future, in the words of Ronald Segal, "Nkrumah has already contributed more to the continent that he so patently loves than any of those—inside and outside Africa—who find it so easy at the moment to belittle him."

Ronald Segal. *African Profiles*, Baltimore, 1962, pp. 216-237; Colin Legum. *Africa: A Handbook to the Continent*, New York, 1962, pp. 217-228. Kwame Nkrumah. *Ghana; the Autobiography of Kwame Nkrumah*, New York, 1957.

Julius Nyerere (1921-   )
TANGANYIKA

Nnamdi Azikiwe (1909-   )
NIGERIA

In Tanganyika he is called *Baba Yetu* (father of the nation). In international circles he is known as Julius Nyerere, president of the newly-independent state of Tanganyika. Long before the country gained its independence in December of 1961, Julius Nyerere had been regarded as the most logical man to lead Tanganyika. Possessed of a first-rate mind, a stable temperament, and a sound education, Nyerere had been in the forefront of his country's struggle for freedom for over a decade. Today few African leaders rank higher on the world scene than he.

The son of the chief of the Zanaki tribe, Nyerere was born in 1921 in the Northern Province of Tanganyika. When he was twelve years of age he began his formal training at the Tabora Government School and finished the four-year course within three years. He then entered Makerere University at Kampala, Uganda and was graduated in 1945 with a degree in education. Desiring to study further, in 1949 he became the first Tanganyikan to attend the University of Edinburgh. Here he developed his general interest in colonial problems and took a Master of Arts degree after studying history and economics. Having entered the teaching profession in 1945 at the St. Mary Mission School in Tabora, Nyerere resumed his teaching career in 1952 in Dar es Salaam but found it impossible to remain aloof from politics.

Indeed, Nyerere had a deep interest in political activity during his student days. At Makerere he had organized a branch of the Tanganyika African Association, then an incipient nationalist study organization. Nyerere became president of the Association and soon gave it a new name, the Tanganyika African National Union (TANU).

TANU became Nyerere's springboard to power. Setting up branches of the organization throughout the country, Nyerere strongly espoused the cause of national independence. Because of Tanganyika's status as a United Nation's Trust Territory under British Administration, it was possible for Nyerere to carry demands for independence directly to the United Nations. In 1955 his UN speech "My People's Hopes" made a most favorable impression on the delegates.

British opposition to Nyerere's agitation for independence served to make him a hero in the eyes of his fellow countrymen. TANU soon became the dominant political force in the country. By October, 1960 it had control of over eighty percent of the seats in the newly-formed Legislative Council and Nyerere was Prime Minister (He later took the post of President.).

Julius Nyerere's motto has been *Uhuru na Kazi* (Freedom and Work). He has attempted to guide the country along democratic non-racial lines. Most seasoned observers feel that under his leadership, Tanganyika will become a leading example of political independence and technological progress.

One day in 1925 Benjamin Nnamdi Azikiwe's favorite uncle said to him, "Now you can go to America. This is all the money (300 pounds) I can give you. From now on it's up to you." With this and the money he had saved as a government clerk in the Nigerian Treasury Department, the young Nigerian set out for America. He entered Storer College in West Virginia, then went on to Howard University in Washington, D.C., Lincoln University and the University of Pennsylvania.

Although America was in the midst of the Roaring Twenties, Nnamdi Azikiwe did not find it a paradise. He worked as a dishwasher, coal miner, farm hand and earned a little money as a boxer. He suffered color discrimination. While he was attending school and earning his way, Azikiwe learned of the Garvey Movement and became aware of the power of the press in arousing a minority's social conscience. After nine years in America, he left for England in 1934 where he wrote *Liberia in World Affairs*.

The lanky young man did not return to his home; instead he went to the Gold Coast (now Ghana) where he spent three years. Resistance to colonial rule was beginning to take shape and when Azikiwe finally returned to his homeland in 1937, he joined a newly organized group called the Nigerian Youth Movement. With the aid of friends he also started a newspaper, the *West African Pilot*, the first of several which were to make him wealthy and to give him a voice in the public life of the country.

In a short time, "Zik" as he was now called, became the focus of resistance to foreign rule. His native Nigerian group, the Ibos of Eastern Nigeria, supported him. When difference within the Nigerian Youth Movement in 1941 proved irreconcilable, "Zik" resigned from it. In 1942 he founded a study group, the Nigerian Reconstruction Group (NRG) devoted to anticipating the problems Nigeria would face at the end of World War II.

In 1944, Azikiwe merged the NRG with a new organization, the National Council of Nigeria and of the Cameroons. Under these combined organizations Azikiwe was able to unite a vast array of organizations, societies, clubs and associations. Seeing this development, the British accelerated their hesitant moves to withdraw from direct control of Nigeria. However, their plans were deemed too conservative. This, plus economic problems arising from World War II, led to a general strike lasting thirty-seven days. Azikiwe strongly supported the strikers and eventually had to go into hiding when he was blamed for allegedly misrepresenting the facts of the strike in his various newspapers.

After the strike ended, the British relented and Azikiwe again became active in Nigerian politics, his influence greater than ever. Over the next decade or more, agitation for independence continued. Finally when full independence was granted Nigeria in 1960, Nnamdi Azikiwe was named Governor-General of the country.

Ronald Segal. *African Profiles*, Baltimore, 1962, pp. 109-116; Roland Oliver and J. D. Fage. *A Short History of Africa*, Balitmore, 1962, p. 249.

Rolf Italiaander. *The New Leaders of Africa*, Englewood Cliffs, New Jersey, 1961, pp. 199-203; Ronald Segal. *African Profiles*, Baltimore, 1962, pp. 199-206.

Léopold Senghor

SENEGAL

(1909-   )

Poet, Philosopher and President, Léopold Sédar Senghor is one of the most brilliant and able of the galaxy of new African leaders. He is a cultivated blend of French training and African nationalism. He is the leading political exponent of the concept of Negritude, that "whole complex of civilized values—cultural, economic, social and political—which characterize the black peoples, or more precisely, the Negro-African world."

While most of Africa's leaders are very able men and possess educated backgrounds, Léopold is perhaps the only African head of state who can truly profess to be an intellectual in the full sense of the term.

Born into a well-off family in Joal, Senegal, Senghor attended schools in N'Gasobil and Dakar and in France where he became the first African to win an agrégation at the Ecole Normal Supérieure. Trained in languages and literary subjects, Senghor wrote important works on Baudelaire. His creative writings include a collection of African poems, *Chants d'Ombre*, which earned him wide notice in Parisian literary circles. At the age of twenty-nine he joined the staff of a lycée (school) at Tours and later the Lycée Berthelot in Paris.

After World War II started Senghor was drafted into a battalion of colonial troops. He became a prisoner of war when the French surrendered to the Germans and was interned until 1942. When the French provisional government regained control over French West Africa, Senghor returned to his teaching duties at Lycée Berthelot.

With the French planning a more liberal relationship with its overseas territories, Senghor became active in politics. In 1945 Senghor formed his own political organization, Bloc Africain. In the same year, he was one of two deputies from Senegal elected to the First Constituent Assembly in Paris. Re-elected in 1946, Senghor became dissatisfied with the policies of many of his adherents in Bloc Africain and felt that the French government was not moving sufficiently rapid in the direction of greater freedom for Senegal.

Leaving the Bloc Africain group, in 1948 Léopold Senghor formed another party, Bloc Démocratique Sénégalais. A year before this he started the journal *Presence Africain* which extols the virtues and glories of African art and culture. In little over a decade under Senghor's leadership Senegal became a republic, owing much of its freedom to Senghor and his political party. On September 11, 1960, Léopold Sédar Senghor was elected president of the Republic of Senegal. Today (July, 1963) his voice is one of the clearest and most influential on the African continent.

Colin Legum, Editor. *Africa: A Handbook to the Continent*, New York, 1962, p. 303; Rolf Italiaander. *The New Leaders of Africa*, Englewood Cliffs, New Jersey, pp. 291-297; Ronald Segal. *African Profiles*, Baltimore, 1962, pp. 273-281.

Tom Mboya

KENYA

(1929-   )

On April 15, 1959 at an African Freedom Day dinner given in New York a young rather handsome, powerfully-built African spoke before an assemblage of dignitaries and on the topic of the emergence of Africa, said:

"My friends, the struggle is simple. It is for political freedom, economic opportunity and human dignity for all African, goals which can only be opposed by those who oppose the very concepts of democracy and human rights. Our struggle for freedom will continue without compromise until the liberation of all Africa is achieved."

At the age of twenty-nine, Tom Mboya had become an international figure. Six years earlier he had been a sanitary inspector in Nairobi, Kenya. Many persons who heard him speak were unaware that this man was not a graduate of Oxford, or the London School of Economics. His keen political insights and polished diction belied the fact that his education ended with his finishing the Kenya Royal Sanitary Institute training school which he entered in 1948 and left in 1951.

The son of a foreman on a sisal farm, Tom Mboya went to Catholic mission school. He was active in the debates and discussions about the economic differences between the whites and blacks in Kenya. As he moved up through the mission schools and the Sanitary Institute, he became ever more aware of the plight of the blacks in their own country. Early he concluded that the best way to do something about the status of his people was to enter politics.

When Mboya informed his government employers in the Sanitary Division of his desire to join the budding Kenya Africa Union, he was bluntly told that this would hamper his career—as a sanitary inspector. Angered by this, he promptly resigned his position to devote all of his considerable energies to the Union. Within two years he was elected Secretary of the Kenya Federation of Labor.

In 1955 Mboya led a successful strike of dock workers at Mombasa. This victory spread his name throughout Kenya, for African workers had long accepted whatever terms their white employers hand down.

Moving from the relative narrow politics of labor to broader issues, Mboya found himself with a political following. In 1958 he was elected Chairman of the All-African Peoples Conference held in Accra in December, 1958. In 1960 he was one of a score of Kenya leaders who drew up in London the outlines of a Kenya Republic to exist within the British Commonwealth. By 1961 he was Secretary of Labor for Kenya and on June 1, 1963, became Minister of Justice in Jomo Kenyatta's government.

Still in his early thirties, most observers feel that, despite his past successes, his best years are yet to come.

Rolf Italiaander. *The New Leaders of Africa*, Englewood Cliffs, New Jersey, 1961, p. 66; Alan Rake. *Tom Mboya: Young Man of Africa*, New York, 1962.

Albert John Luthuli
(1899-   )

1960 NOBEL PEACE PRIZE WINNER

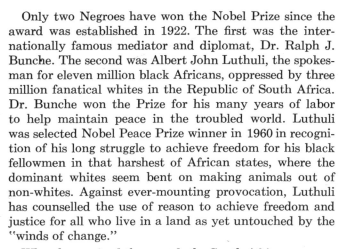

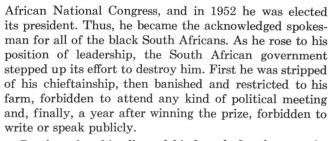

Only two Negroes have won the Nobel Prize since the award was established in 1922. The first was the internationally famous mediator and diplomat, Dr. Ralph J. Bunche. The second was Albert John Luthuli, the spokesman for eleven million black Africans, oppressed by three million fanatical whites in the Republic of South Africa. Dr. Bunche won the Prize for his many years of labor to help maintain peace in the troubled world. Luthuli was selected Nobel Peace Prize winner in 1960 in recognition of his long struggle to achieve freedom for his black fellowmen in that harshest of African states, where the dominant whites seem bent on making animals out of non-whites. Against ever-mounting provocation, Luthuli has counselled the use of reason to achieve freedom and justice for all who live in a land as yet untouched by the "winds of change."

When he received the award, the South African government was extremely reluctant to permit him to journey to Oslo, Norway for the presentation ceremony. High white officials declared that the Nobel Prize Committee made Luthuli a Nobel Laureate only to embarrass the government of South Africa. Luthuli himself saw the prize as recognition of the efforts of many people also fighting for freedom and reason, and justice and equality in his home land. Of the prize he said, "Thank God for it; God has answered the call of the oppressed people of South Africa."

Born in 1899, Albert Luthuli was elected chief of his tribe in 1935. Ten years later he joined the non-violent African National Congress, and in 1952 he was elected its president. Thus, he became the acknowledged spokesman for all of the black South Africans. As he rose to his position of leadership, the South African government stepped up its effort to destroy him. First he was stripped of his chieftainship, then banished and restricted to his farm, forbidden to attend any kind of political meeting and, finally, a year after winning the prize, forbidden to write or speak publicly.

Gentle, calm, friendly and kind, as befits the son of a Seventh Day Adventist missionary, Luthuli has continued to remain a symbol of reason and hope. Though deposed as chief and barred from political activity, his followers still call him "Chief Luthuli." His children, including one physician, two nurses and others securing higher education, are all dedicated to bringing freedom to this race-wracked land. Luthuli and his wife live on his small sugar farm near Natal, quite confident that the cause they serve and the God they worship will prevail.

Albert John Luthuli, *Let My People Go*. 1962, McGraw-Hill. *Time*, August 10, 1962, p. 20.

Sekou Touré (1922-   )

GUINEA

The flag of Guinea, adopted Nov. 1958 has three vertical bars which are red, green and gold like many African states

In 1958 the world became familiar with the name of Sekou Toure, the first president of the Republic of Guinea. When his country gave a resounding "no" to the proposal that it remain in the French political community as a part of the French federation of former colonial states, it was voicing the thoughts and ideas of one man, Sekou Toure. There were, naturally, other men and other voices in Guinea but Sekou Toure's was by far the loudest and clearest. When cautioned that Guinea would face economic collapse as a result of complete independence, Toure declared that "We prefer poverty in freedom to riches in slavery."

Three years later Sekou Toure was described as "perhaps the single most influential and significant figure on the (African) continent for the younger and more radical African." Observers of African politics feel that he has tried to steer a political course independent of the East and the West, thus making his small country a prime example of African neutralism in world affairs. In addition to his strong desire for African independence, he has been an eloquent advocate of African self-help. He once said "Africans must work hard because (in) the underdeveloped countries, the only capital is human energy." Toure's prodigious labors in Guinea earned him the nickname "The Elephant."

Sekou Toure was born in poverty in the Guinea of Faranah in 1922. His formal education ended when he was fifteen. After earlier study in a Koranic school at Kankan, he entered the George Poiret Technical School in 1936 but was expelled during his second year for leading a food strike. He completed his secondary course by correspondence.

In 1941, Toure passed an examination for a minor government job. About the same time he manifested two qualities which were to lay the foundation of much of his later success: a great interest in the African trade union movement and a distinctive flair for organizing men. He once stated that "trade unionism is a faith, a calling, an engagement to transform fundamentally a given economic and social regime, always in the search for the best, the beautiful and the just." He developed into a spellbinding orator in three languages: his native Malinke, Soussou and French.

The trade union movement carried Toure to the top of the political structure within the country. The year 1950 found him in the Guinean legislative assembly. In 1953 he was territorial councilor for the province of Beyla. In 1955, Toure, now the most popular figure in the land, was elected mayor of Conakry, the capital city. Having re-aligned the local political parties in 1956, he was ready and able to take Guinea out of the French political community in 1958. In the same year he became the first president of Guinea. At the date of writing (August, 1963), he was still the leader of his people.

Rolf. Italiaander. *The New Leaders of Africa*, Englewood Cliffs, New Jersey 1961, p. 276; Ronald Segal *African Profiles*, Baltimore, 1962, pp. 262-271.

EPILOGUE

GREAT NEGROES—Past and Present is the first of a proposed series of illustrated volumes on the Negro planned by the AFRO-AM PUBLISHING COMPANY, INC. We believe that this volume will provoke considerable interest and comment. Readers are invited to submit their opinions, reactions and criticisms. We welcome information regarding documents and factual data relating to important individuals and historical events which might be used as material to be incorporated in future publications.

During the production of this book we received many inquiries and requests from teachers, students, librarians and individuals for pictorial material on significant Negro contributors, to be used for educational displays. To fill this demand, we will soon make available large, two-color, 11"x14" plates suitable for mounting.

AFRO-AM PUBLISHING COMPANY, INC.

CHICAGO , ILLINOIS

We can assume no responsibility for unsolicited material.

BIBLIOGRAPHY

Anderson, Marian. *My Lord, What a Morning; An Auto-biography*. New York: The Viking Press, 1956.

Andreas, A. T. *History of Chicago*. Chicago: A. T. Andreas, 1884.

Armstrong, Louis. *Satchmo; My Life in New Orleans*. New York: Prentice-Hall, Incorporated, 1954.

Aptheker, Herbert (ed). *A Documentary History of the Negro People in the United States*. New York: The Citadel Press, 1951.

Aptheker, Herbert. *The Negro in the Civil War*. New York: International Publishers, 1938.

Baldwin, James. *Notes of a Native Son*. Boston: The Beacon Press, 1955.

Bennett, Jr., Lerone. *Before the Mayflower: A History o the American Negro*. Chicago: The Johnson Publishing Company, 1962.

Bond, Frederick. *The Negro and the Drama*. Washington, D.C.: The Associated Publishers, 1940.

Bone, Robert. *The Negro Novel in America*. New Haven: The Yale University Press, 1958.

Bontemps, Arna. *One Hundred Years of Negro Freedom*. New York: Dodd, Mead and Company, 1961.

Bontemps, Arna. *We Have Tomorrow*. Boston: Houghton, Mifflin Company, 1945.

Bradford, Sarah. *Harriet Tubman: The Moses of Her People*. New York: Corinth Press, 1961.

Breyfogles, William. *Make Free: The Story of the Underground Railroad*. New York: J. B. Lippincott Company, 1958.

Brawley, Benjamin. *A Short History of the American Negro*. New York: The Macmillan Company, 1931.

Brawley, Benjamin. *Early Negro American Writers*. Chapel Hill: The University of North Carolina Press, 1936.

Brawley, Benjamin. *Negro Builders and Heroes*. Chapel Hill: The University of North Carolina Press, 1937.

Brawley, Benjamin. *Paul Laurence Dunbar, Poet of his People*. Chapel Hill: The University of North Carolina Press, 1936.

Brawley, Benjamin. *The Negro Genius*. New York: Dodd, Mead and Company, 1937.

Brazeal, Brailsford, R. *The Brotherhood of Sleeping Car Porters*. New York: Harper and Brothers, 1946.

Broderick, Francis L. *W. E. B. DuBois: Negro Leader in a Time of Crisis*. Stanford (California), Stanford University Press, 1959.

Brooks, Gwendolyn. *The Bean Eaters*, New York: Harper and Row Publishers, Incorporated, 1960.

Brown, Sterling et al. *The Negro Caravan*. New York: Dryden Press, 1941.

Buckler, Helen. *Doctor Dan: Pioneer American Surgeon*. Boston: Little, Brown and Company, 1954.

Bullock, Ralph. *Inspite of Handicaps*. New York: Association Press, 1927.

Butcher, Margaret Just. *The Negro in American Culture*. New York: New American Library, 1957.

Cannon, Poppy. *A Gentle Knight: My Husband, Walter White*. New York: Rinehart, 1956.

Carter, Gwendolen M. *Independence For Africa*. New York: Praeger, 1960.

Chambers, Lucille Arcola. *America's Tenth Man*. New York: Twayne Publishers, 1957.

Chestnutt, Helen M. *Charles Waddell Chestnutt: Pioneer of the Color Line*. Chapel Hill: The University of North Carolina Press, 1962.

Cornish, Dudley Taylor. *The Sable Arm; Negro Troops in the Union Army*. New York: Longmans, Green, 1956.

Cross, Samuel H. and Simmons, Ernest J. *Alexander Pushkin, 1799-1837: His Life and Literary Heritage*. Washington, D. C.: The American-Russian Institute, 1937.

Cuney-Hare, Maud. *Negro Musicians and Their Music*. Washington, D. C.: The Associated Publishers, Incorporated, 1936.

Cunningham, Virginia. *Paul Laurence Dunbar and his Song*. New York: Dodd, Mead and Company, 1947.

Cronon, Edmond D. *The Story of Marcus Garvey and the Universal Negro Improvement Association*. Madison: The University of Wisconsin Press, 1955.

Daly, John J. *A Song in his Heart*. Philadelphia: The John C. Winston Company, 1951.

Davidson, Basil. *The Lost Cities of Africa*. Boston: Little, Brown and Company, 1959.

Douglass, Frederick. *Narrative of the Life of Frederick Douglass, An American Slave*. Hartford: Miller, 1845.

Douglass, Frederick. *Narrative of the Life of Frederick Douglass*. Benjamin Quarles, Ed. Cambridge (Massachusetts): Belknap Press, 1960.

Dover, Cedric. *American Negro Art*. Greenwich (Conn.), New York Graphic Society, 1960.

Dreer, Herman. *American Literature by Negro Authors*. New York: The Macmillan Company, 1950.

DuBois, W. E. B. *The Souls of Black Folk*. New York: Blue Heron Press, 1953.

Dunham, Katherine. *A Touch of Innocence*. New York: Harcourt, Brace and Company, 1959.

Eipsky, George A. *Ethiopia: Its People, Its Society, Its Culture*. New Haven: The Yale University Press, 1962.

Essien-Udom, E. U. *Black Nationalism: A Search for an Identity in America*. Chicago: The University of Chicago Press, 1962.

Ethridge, James M. *Contemporary Authors*. Detroit: Gale Research Company, 1962.

Ewen, David (ed). *Popular American Composers*. New York: The H. W. Wilson Company, 1962.

Flemming, Beatrice and Pryde, Marion. *Distinguished Negroes Abroad*. Washington, D. C., The Associated Publishers, 1946.

Foley, Albert S. *God's Men of Color: The Colored Catholic Priests of the United States: 1854-1954*. New York: Farrar, Straus and Young, 1954.

Franklin, John Hope. *From Slavery to Freedom: A History of American Negroes*. 2nd edition. New York: Alfred A. Knopf, 1961.

Franklin, John Hope. *Reconstruction After the Civil War*. Chicago: The University of Chicago Press, 1961.

Gammond, Peter (ed.). *Duke Ellington: His Life and Music*. New York: Roy, 1958.

Gloster, Hugh. *Negro Voices in American Fiction*. Chapel Hill: The University of North Carolina Press, 1948.

Goffin, Robert. *Horn of Plenty: The Story of Louis Armstrong*. New York: Allen, Towne and Heath, Incorporated, 1947.

Gosnell, Harold F. *Negro Politicians*. Chicago: The University of Chicago Press, 1935.

Graham, Shirley. *Paul Robeson, Citizen of the World*. New York: Julian Messner, Incorporated, 1946.

Graves, Anna Melissa. *Africa: The Wonder and the Glory*. Baltimore, 1961.

Harris, Abram. *The Negro as Capitalist*. Philadelphia: The American Academy of Political and Social Science, 1936.

BIBLIOGRAPHY

Helm, McKinley. *Angel Mo' and Her Son, Roland Hayes*. Boston: Little, Brown and Company, 1942.

Henson, Matthew A. *A Negro Explorer at the North Pole*. New York: Stokes, 1912.

Hughes, Langston. *Famous Negro Music Makers*. New York: Dodd, Mead and Company, 1955.

Hughes, Langston, *Fight for Freedom: The Story of the NAACP*. New York: Berkley Publishing Company, 1962.

Isaacs, Edith J. R. *The Negro in the American Theatre*. New York: Theatre Arts, Incorporated, 1947.

Isaacs, Harold. *The New World of American Negroes*. New York: John Day, 1963.

Johnson, James Weldon. *Along This Way*. New York: The Viking Press, 1945.

Johnson, James Weldon. *Black Manhattan*. New York: Alfred A. Knopf, 1930.

Jordan, Lewis G. *Negro Baptist History U. S. A.* Nashville: The Sunday School Publishing Board, 1930.

Judd, Peter (ed.). *African Independence*. New York: Dell Publishing Company, 1963.

King, Martin Luther. *Stride Toward Freedom: The Montgomery Story*. New York: Ballantine Books, 1960.

Legum, Colin. *Africa: A Handbook to the Continent*. New York: Frederick A. Praeger, 1962.

Lewinson, Paul. *Race, Class and Party*. New York: Oxford University Press, 1932.

Lincoln, C. Eric. *The Black Muslims in America*. Boston: Beacon Press, 1961.

Litwack, Leon. *North of Slavery: The Negro in the Free States, 1790-1860*. Chicago: The University of Chicago Press, 1961.

Locke, Alain L. *The Negro in Art*. Washington, D. C., Associates in Negro Folk Education, 1940.

Locke, Alain L. *The New Negro: An Interpretation*. New York: Albert and Charles Boni, 1925.

Melady, Thomas. *Profiles of African Leaders*. New York: The Macmillan Company, 1961.

Morris, Saurian. *A Sketch of the Life of Benjamin Banneker: Own Notes Taken in 1836*. Baltimore: Proceedings of the Maryland Historical Society, 1854.

Nichols, Lee. *Breakthrough on the Color Front*. New York: Random House, 1954.

Nordholt, J. W. Schulte. *The People That Walk in Darkness*. New York: Ballantine Books, Incorporated, 1960.

Oak, Vishnu V. *The Negro's Adventure in General Business*. Yellow Springs (Ohio): The Antioch Press, 1949.

Oliver, Roland and Fage, J. D. *A Short History of Africa*. Baltimore: Penguin Books, Incorporated, 1962.

Ottley, Roi. *New World A-Coming; Inside Black America*. New York: Houghton Mifflin Company, 1943.

Ottley, Roi. *The Lonely Warrior: The Life and Times of Robert S. Abbott*. Chicago: Henry Regnery Company, 1955.

Ovington, Mary White. *Portraits in Color*. New York: The Viking Press, 1927.

Owens, William A. *Slave Mutiny: The Revolt on the Schooner Amistad*. New York: John Day Company, 1953.

Pauli, Hertha E. *Her Name was Sojourner Truth*. New York: Appleton-Century-Crofts, 1962.

Peare, Catherine O. *Mary McLeod Bethune*. New York: The Vanguard Press, 1951

Pierce, Joseph. *Negro Business and Business Education*. Harper and Brothers, 1947.

Porter, James *Modern Negro Art*. Washington, D.C.: The Associated Publishers, 1943.

Rake, Alan. *Tom Mboya: Young Man of New Africa*. Doubleday and Company, 1962.

Range, Willard. *The Rise of Progress of Negro Colleges in Georgia: 1865-1949*. Athens (Georgia): The University of Georgia Press, 1951.

Reddick, L. D. *Crusader Without Violence*. New York: Harper and Brothers, 1959.

Robinson, Bradley. *Dark Companion*. New York: R. M. McBride, 1947.

Rogers. J. A. *World's Great Men of Color, 3,000 B.C. to 1946 A.D.* New York: Futuro Press, 1946.

Richardson, Ben Albert. *Great American Negroes*. New York: Thomas Y. Crowell Company, 1945.

Ritter, E. A. *Shaka Zulu: The Rise of the Zulu Empire*. New York: G. P. Putnam's Sons, 1955.

Sayers, W. C. Berwick. *Samuel Coleridge-Taylor: Musician*. New York: Cassell and Company, 1915.

Segal, Ronald. *African Profiles*. Baltimore: Penguin Books, Incorporated, 1962.

Segal, Ronald. *Political Africa: A Who's Who of Personalities and Parties*. New York: Frederick A. Praeger, 1961.

Sherwood, H. N. *Paul Cuffe*. Washington, D.C.: Association for the Study of Negro Life and History, 1923.

Simmons, William J. *Men of Mark*. Cleveland: George M. Rewell, 1887.

Singleton, George A. *The Romance of Methodism: A Study of the African Methodist Episcopal Church*. New York: Exposition Press, 1952.

Stampp, Kenneth. *The Peculiar Institution; Slavery in the Ante-Bellum South*. New York: Alfred A. Knopf, 1956.

Stearns, Marshall W. *The Story of Jazz*. New York: The New American Library, 1958.

Sterling, Dorothy. *Captain of the Planter: The Story of Robert Smalls*. New York: Doubleday Company, 1958.

Sterling, Dorothy. *Freedom Train; The Story of Harriet Tubman*. New York: Doubleday Company, Incorporated, 1954.

Taylor, Julius H. (ed.). *The Negro in Science*. Baltimore: Morgan State College Press, 1955.

Terrell, Mary Church. *A Colored Woman in a White World*. Washington, D.C., Ransdale Publishers, 1940.

Torrence, Ridgely. *The Story of John Hope*. New York: The Macmillan Company, 1948.

Vandercook, John. *Black Majesty*. New York: Harper and Brothers, 1928.

Vehanen, Kosti. *Marian Anderson; A Portrait*. New York: McGraw-Hill Book Company, Incorporated, 1941.

Voorhis, Harold van Buren. *Negro Masonry in the United States*. New York: Harry Emmerson, 1940.

Wallerstein, Immanuel. *Africa: The Politics of Independence*. New York: Random House, 1961.

Waters, Ethel and Samuels, Charles. *His Eye is on the Sparrow*. New York: Doubleday Company, Incorporated, 1951.

White, Walter. *A Man Called White, The Autobiography of Walter White*. New York: The Viking Press, 1948.

Woodson, Carter G. *The Negro in Our History*. Washington, D.C., The Associated Publishers, 1941.

Woodson, Carter G. and Wesley, Charles H. *The Negro in Our History* (10th Ed.).

Woodson, Carter G. *The History of the Negro Church*. Washington, D.C.: The Associated Publishers, 1945.

INDEX

INDEX

INDEX